IBM® SPSS® by Example

Second Edition

For E'Lynne and Beverly

IBM® SPSS® by Example

A Practical Guide to Statistical Data Analysis

Second Edition

Alan C. Elliott

Southern Methodist University

Wayne A. Woodward

Southern Methodist University

Los Angeles | London | New Delhi
Singapore | Washington DC | Boston

Los Angeles | London | New Delhi
Singapore | Washington DC | Boston

FOR INFORMATION:

SAGE Publications, Inc.
2455 Teller Road
Thousand Oaks, California 91320
E-mail: order@sagepub.com

SAGE Publications Ltd.
1 Oliver's Yard
55 City Road
London EC1Y 1SP
United Kingdom

SAGE Publications India Pvt. Ltd.
B 1/I 1 Mohan Cooperative Industrial Area
Mathura Road, New Delhi 110 044
India

SAGE Publications Asia-Pacific Pte. Ltd.
3 Church Street
#10-04 Samsung Hub
Singapore 049483

Reprints Courtesy of International Business Machines Corporation, © International Business Machines Corporation, pages 6, 26, 28, 29, 33, 34, 37, 39, 40-42, 44-46, 51-61, 63-69, 71, 73, 78-81, 89-93, 97-98, 103-106, 117-118, 125, 127-129, 139-140, 142-143, 150-152, 154, 157, 158, 166-167, 169-172, 175-176, 180-181, 190-191, 193, 195-196, 197-202, 207-211, 215-221, 225-230, 234-235, 237-238, 240-242, 245-247, 249-251, 256-259, 262-265, 267, 275-284, 286-292, 296, 297, 299-304, 306-309, 312-316.

Printed in the United States of America

Cataloging-in-publication data is available for this title from the Library of Congress.

ISBN 978-1-4833-1903-2

This book is printed on acid-free paper.

Acquisitions Editor: Vicki Knight
Assistant Editor: Katie Bierach
Editorial Assistant: Yvonne McDuffee
Production Editor: Laura Barrett
Copy Editor: Beth Hammond
Typesetter: C&M Digitals (P) Ltd.
Proofreader: Jennifer Grubba
Indexer: Molly Hall
Cover Designer: Scott Van Atta
Marketing Manager: Nicole Elliot

15 16 17 18 19 10 9 8 7 6 5 4 3 2 1

Brief Contents

Detailed Contents

List of Tables and Figures

SAGE was founded in 1965 by Sara Miller McCune to support the dissemination of usable knowledge by publishing innovative and high-quality research and teaching content. Today, we publish more than 750 journals, including those of more than 300 learned societies, more than 800 new books per year, and a growing range of library products including archives, data, case studies, reports, conference highlights, and video. SAGE remains majority-owned by our founder, and after Sara's lifetime will become owned by a charitable trust that secures our continued independence.

Los Angeles | London | Washington DC | New Delhi | Singapore | Boston

Preface & Acknowledgments

We consulted with a number of colleagues for ideas and suggestions on how to meet our goals for creating a data analysis guidebook that would be useful to students and researchers using IBM® SPSS® Statistics software[1]. Our hope is that this book will be a practical guidebook for SPSS users in a wide variety of disciplines. Additionally our goal is to also provide readers with a good foundation of statistical concepts. We thank all of our colleagues who provided suggestions for both the first and now second edition of the book. These include Paul Witt, PhD (Texas Christian University); Doug Pollock (Tyco Electronics); Linda Hynan, PhD (UT Southwestern); and Charles South (Southern Methodist University).

We are also indebted to the fine editorial and production staff at SAGE Publications and for the reviewers who provided valuable insights and suggestions, H. Colleen Sinclair (Mississippi State University), Philip J. Murphy (Monterey Institute of International Studies), Tyrone Bynoe (University of the Cumberlands), Jonah Schlackman (California State University, Northridge), Richard Feinn (Southern Connecticut State University), Alan Davis (University of Colorado), and Shlomo S. Sawilowsky (Wayne State University). In particular, we'd like to thank Vicki Knight for her efforts that made this second edition possible.

Above all, we wish to thank our wives, E'Lynne and Beverly, for their patience and support through this long process of writing and rewriting the book.

What's New in the Second Edition?

Two new chapters have been added to the second edition: Creating and Using Graphs (Chapter 3) and Factor Analysis (Chapter 10). The Graphs chapter includes tutorials for creating SPSS graphs using the three major techniques available: Chart Builder, Graphboard Template Chooser, and Legacy Dialogs. In addition, a new section on SPSS Syntax is included in the appendix. All chapters have been updated to reflect current menu options. Each chapter includes expanded and reorganized step-by-step instructions and additional figures make analysis steps easier to follow. Also, additional information has been added on how to write up results.

We'd like to thank second edition reviewers for their insights and suggestions on how to make this edition more understandable and useful to SPSS users.

1. SPSS is a registered trademark of International Business Machines Corporation. SPSS Inc. was acquired by IBM in October, 2009.

About the Authors

Alan C. Elliott is the Director of the Statistical Consulting Center at Southern Methodist University, Dallas, Texas, within the Department of Statistical Science. Previously he served as a statistical consultant in the Department of Clinical Science at the University of Texas Southwestern Medical Center at Dallas for over 30 years. Elliott holds master's degrees in Business Administration (MBA) and Applied Statistics (MAS). He has authored or coauthored over 35 scientific articles and over a dozen books including the *Directory of Microcomputer Statistical Software, Microcomputing With Applications, Using Norton Utilities, SAS Essentials, Applied Time Series Analysis,* and *Statistical Analysis Quick Reference Guidebook With SPSS Examples.* Elliott has taught university-level courses in statistics, statistical consulting, and statistical computing for over 25 years.

Wayne A. Woodward, PhD, is a Professor of Statistics and chair of the Department of Statistical Science at Southern Methodist University, Dallas, Texas. In 2003, he was named a Southern Methodist University Distinguished Teaching Professor by the university's Center for Teaching Excellence, and he received the 2006–2007 Scholar/Teacher of the Year Award at SMU, an award given by the United Methodist Church. He is a fellow of the American Statistical Association and was the 2004 recipient of the Don Owen Award for excellence in research, statistical consulting, and service to the statistical community. In 2007, he received the Outstanding Presentation Award given by the Section on Physical and Engineering Sciences at the 2007 Joint Statistical Meetings in Salt Lake City, Utah. Over the last 35 years, he has served as statistical consultant to a wide variety of clients in the scientific community and has taught statistics courses ranging from introductory undergraduate statistics courses to graduate courses within the PhD program in Statistics at Southern Methodist University. He has been funded on numerous research grants and contracts from government and industry to study such issues as global warming and nuclear monitoring. He has authored or coauthored over 70 scientific papers and four books.

CHAPTER 1

Introduction

Performing a statistical analysis is a little like jumping off the high board into a swimming pool. You may be a little unsure the first few times, but the more you do it, the easier it becomes. Although this book doesn't help with swimming, it does provide you with information that will help you make those initial jumps into data analysis, and we hope the more you do it, the easier it will become. With over 60 combined years (egad!) of consulting and teaching experience behind us, our goal is to help students and researchers jump into the waters of statistical data analysis with confidence.

IBM SPSS by Example is a practical handbook that "cuts to the chase" and explains the when, where, and how of statistical data analysis as it is used for real-world decision making in a wide variety of disciplines. It is designed to assist students and data analysts who have general statistical knowledge to apply the proper statistical procedure to their data and reporting results in a professional manner consistent with commonly accepted practice. Each upcoming chapter discusses the following aspects of performing a statistical analysis and interpreting your experimental data:

- How to make sure you are using an appropriate application of the statistical procedure
- What design considerations you should consider when using a particular statistical procedure
- An explanation of the hypotheses tested by the procedure
- A description of tips and caveats you should know about the procedure
- An example (or two) illustrating the use of the procedure on a data set using step-by step directions on how to perform the analysis in SPSS.
- How to report the analysis results using standard American Psychological Association (APA) and Modern Language Association (MLA) compatible formats (APA, 2013; Gibaldi, 2006)

Before moving on to chapters that discuss specific statistical procedures, the next few sections in this chapter contain general information that pertains to the data analysis process. We cover this information here in part, so it will not have to be repeated individually for later analyses. We encourage you to review the information in this chapter before moving on to the subsequent chapters.

Getting the Most Out of
IBM SPSS by Example

The primary purpose of *IBM SPSS by Example* is to provide you with information about how to use and understand the statistical data analysis process. The analysis topics covered in the book are as follows:

- *Chapter 2: Describing and Examining Data*. Explains how to use descriptive statistics to understand and report information about your data.
- *Chapter 3: Creating and Using Graphs*. Explains how to use the SPSS Chart Builder, Graphboard Template Chooser, and Legacy graphs to describe your data.
- *Chapter 4: Comparing One or Two Means Using the t-Test*. Explains the one-sample *t*-test, two-sample *t*-test, paired *t*-test, and appropriate confidence intervals.
- *Chapter 5: Correlation and Regression*. Explains correlation and simple linear regression with a brief discussion of multiple linear regression.
- *Chapter 6: Analysis of Categorical Data*. Explains methods that are applicable to count or categorical data, including contingency table analysis, measures of risk (including relative risk), odds ratios, and goodness of fit.
- *Chapter 7: Analysis of Variance and Covariance*. Explains several methods of comparing means, including one-way analysis of variance (ANOVA), two-way ANOVA, repeated-measures ANOVA, and analysis of covariance (ANCOVA).
- *Chapter 8: Nonparametric Analysis Procedures*. Explains nonparametric statistical procedures, including Spearman's correlation, sign test, the Mann-Whitney *U*, Kruskal-Wallis, and Friedman's test.
- *Chapter 9: Logistic Regression*. Explains logistic regression analyses, including the cases of single or multiple independent variables, variable selection, and evaluation of the model.
- *Chapter 10: Factor Analysis*. Explains how to use Factor Analysis to examine data sets and identify underlying components of the information.

Along with each analysis in these chapters, we include examples along with "step-by-step" instructions describing how to perform the calculations using IBM SPSS. Additional information that may be helpful to you in analyzing the example data sets and selecting an appropriate analysis for your data is included in the following appendices:

- *Appendix A: A Brief Tutorial for Using SPSS for Windows.* This tutorial gets you started with the essential information needed to work through the examples in this book. We recommend that if your SPSS is rusty, if you have limited experience using SPSS, or if you are new to SPSS, you should go through the examples in this appendix before working the examples in the book. For the more adventurous, it also includes a tutorial for using the SPSS Code Language that describes how you can use the SPSS Syntax Editor to modify existing analyses.
- *Appendix B: Choosing the Right Procedure to Use.* This appendix includes a decision chart that can help you decide which statistical procedure is appropriate to address your research question.

The remainder of this chapter contains material that we believe is important for understanding the examples contained in this book. We know you are in a hurry, maybe faced with a deadline, and anxious to get to your analysis. Take a breath. Relax. Slow down. This chapter provides you with basic refresher information about research methods that can help you successfully navigate your way through the analysis process . . . if you take a few minutes to read the rest of the chapter. Doing so may save you hours of frustration down the road and provide you with the ability to do a quicker and better job with your analysis. The remaining topics covered in the rest of this chapter are as follows:

- A Brief Overview of the Statistical Process
- Understanding Hypothesis Testing, Power, and Sample Size
- Understanding the *p*-Value
- Planning a Successful Analysis
- Guidelines for Creating Data Sets
- Preparing Excel Data for Import
- Guidelines for Reporting Results
- Downloading Sample SPSS Data Files
- Opening Data Files for Examples

A Brief Overview of the Statistical Process

Perhaps you are currently taking a statistics course or you struggled through a statistics course in the past and the concepts you once knew are a bit fuzzy. In this review, we remind you of the issues that typically motivate the use of statistical data analysis and illustrate the types of analyses that are most commonly used to describe data or make a decision based on observed data. Even if you have studied these concepts before, you might learn something new or gain some insights that hadn't occurred to you previously. In either case, we hope this review is helpful.

Most analyses can be categorized into one of these types:

- Description
- Comparison
- Association/correlation

Using Descriptive Statistics

In today's world, information is being accumulated at a dizzying pace that makes it impossible for anyone to comprehend it all. However, computer software, such as SPSS, enables us to summarize vast quantities of this information into numbers and graphs that can help us understand trends, make decisions, and predict future behavior. The challenge for the data analyst is to interpret this tsunami of information in some logical and practical manner based on accepted statistical practice.

For example, suppose you have been funded by a government agency to evaluate the operation of two charity-sponsored counseling centers. As a part of the analysis, a satisfaction survey is given to 109 clients over a period of 1 month and measured on a scale of 1 to 100. In order to describe the results of the survey, you wouldn't want to present a list of raw results (109 scores). Instead, it would be more informative to report several summaries, such as the following:

Average satisfaction score: 80.3 (on a scale of 0 to 100)

Lowest score: 58.6

Highest score: 94.1

This descriptive information gives you an idea about the average level of satisfaction and something about the variability of scores.

Using Comparative Statistics

Since there are two counseling center locations, your research group might be interested in knowing if there is a difference in level of satisfaction among clients at the two locations. This could be important in deciding which center receives additional funding. Suppose you have the following summary data grouped by location:

Average satisfaction score at the uptown location was 82.4 (based on 54 client scores).

Average satisfaction score at the downtown location was 78.5 (based on 55 client scores).

Assuming that the clients are representative at each location, you have some evidence to make a decision about which center is more effective in terms of satisfaction score. Your data suggest that the uptown location may do a better job as far as the satisfaction score is concerned since the score for uptown is 3.9 points higher than the score for the downtown location. However, what if the average scores were only 1 point apart? Or 10 points apart? What level of difference would it take for you to conclude that the average score for one location was significantly higher than for the other? Could the difference in scores be due to random fluctuation? If you did the survey again during some other time period, is there a reasonable chance that the downtown location would produce a better score? These questions are addressed with a properly designed and executed statistical analysis.

Using Correlational Statistics

To learn more about your survey results, you could examine your data in another way. Ignoring for a moment the location of the center, you may want to compare the relationship between educational level of clients and satisfaction scores. The variables *survey scores* and *years of schooling* are plotted on a scatterplot in Figure 1.1, and a measure of how they are related is summarized in a number called the correlation coefficient, which is found to be $r = 0.37$. From this measure of association, you have evidence that suggests there is a mild positive linear relationship between years of schooling and satisfaction score. There is a tendency for clients with a higher education to have a higher satisfaction score. (Correlation is discussed in more detail in Chapter 5: Correlation and Regression.)

In each of these example analyses, the raw data are summarized into summary statistics or a graph that allows you to discover important information about the data and to provide the basis for making informed decisions. *IBM SPSS by Example* provides you with the information needed to use these and other types of statistical procedures and to interpret the results.

Understanding Hypothesis Testing, Power, and Sample Size

To properly interpret a statistical analysis, you must understand the concept of hypothesis testing. Otherwise, most SPSS output will be so much gibberish. This brief discussion is designed to refresh your memory about these concepts.

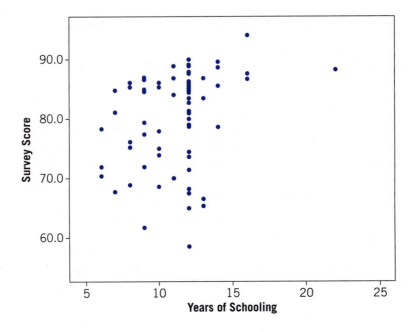

Figure 1.1   Scatterplot of Schooling by Survey Score

Many people have likened hypothesis testing to a criminal jury trial. In the U.S. judicial system, we make an initial assumption that the defendant is innocent (not guilty). Evidence is then presented to show guilt. If there is a preponderance of evidence of the defendant's guilt, you should conclude that the defendant is indeed guilty (you reject innocence). In the same way, a statistical analysis is based on a "null" hypothesis (labeled H_0) that there is "no effect" (e.g., no treatment differences). In research terms, the null hypothesis will typically be a statement such as the following: There is no difference in group means, no linear association between two variables, no difference in distributions, and so on.

An experiment is designed to determine whether evidence refutes the null hypothesis. If your evidence (research results) indicates that what you observed was extreme enough, then you would conclude that you have "significant" evidence to reject the null hypothesis. However, if you do not gather sufficient evidence to reject H_0, this does not prove that the null hypothesis is true, only that we did not have enough evidence to "prove the case." Back to the criminal trial example, failure to prove guilt beyond a reasonable doubt does not prove the "innocence" of the defendant. In fact, we use the terminology "We find the defendant not guilty" as a subtle way to distinguish from a verdict of innocence.

In general, null and alternative hypothesis are of the following form:

- A "null hypothesis" (H_0) is the hypotheses of "no effect" or "no differences" (i.e., the observed differences are only due to chance variation).
- An alternative hypothesis (H_a) states that the null hypothesis is false and that the observed differences, relationships, etc. are real.

In the following chapters, the null and alternative hypotheses related to each statistical test will be presented. They appear in the following form:

H_0: $\mu_1 = \mu_2$ (the population means of the two groups are the same).

H_a: $\mu_1 \neq \mu_2$ (the population means of the two groups are different).

These particular hypotheses are for a two-sample t-test as described in Chapter 4: Comparing One or Two Means Using the t-Test. In most cases, we will present the hypotheses in both a mathematical form (such as $\mu_1 = \mu_2$) and in words.

The alternative hypothesis is usually what the investigator wants to show or suspects is true. The alternative in the example above is called a two-tailed alternative (also called a two-sided alternative). That is, we would reject H_0 if there is sufficient evidence that the null is not true. For a one-tailed alternative (e.g., H_a: $\mu_1 > \mu_2$), we would reject H_0 only if the evidence against H_0 tends to support H_a. Further discussion of one- and two-tailed alternatives will be given when appropriate for the discussion of various tests in future chapters.

In hypothesis testing, two types of errors can occur, as illustrated in Table 1.1. The top classification is the "truth" that you do not know. The left categories are your decisions. For example, if you reject H_0 when it is false, you've made a correct decision. However, if you reject H_0 when it is true, you've made a "Type I error." Notice that of the four possible outcomes summarized in the table, two are errors.

The Type I error is controlled by your choice of a decision-making criterion, called alpha (α) or the level of significance. It is commonly set small, at 0.05, which means you are willing to risk making a Type I error 5% of the time, or 1 in 20 times.

If H_0 is false and you do not reject H_0, you commit a Type II error. The probability of committing a Type II error is called beta (β). The power of the test is defined to be one minus β. When a test has low power, it increases the chance of making a Type II error (i.e., failing to reject H_0 when it is actually false). Looking at it the other way, the higher the "power," the better your chance of rejecting H_0 when it is false—the better your chance of finding a difference when it in fact exists. Other factors that we have not discussed here that may be related to power include sample size, effect size (or size of the smallest important difference), whether your test is one or two-tailed, your selection of the alpha-level (α), correlations among samples, and type of distribution (e.g., normal), etc.

An important point is that there are many ways in which a null hypothesis can be "not true." For example, if the null hypothesis is that there is no difference in two population means (measured in inches), then, for example, this hypothesis is "not true" if the actual difference between the two means is 1 in., 5 in., or 50 in. It may be very difficult to develop a test for which we are able to detect a difference in population means of 1 inch. In fact, such a difference may be of no practical importance. On the other hand, it will likely be the case that a true difference of 50 in. may be very easy to detect. That is, if the true difference is 50 in., the power of the test will be large.

Another important point is that for any given level of significance (α), power can be increased by increasing the sample size. Thus, sample size should be a consideration when embarking on an experiment. Many negative (nonsignificant) studies reported in the literature are the result of inadequate sample size resulting in poor power (Friedman, Chalmers, Smith, & Kuebler, 1978). Therefore, the process of selecting a sample size for your analysis should begin early in your study. To follow with this example, the experimenter should determine the level of difference it is desirable to detect and then select a sample size that will detect this difference with an acceptable power (say, at least 0.80). Often, a pilot study will be undertaken to help determine the necessary sample size. SPSS offers a separate program called SamplePower that allows you to calculate a sample size for a given power or range of powers you select. Other commercial programs (PASS, nQuery, and SAS) are also available for these purposes. Or consult your friendly local statistician for help. For more concerning hypothesis testing, see a standard statistical text such as Moore and McCabe (2012). For a good discussion of power and sample size, see Keppel and Wickens (2004). References for effect size are Nakagawa and Cuthill (2007) and Ferguson (2009).

Table 1.1   Hypothesis Test Decisions

Our Decision	Truth	
	H_0 True	H_0 False
Reject H_0	Type I error (α)	Correct decision ($1 - \beta$ or power)
Do not reject H_0	Correct decision ($1 - \alpha$)	Type II error (β)

Understanding the p-Value

The "evidence" used to reject a null hypotheses is summarized in a probability called a p-value. The p-value is the probability of obtaining results as extreme or more extreme than the ones observed given that the null hypothesis is true. Thus, the smaller the p-value, the more evidence you have to reject the null hypothesis.

When your rejection criterion, α, is set at 0.05, then if your p-value for that test is 0.05 or less, you reject H_0. All of the examples illustrating statistical tests in *IBM SPSS by Example* use the criterion that a p-value less than 0.05 indicates that the null hypothesis should be rejected.

However, don't base your entire decision-making criteria on the p-value. For example, suppose two sample means for systolic blood pressure (SBP) differ by 1 point and are found to be statistically significantly different (i.e., $p < 0.05$). This could occur if the sample sizes are large, but such a finding may have no practical or therapeutic importance, even though the results are statistically significant. On the other hand, an observed difference in mean SBP of 20mm Hg based on small sample sizes may not be statistically significant (i.e., $p > 0.05$). However, such a finding may be of sufficient practical importance that this (nonsignificant) result may indicate the need for further investigation with larger sample sizes to increase the power to the extent that you would have a good chance of detecting a difference of 20mm Hg if it really exists. The point here is that the p-value is a valuable decision-making tool, but it should not be the only criterion you use to judge the results of your research. Another approach to interpreting results is to make use of *effect size* reporting which provides wording you can use to express the magnitude of a difference.

A word of warning: If you perform multiple statistical tests within the same analysis, you should adjust your α level for individual tests to protect your overall Type I error rate. For example, if 10 independent statistical tests are reported for the same analysis (such as in a table comparing baseline values between two groups), each conducted at the 0.05 significance level, there is about a 40% chance that one or more significant differences would be found even if there are no actual differences. That should be unacceptable to you—and is usually unacceptable to journal reviewers. The proper response to this problem is to adjust p-values in multiple tests using a standard technique such as the Bonferroni correction. (SPSS offers several other techniques for p-value adjustments. For simplicity, we're only mentioning the Bonferroni technique here.) To perform this simple adjustment, divide your rejection criterion value (α) by the number of tests performed. For example, if you are testing at the $\alpha = 0.05$ level and 10 tests are performed, then your rejection criterion for each test should be $0.05/10 = 0.005$ in order to maintain your 0.05 overall Type I error rate (Miller, 1981). To report these results in your paper, use wording such as "$p < 0.005$ was considered statistically significant for baseline comparisons according to a Bonferroni correction. . . ."

Planning a Successful Analysis

Statistical data analysis begins with planning. Entire university courses are devoted to properly designing experiments. An improperly designed experiment can make data analysis a nightmare. Therefore, it is to the researcher's advantage to spend some up-front time considering how an experiment will be analyzed before collecting the data. Although this book cannot cover all the aspects of good experimental planning, a few important considerations are provided here. And although there are times when plans need to be adjusted once you know more about your experiment, having a solid up-front plan will provide you with the best process to deal with any subsequent issues.

Formulate a Testable Research Question (Hypothesis)

You should formulate a testable research question (hypothesis) before collecting your data and formulating your research question in a way that is statistically testable. For example, you might test the null hypothesis that there is no difference in satisfaction scores from the two counseling centers in the previous example. You "test" this assumption by gathering data and determining if there is enough information to cast sufficient doubt on your null hypothesis. If there is such evidence, then you may reject the null hypothesis in favor of the alternative (one location has a better satisfaction score than the other, or they are different).

Collect Data Appropriate to Testing Your Hypotheses

Consider the types of variables you will need to answer your research question:

An outcome variable. (Sometimes also called the dependent or response variable.) The outcome variable measures the characteristic that you want to test or describe in some way. It could be some measure such as death, sales amounts, growth rate, test score, time to recovery, and so on.

Predictor variable(s). (Sometimes called independent or explanatory variables, or factors.) The predictor variables are often manipulated by the experimenter (e.g., level or dosage, color of package, type of treatment), although they may also be observed (such as cigarette smoking, blood pressure, gender, amount of rainfall).

For correlational studies. If you are performing a correlational study (examining the association between variables), you may not have a specific outcome variable. Keep in mind, however, that a correlational study by itself cannot be used to conclude cause and effect.

Scales of measurement. The method you use to measure an observation affects the type of analysis that may be performed. Table 1.2 describes three measurement types used by SPSS. As you design your study, keep in mind these general ways of measuring data.

As various statistical analyses are discussed in this text, reference will be made to the measurement types appropriate for the analysis.

SIDEBAR
SPSS makes a distinction between **measurement types** described in Table 1.2 and **data types**, which refer to the way actual values are displayed in the data set. Data types include numeric, comma, dot, scientific notation, date, dollar, custom currency, string, and restricted number. These data types are described more thoroughly in Appendix A: A Brief Tutorial for Using SPSS for Windows.

Decide on the Type of Analysis Appropriate to Test Your Hypothesis

Do you need a descriptive, comparative, or association/correlation analysis? See Appendix B: Choosing the Right Procedure to Use for help in deciding which type of data analysis to use for testing your hypotheses. Wilkinson and the Task Force on Statistical Inference (1999) state,

> The enormous variety of modern quantitative methods leaves researchers with the nontrivial task of matching analysis and design to the research question. Although complex designs and state-of-the art methods are sometimes necessary to address research questions effectively, simpler classical approaches often can provide elegant and sufficient answers to important questions. Do not choose an analytic method to impress your readers or to deflect criticism. If the assumptions and strength of a simpler method are reasonable for your data and research problem, use it. (p. 598)

Table 1.2   SPSS Measurement Types

SPSS Measurement Type	Interpretation	Other Notes
Scale	Scale data has an order and a metric so that a comparison of distance between numbers is appropriate. Examples are measurements such as height, age, income in dollars, etc.	SPSS scale variables include both interval data (data without a fixed origin) and ratio data (data with a fixed origin). We will sometimes refer to scale variables as quantitative.
Categorical/ Nominal	Nominal categorical variables do not have any implied order (e.g., gender, race, eye color, etc.).	Categorical results are generally reported as counts—that is, how many of each category is observed. We will also refer to categorical variables as qualitative.
Categorical/ Ordinal	Ordinal categorical variables have an implied order (e.g., level of difficulty, easy, hard; or box size, small, medium, large; or cancer grade, 1, 2, 3, 4).	Although cancer grades are numbers, they cannot be assumed to be an equal distance apart, and so cannot be considered to conform to a metric (see scale).

A practical interpretation of this is that you need to be able to understand and defend whatever analysis technique you use. In general, select the simplest statistical procedure that adequately answers your research question. How do you know what technique is the simplest and best? Frankly, only experience can provide you with a good answer.

Properly Interpret and Report Your Results

As a part of the discussion of each analysis method in *IBM SPSS for Example*, suggestions for interpreting your results and reporting them in a professional manner are presented.

> The above items are important considerations for your data analyses. The discussion here is not comprehensive and cannot substitute for the expertise of a professional statistician. If you do not understand the relevance of these issues to your own analysis, we recommend that you consult a professional statistician.

Guidelines for Creating Data Sets

Information that consists of thousands (or millions) of raw numbers and codes provides little information useful for decision making. Like a builder who transforms raw materials into a functional skyscraper, statistical data analysis transforms raw data into meaningful and useful information. However, before you can begin to perform your data analysis, you must get that raw data into the software program.

Before entering data for analysis, there are several data issues you should address. The following discussion describes how to prepare a data set for use in any statistical software program. For specific requirements in SPSS, see Appendix A: A Brief Tutorial for Using IBM SPSS for Windows. Also, for a general discussion of this topic, see Elliott, Hynan, Reisch, and Smith (2006).

1. Decide What Variables You Need and Document Them

Your research question determines which variables are needed for your analysis. Researchers should document their variables in a "data dictionary" that contains the important information defining the variables. (Some texts refer to this as a data codebook.) For an example of a data dictionary, see Table 1.3. This table is created during your planning stage. It can be created using a spreadsheet or a word processor. Creating this simple "dictionary" before you collect your data not only forces you to consider which variables you will need in your data set, their types, and how they will be named but it also provides documentation that can be a valuable tool to you and others in performing and interpreting your analyses later on.

Variables may contain values (data types) that are either represented by alphabetic characters called strings (such as M and F or A, B, and C) or numbers (such as 0 and 1) whose meaning may not be completely clear. For example, if you coded a *female* variable as 1 and 0 (1 = female gender, and 0 = not female) and *race* as AA, C, H, and O, you will want to define those codes in your data dictionary, as illustrated for the *female* and *race* variables in Table 1.3.

Note that when you create a categorical variable, you may need to also include an "other" designation when the list does not include an exhaustive collection of possibilities. For example, the *race* variable includes an "O" for other or unknown.

Missing value codes are used to indicate that the information is not available for that variable. It is recommended that you use a proactive code rather than leaving missing data as blanks. See the section "Define Missing Value Codes" below for more information.

Table 1.3   Sample Data Dictionary

Variable Name	Label	Data Type (Width)	Value Codes	Missing Code
id	Identification number	String (4)	0001 to 9999	Not allowed
age	Age January 1, 2015	Numeric (3.0)	None	−9
female	Female Gender	Numeric (1.0)	1 = Female 0 = Not Female	9
tdate	Test date	Date (10) (mm/dd/yyyy)	None	11/11/1111
score	Initial test score	Numeric (6.2)	None	−9
race	Indicated Race	String (2)	AA = African American C = Caucasian H = Hispanic	O = Other or Unknown

One reason to code gender as *female* (1 = yes, 0 = no) rather than (Gender) M and F or (Gender) 1 and 2 is that a 0, 1 variable is easier to interpret in some analyses such as regression, and since 1 is typically set as Yes and 0 as No, the meaning of the variable is easy to interpret. (You could also call the variable *male* with 1 = Yes, is male, and 0 = No, is not male, but you do not need both variables.) You might also use this technique with other categorical variables. Suppose you record race as Caucasian, Hispanic, African-American, and Other. You could create the variable Caucasian as 0, 1; Hispanic as 0, 1; and African-American as 0, 1. The number of variables needed to define all groups is the number of categories minus 1. This allows you to make comparisons such as Hispanic versus all others in an analysis, which is sometimes preferred over using a (nominal) variable containing four categories. On the other hand, for a contingency table analysis, you might want to keep the four categories.

2. Design Your Data Set With One Subject (or Observation) Per Line

The vast majority of data analyses require your data set to contain one subject (or entity) per row. A properly designed data set should look something like Table 1.4.

Notice how this data set is designed. Each row contains data from a single subject. Each column contains the data from a single variable. You may be tempted to have multiple rows per subject or to design your data set with subjects as columns, but if you enter your data in that manner, you are only asking for problems later on in most cases. If your data are already in a data set where the subjects are in columns and your variables are in rows, see the transpose example in Appendix A: A Brief Tutorial for Using IBM SPSS for Windows for a way to realign your data file.

3. Each Variable Must Have a Properly Designated Name

Variable names are often short designations such as ID for subject identification number, SSBP (supine systolic blood pressure), and so on. Each statistical package has a set of restrictions for naming variables. The guidelines given here will help you design your data dictionary with variable names that are acceptable to most statistical programs:

- Variable names should begin with a letter but may also include numbers.
- Keep variable names short. Some programs require variable names of eight or fewer characters, although many allow names up to 64 characters in length.
- Do not use blanks or special characters (e.g., !, ?, ', and *).
- Variable names must be unique; no duplicate names are allowed.
- Case usually does not matter. Use any mixture of uppercase and lowercase characters when naming or referring to your variables. (Case does not matter in SPSS but it may matter in other statistical software, e.g., the R language.)

Table 1.4   Table Showing the First Three Records in a Typical Data Set

ID	Age	Female	Tdate	Score
1001	45	0	07/10/2015	60
1002	34	1	06/12/2015	55
1003	65	0	12/02/2015	62

4. Select Descriptive Labels for Each Variable

Creating a variable label allows you to associate a descriptive label with each variable name. Variable labels are important because they help you more clearly understand and interpret statistical output, particularly if the variable names are ambiguous, similar, or difficult to decipher. Typical names and labels might be the following:

age: Age on January 1, 2015

sbp: Systolic blood pressure

s1 to *s50*: Answers to a satisfaction survey

female: Female or non-female (male)

swq1: Sales for the southwest region during the first quarter

5. Select a Data Type for Each Variable

Each variable designates a particular type of information. The most commonly used variable types are numeric (a quantitative value) and string (also called character or text and often used for categorical-type data). (Numeric variables may also be indicated with the data types comma, dot, scientific notation, date, dollar, or custom currency.) A good rule of thumb is to designate as numeric only those variables that could be used in a calculation or that are factor or grouping codes for categorical variables. For example, a Social Security number, an ID number, and a telephone number are not really "numbers" that are used in calculations, and they should be designated as string values. This prevents the program from accidentally using that "number" in a calculation. However, it is common to designate dichotomous or grouping variables using numeric codes such as 0 and 1 or 1, 2, and 3, but care must be taken if you use these numbers in calculations. Also, never use codes such as "NA," "Missing," "> 100," or "10 to 20" as entries in numeric fields (which may occur if you first enter your data into a spreadsheet such as Excel and then import the data into your statistics program). For a list of specific data types in SPSS, see the section in Appendix A titled "Working With Data in SPSS."

6. Additional Tips for Categorical (String) Variables

Keep Case Consistent. For coded variables that are of the string (character or text) type, it is always good advice to maintain consistent case in data values. For example, use all uppercase ("Y" and "N") or all lowercase ("y" and "n") for a string type variable that is coded to represent yes or no. Even when case does not matter for variable names, it does matter for the data contents of the variables. The computer recognizes uppercase *Y* as a different character than lowercase *y*. Therefore, if you haphazardly use *Y, y, N,* and *n* as data entries, your program may recognize the data as having four categories instead of two.

Avoid Long Data Codes. Avoid long (and easy to misspell) string variables such as Influenza or Timer Clock Malfunction. Use shortened codes such as FLU and TCM instead. The Label field (see item number 4) can be used for a more complete description of the variable if needed.

Consider Binary Coding. If your data are binary (having only two levels such as diabetic or non-diabetic), creating a numeric variable that uses the values 0 and 1 may save time later since some analyses (such as regression) require numeric data.

7. Define Missing Values Codes

Sometimes data are lost or never collected. For example, a test tube is broken, a subject refuses to answer, or a patient fails to show up for an appointment. This type of data should be coded using a missing value code. Always select a missing value code that is an "impossible value" for the particular variable. For example, a –9 (negative 9) is an appropriate missing value code for *age, weight,* or *height* since that value would never be observed for those variables. Specifically, avoid using a blank or a 0 as a missing value code since that may cause confusion as to whether the data value was ever recorded and may cause an incorrect number to be used in a calculation. For a date variable, you can use a legitimate but highly unlikely date such as 11/11/1111 or 1/1/1800 as a missing value code (assuming your data do not include observations from the 12th or 19th century!). Once you specify a missing value code in your statistics program, the program will take that missing value into account when performing an analysis.

8. Consider the Need for a Grouping Variable

A grouping variable is a code that tells the statistical program how to separate records into groups—such as control group and experimental group. Therefore, if your data set contains information on two or more groups, you should include a variable that specifies the group membership of each observation. A grouping specification could be a single character (A, B, C), numeric (1, 2, 3), or names (CONTROL, TRT1, TRT2). For example, suppose you will be comparing the mean heights of 24-month-old males who were fed regularly with breast milk and those who were fed on formula. You could choose numeric grouping codes to be 1 and 0, where 1 means breast-fed and 0 means formula-fed. Or you could use string grouping codes such as B and F or BREAST and FORMULA or any other designation that makes sense to you. For example, Table 1.5 contains a grouping variable (named *group*) as well as two other variables, *subject* and *height*.

From this example, you can see how the program can tell that the height 30.4 belongs to Subject 1001 in Group B, the height 35.9 belongs to a subject in Group F, and so on.

Table 1.5 Sample Grouped Data

Subject	group	height
1001	B	30.4
1002	F	35.9
1003	B	30.2
1004	B	38.0
1005	F	34.3
etc. . . .		

Preparing Excel Data for Import

A number of researchers choose to first enter data using the Microsoft Excel program and then subsequently import that data set into a statistical program. This section describes how you should prepare your data in Excel (or any other spreadsheet or database program) for importation into a statistics program such as SPSS. Using the guidelines in the previous section, here are several additional items you should keep in mind. (The procedure for importing an Excel spreadsheet into SPSS is illustrated in Appendix A: A Brief Tutorial for Using IBM SPSS for Windows.)

1. Row 1 of your Excel spreadsheet should contain only variable names. Do not extend names to row 2.

2. Each subsequent row (line) in the Excel spreadsheet should contain data for a single subject or observed entity (in almost all cases).

3. Avoid blank rows—it will complicate your import and analysis.

4. If you have missing data in your data set, define a missing value code and place that code in any cell that contains missing data.

5. Always use date variables with four-digit year formats in Excel. That is, enter the date in Excel using the format 01/01/2015 and not 01/01/15. Otherwise, the old Y2K gotcha can still be a problem for date calculations because the date 1/1/15 could either represent the year 1915 or 2015.

6. Use your data dictionary (previously discussed), making sure to include all of the variables you will need. Use the specifications in the data dictionary such as codes, formats, and data ranges to determine how you will enter your data into Excel.

7. If you have the time or resources, enter your data twice (preferably using two different data entry people) and compare the two files. See Elliott et al. (2006) for an example of how to do a simple double-entry comparison in Excel.

8. Avoid putting any extraneous text into your spreadsheet. Instead, put explanatory information in other sheets in the same spreadsheet file. Extraneous data in your primary spreadsheet can make importing the data more difficult.

Guidelines for Reporting Results

All the statistics in the world will not get your point across unless you properly report your results. Most journals and publications have guidelines that you must follow when submitting your results. Along with each example in *IBM SPSS by Example*, we illustrate how you might report your findings using statements that are compatible with generally accepted formats. Since certain guidelines are commonly adopted when reporting statistical results, we present these general rules:

- Computer programs tend to report statistics (such as means, medians, standard deviations, etc.) to more digits than are necessary or meaningful. A generally accepted practice is to report statistics to one decimal place more than the resolution of the original measurements. For example, if age is measured as integer, report the average *age* using one decimal place. Occasionally, if precision is important, you may report more decimals. APA guidelines state that two or three significant digits (e.g., digits that convey information and are not merely placeholders) are usually sufficient for reporting any statistic. (However, you should use all decimal places reported in the computer output when using these results in further calculations.)

- For very large numbers, you may want to limit the number of significant digits depending on the nature of the measure. For example, if you are reporting the average salary of corporate presidents, you might report a mean of $723,000 and a standard deviation of $59,000 rather than $723,471.20 and $59,356.10.

- Whenever a number is less than 0, place a zero before the decimal. For example, use 0.003 instead of .003.

- When reporting percentages, include the counts as well. For example, "There were 19% males (12 of 64) represented in the sample." Note also that the percentage was rounded. In general, give percentages as whole numbers if the sample size is less than 100 and to one decimal place if the sample size is larger than 100 (Lang & Secic, 1997, p. 41).

- When using the APA format for reporting statistical results, use the appropriate abbreviations for common statistical measures. Examples are the following:

Mean: $M = 1.34$

Standard deviation: $SD = 3.21$

Sample size: $N = 203$

p-value: $p = 0.03$ or $p < 0.001$

t-statistic with degrees of freedom: $t(13) = 2.12$

Chi-square results: $\chi^2(2, N = 97) = 7.6, p = 0.02$

F-test: $F(2, 21) = 3.33, p = 0.04$

- Information on creating and reporting results using graphs is covered in Chapter 3: Creating and Using Graphs.

Downloading Sample SPSS Data Files

This *IBM SPSS by Example* uses a number of data files that are used to illustrate the procedures described in this book. These data files are available for you to download from the Internet. To download these files onto your local hard drive, point your browser to the following site (enter in all lowercase):

http://www.alanelliott.com/spss2

Follow the instructions on this Web page to download and install the files onto your computer.

Opening Data Files for Examples

Once you have downloaded the sample data onto your hard drive, you can open these data files in the IBM SPSS program using the following steps:

1. Begin IBM SPSS.

2. From the main menu select **File/Open/Data**. . . .

3. In the "Look In" option on the Open Data dialog box, drill down to the C:\SPSSDATA folder on your computer (or wherever you stored your data).

SIDEBAR

Examples in the subsequent chapters assume that the data files have been downloaded and stored in a directory (folder) on your computer and that you know the name of the directory where the files are stored. The examples in this book use the convention that data files are stored in the C:\SPSSDATA folder.

SIDEBAR

To designate a series of menu selections using the SPSS drop down dialogs, we used the convention that a slash (/) means the next menu item selection. For example, **File/Open/Data** . . . indicates to select the File menu option from the main SPSS data screen. From the File menu options, select Open, and from the Open options, select Data. . . .

4. Select the file to open (such as EXAMPLE.SAV) and click OK. (Or simply double-click on the file name.) The data will be opened into the SPSS data grid.

5. You are now ready to use that data in an analysis.

In the examples referenced in subsequent chapters, you should use the above steps to open designated data files to perform the analyses under discussion.

SUMMARY

This chapter includes a description of the goals of this book, a brief review of statistical concepts, guidelines for creating a data set, entering data into Excel, presenting results, and instructions on how to download example data. The next chapter plunges you into the analysis process, beginning with a look at how to describe your data.

REFERENCES

American Psychological Association (APA). (2013). *Publication manual of the American Psychological Association* (6th ed.). Washington, DC: Author.

Elliott, A. C., Hynan, L. S., Reisch, J. S., & Smith, J. P. (2006). Preparing data for analysis using Microsoft Excel. *Journal of Investigative Medicine, 54*(6), 334–341.

Ferguson, Christopher J. (2009). An effect size primer: A guide for clinicians and researchers. *Professional Psychology: Research and Practice, 40.5*, 532.

Friedman, J. A., Chalmers, T. C., Smith, H., & Kuebler, R. R. (1978). The importance of beta, the Type II error and sample size in the design and interpretation of the randomized control trial. *NEJM, 299*, 690–696.

Gibaldi, J. (2006). *MLA handbook for writers of research papers* (7th ed.). New York, NY: Modern Language Association of America.

Keppel, G., & Wickens, T. D. (2004). *Design and analysis: A researcher's handbook* (4th ed.). Mahwah, NJ: Pearson Prentice Hall.

Lang, T. A., & Secic, M. (1997). *How to report statistics in medicine*. Philadelphia, PA: American College of Physicians.

Miller, R. G. (1981). *Simultaneous statistical inference* (2nd ed.). New York, NY: Springer Verlag.

Moore, D., & McCabe, G. (2012). *Introduction to the practice of statistics* (7th ed.). New York, NY: Freeman.

Nakagawa, Shinichi, & Cuthill, Innes C. (2007). Effect size, confidence interval and statistical significance: A practical guide for biologists. *Biological Reviews, 82.4*, 591–605.

Wilkinson, L., & the Task Force on Statistical Inference, APA Board of Scientific Affairs. (1999). Statistical methods in psychology journals: Guidelines and explanations. *American Psychologist, 54*(8), 594–604.

2

Describing and Examining Data

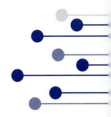

Information is the currency of research. However, unlike real money, there is often too much information. In most cases, data must be summarized to be useful.

The most common method of summarizing data is with descriptive statistics and graphs.

Even if you're planning to analyze a set of data using a statistical technique such as a *t*-test, analysis of variance, or logistic regression, you should always begin by examining the data. This preliminary step helps you determine which statistical analysis techniques should be used to answer your research questions.

In fact, this process of examining your data often reveals information that will surprise or inform you. You may discover unusually high or low values in your data. Perhaps these "outliers" are caused by incorrectly coded data, or they may reveal information about your data (or subjects) that you have not anticipated. You might observe that some observations are not normally distributed. You might notice that a histogram of observations shows two distinct peaks, causing you to realize that your data show a difference between genders. Insights such as these often result from the proper use of descriptive techniques.

The following sections of this chapter discuss the most commonly used tactics for understanding, describing, or preparing your data for further analysis. The two major topics discussed in this chapter are as follows:

- Describing quantitative data using statistics
- Describing categorical data using statistics

Each section includes, where appropriate, methods for reporting results in a standard manner for a report or journal article using APA guidelines (2013). Chapter 3: Creating and Using Graphs continues with the concept of describing data, but with an emphasis on graphs.

Example Data Files

SIDEBAR

Recall that the purpose of *IBM SPSS by Example* is to "cut to the chase" and discuss only material that is typically important in performing a well-planned and -analyzed experiment. Therefore, some statistics, tests, and graphs that are presented in standard computer output are not discussed.

Before continuing, there is one bit of housekeeping we need to cover; we assume that you've installed the sample data sets on your computer, as described in Chapter 1 in the section "Downloading Sample SPSS Data Files." What? You haven't installed the sample data? Go back. "Do not pass Go. Do not collect $200."

You've installed the sample data files now? Great! Welcome back. Now that you have the sample data stored on your computer, you are ready to proceed.

Describing Quantitative Data

Quantitative data are numeric data on which computations such as addition and subtraction make sense. In SPSS terminology, quantitative data is called "scale" data. Statisticians usually use the word quantitative instead of scale to refer to this type of numeric data, and in this description, we use them interchangeably. Furthermore, there are additional delineations of quantitative data that SPSS does not mention or use. For example, quantitative data are often characterized as the following:

- *Continuous values*: Data values fall along a continuum. Examples are weight or length.

- *Discrete values*: Data are defined as a countable number of possible outcomes. Examples are number of children in your family, number of years of schooling, and so on.

- *Interval values*: Data where the difference between two observed values is meaningful. For example, in the Fahrenheit temperature scale, the difference between 0 and 10 degrees is the same "distance" as the difference between 90 and 100 degrees.

- *Ratio Values*: Interval data with the additional restriction that it has a natural zero (0) value. For example, the weight of an object has a natural value of 0, meaning no weight (absence of any weight). (Whereas a 0 temperature, in Celsius or Fahrenheit, does not mean the absence of temperature.)

Examples of the types of data that would fall into the quantitative (scale) category include the following:

- Rainfall (continuous, ratio)
- Child's temperature recoded upon arrival at an Emergency Room (continuous, interval)

- Number of peaches harvested from each tree (discrete, ratio)
- Years of smoking (discrete, ratio)

It makes sense to talk about the average value of each of these variables (even if there is no such thing as a part of a peach growing on a tree).

SIDEBAR
The determination of whether arithmetic computation for the data makes sense is a key component in the decision regarding whether your data are quantitative or not.

Observe the Distribution of Your Data

Since many common statistical procedures assume normally distributed data, you may want to examine your data set to determine whether it fits this criterion. There are a number of ways to check the normality of a set of observed values. These include both numerical and graphical techniques. This chapter discusses several numerical methods used to understand your data's distribution, and graphical techniques are discussed in Chapter 3: Creating and Using Graphs.

Testing for Normality

SPSS provides the Kolmogorov-Smirnov and Shapiro-Wilk tests in the Explore procedure to test the hypothesis that the distribution of a set of data is normal. The hypotheses used in testing for normality are as follows:

H_0: The data follow a normal distribution.

H_a: The data do not follow a normal distribution.

If a test does not reject normality, this suggests that a parametric procedure that assumes normality (e.g., a t-test) can be safely used. However, it is always a good idea to also examine data graphically in addition to the formal tests for normality.

SIDEBAR
The term *normal distribution* used here and in the remainder of the book indicates that histograms of data sampled from this distribution will approximate a bell-shaped curve. The normal distribution is also referred to as a Gaussian distribution (after the mathematician Karl Friedrich Gauss). We will refer to data from a normal distribution as "normal data." Figure 2.6 shown in a later example in this chapter, shows a bell-shaped curve fitted to data.

Tips and Caveats for Quantitative Data

How to Use the Information About Normality

Given the fact that there is a normality assumption associated with many statistical procedures (e.g., the t-test), you'd think it was a "make-or-break" criterion for your analysis. This is not necessarily the case. In fact, true normality is usually a myth. What is important is to ascertain whether your data show a serious departure from normality. Data showing a moderate departure from normality can usually be used in parametric procedures without loss of integrity. However, if your data are not close to normal and your sample sizes are small, you should consider using a nonparametric statistical test that does not assume normality. Nonparametric tests are discussed in Chapter 8: Nonparametric Analysis

Procedures. For further discussion of the normality assumption in the context of the *t*-test, see Chapter 4: Comparing One or Two Means Using the *t*-Test. Other reasons you might choose a nonparametric procedure are given by Fay and Proschan (2010) and Sawilowsky (2005).

If Data Are Not Normally Distributed, Don't Report the Mean

Describe distinctly nonnormal data with the median and range or interquartile range (Lang & Secic, 1997). Another way to report this type of data is by using a Tukey five-number summary consisting of the minimum, 25th percentile, 50th percentile, 75th percentile, and maximum. This five-number summary is the basis for the boxplot (illustrated in Chapter 3: Creating and Using Graphs).

When in Doubt, Report the *SD* Rather Than the *SEM*

When reporting descriptive statistics, there is sometimes a dilemma regarding whether to report the standard deviation (*SD*) or standard error of the mean (*SEM*), which is the *SD* divided by the square root of the sample size. You should report the *SD* if you are describing the variability of the data and the *SEM* if you are reporting the variability of the mean. Some texts and journals recommend that you always report the *SD* since the *SEM* can be calculated easily from the *SD* and sample size and the *SEM* may give an uninformed reader a false impression about the variability of the data. If you are unsure, the safe bet is to report the *SD*. (In either case, you should make it clear which statistic you are reporting.)

Use Tables and Figures to Report Many Descriptive Statistics

If you are reporting two or three descriptive measurements in a report or article, we recommend that you include the statistics in the text. However, if you have more than two or three measurements, consider using a table or graph.

Break Down Descriptive Statistics by Group

Descriptive statistics should be broken down by group (i.e., calculated separately for each group) for populations composed of distinct groups rather than looking at aggregate data. For example, a mixture of normal subpopulations will usually not have a normal appearance, and an overall mean or standard deviation may be meaningless.

Quantitative Data Description Examples

The following examples illustrate techniques for describing quantitative data. The results include both statistics and graphs (when the techniques covered include a graph or graphs). More detailed information on creating graphs is included in the upcoming Chapter 3: Creating and Using Graphs.

Example 2.1

Quantitative Data With an Unusual Value

Describing the Problem

Hypothetical data from several branch banks in Southern California contain information on how many IRAs (individual retirement accounts) were set up in 19 locations during a 3-month period. The variable is called *IRASetup* (labeled IRA Setup). These data are counts and are appropriately classified as quantitative data since, for example, it makes sense to calculate a mean number of accounts per bank. Before calculating and reporting the mean or other parametric measures of these values, you may want to assess the normality of the data. One way to do that is to perform a statistical test.

SPSS Step-By-Step. EXAMPLE 2.1: Quantitative Data With an Unusual Value

Use the following steps to obtain the output for the IRA data analysis:

1. Open the data set IRA.SAV (**File/Open**). The data for this example are shown in Table 2.1.

2. Select **Analyze/Descriptive Statistics/Explore**. . . .

3. Select the *IRASetup* variable from the dependent list by clicking on the variable name *IRASetup* and then clicking on the arrow next to the Dependent List box (or click on the variable name, *IRASetup*, and drag it into the Dependent List box). (See Figure 2.1.)

4. Click on the Plots . . . button and select the "Normality plots with tests" checkbox and "Histogram" and click Continue. (See Figure 2.2.)

5. Click OK. Table 2.2 is displayed (along with other output).

The "Sig." values in the "Tests of Normality" table are the *p*-values based on testing the null hypothesis that the data are normally distributed. Both tests are designed to determine whether the observed data closely fit the shape of a normal curve. The Shaprio-Wilk test result is significant ($p = 0.019$), which suggests that the data are not normal, while the Kolmogorov-Smimov test result is nonsignificant ($p = 0.136$). This leaves you without a convincing argument one way or another.

To further examine these data (and perhaps understand the reasons for the discrepancy), you can visualize the distribution of the data

Table 2.1 Data in the IRA.SAV Data Set

Location	IRASetup
U	10
U	12
U	15
R	14
U	16
U	14
R	13
U	12
U	16
R	12
U	13
R	14
R	15
R	17
R	5
R	14
U	13
R	14
U	11

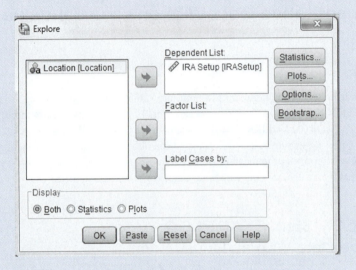

Figure 2.1 Select IRASetup for the Dependent List

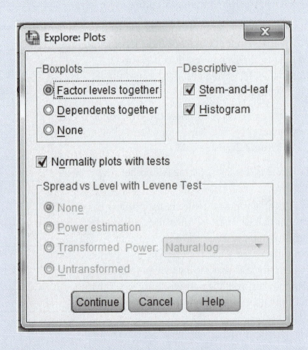

Figure 2.2 Completed Dialog Box for Normality Tests

Table 2.2   Test for Normality on IRA Data

	Tests of Normality					
	Kolmogorov-Smirnov[a]			Shapiro-Wilk		
	Statistic	df	Sig.	Statistic	df	Sig.
IRA Setup	.173	19	.136	.878	19	.019

[a]Lilliefors Significance Correction

using graphical displays such as a histogram, a normal Q-Q plot, a detrended normal Q-Q plot, and a box-and-whiskers plot. (See Figure 2.3.)

Here is a brief explanation of how to interpret each of these plots in the context of normality:

- *Histogram* (upper left). When a histogram's shape approximates a bell curve, it suggests that the data may have come from a normal population.

- *Q-Q plot* (upper right). A quantile-quantile (Q-Q plot) is a graph used to display the degree to which the quantiles of a reference (known) distribution (in this case, the normal distribution) differ from the sample quantiles of the data. When the data fit the reference distribution, then the points will lie in a tight random scatter around the reference line. For the IRA data, the curvature of the points in the plot indicates a possible departure from normality, and the point lying outside the overall pattern of points indicates a possible outlier.

- *Detrended normal Q-Q plot* (lower left): A version of the Q-Q plot that shows the differences between the observed normal and observed values under the assumption of normality. When the data are normal, the points cluster in a random horizontal band around zero. As in the Q-Q plot, the curve, and the one outlying point may be of concern when assessing normality for these data.

- *Boxplot* (lower right). A boxplot that is symmetric with the median line in approximately the center of the box and with symmetric whiskers somewhat longer than the subsections of the center box suggests that the data may have come from a normal distribution.

All four of these plots for *IRASetup* indicate something unusual. There is one small value (Case 15, as indicated by the boxplot) that is a potential outlier (unusually small). Suppose that after carefully examining the source documentation for these data, you discover that the branch location for Case 15 was closed for 21 days because of localized wildfires. After this type of discovery, and observing that *IRASetup* = 5 for that branch you might be justified in excluding this branch location from your analysis.

6. To eliminate the outlying value (*IRASetup* = 5), return to the data editor by clicking Windows and IRA.SAV or choosing the IRA.SAV window using the SPSS icon at the bottom of your screen and select **Data/Select Cases** . . . and select the option "If condition is satisfied. . . ." Click on the "If . . ." button. In the formula text box, enter the expression "*IRASetup* > 5" (without quotes). (See Figure 2.4.)

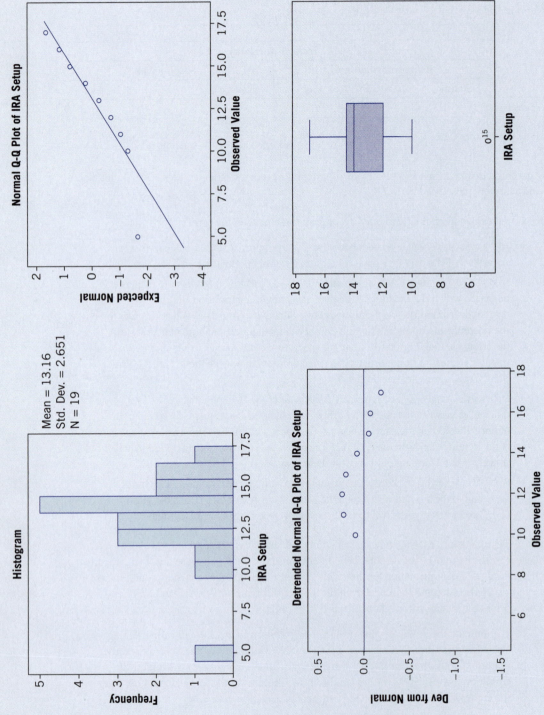

Figure 2.3 Plots Used to Assess Normality Using *IRA Setup* Data

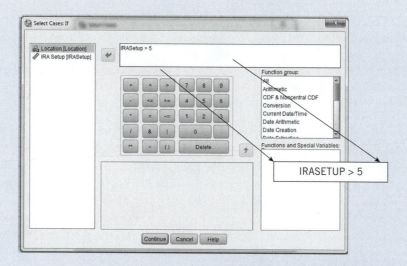

Figure 2.4 Select if Condition Is Satisfied

Click Continue and OK. A slash appears in the IRA data file next to record 15, indicating that the record will not be included in subsequent analyses. (See Figure 2.5.) (For more information about filtering cases, see "Transforming, Recoding, and Categorizing Your Data" in Appendix A.)

27 :		Location	IRASetup	filter_$	
1		U	10	1	
2		U	12	1	
3		U	15	1	
4		R	14	1	
5		U	16	1	
6		U	14	1	
7		R	13	1	
8		U	12	1	
9		U	16	1	
10		R	12	1	
11		U	13	1	
12		R	14	1	
13		R	15	1	
14		R	17	1	
15		R	5	0	
16		R	14	1	
17		U	13	1	
18		R	14	1	
19		U	11	1	

Note the slash on record 15 indicating that it will be ignored during subsequent analyses.

Figure 2.5 Slash Indicates Item 15 Will Not Be Used in Analyses

7. To display the output based on the revised data select **Analyze/Descriptive Statistics/Explore** . . . and OK. (SPSS remembers your previous selection of the variable and options.) Locate the histogram in the output and double-click on it. A Chart Editor will appear. From this editor, select the menu options **Elements/Show Distribution Curve**, and Close. Select **File/Close** to close the Chart Editor. The revised histogram with a superimposed normal curve is displayed in Figure 2.6.

When the outlying data value is excluded from the data set and the data are reanalyzed, the Shapiro-Wilk test yields a *p*-value of 0.73, and the Kolmogorov-Smirnov *p*-value is greater than 0.2, indicating that there is no reason to be concerned about the normality assumption. Furthermore, after the removal of the extreme data value, the revised histogram looks considerably more normal (as does the boxplot). The histogram for the revised data is shown in Figure 2.6. The superimposed normal curve helps you assess the normality assumption. Although not a perfect fit, the histogram suggests that it is reasonable to assume that the data are from a normal population. The boxplot, not shown here, is relatively symmetric and typical of normally distributed data containing no outliers or extreme values. The other plots also suggest normality. The point of this example is to show that it is important to not only look at statistics and tests but also to look at graphical displays based on your data.

8. To remove the "Select cases" criterion select **Data/Select Cases** . . . and select the option "All cases" and OK.

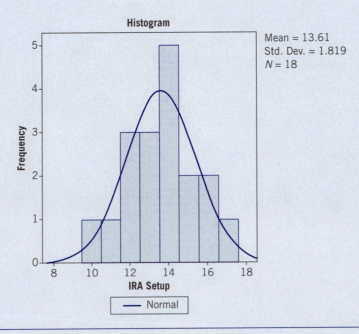

Histogram

Mean = 13.61
Std. Dev. = 1.819
N = 18

Figure 2.6   Revised Histogram With Normal Curve to Assess Normality in the *IRA Setup* Data

Once you are satisfied that a normality assumption makes sense for your data, you can use statistics such as means, standard deviations, and so on to describe your data. In the example here, note that we were justified in removing the extreme value. In addition to reporting the sample mean of the data, you may also want to report a confidence interval. For the modified dataset in this example, a 95% CI (confidence interval) on the mean is given in the Descriptives table as (lower bound, upper bound) or [12.71, 14.52]. Alternatively, you may also choose to report 13.6 ± 1.8 (mean ± *SD*). Why should you choose one over the other? If you wish to report the *precision* of your estimate, you should report the 95% CI. The interpretation of the 95% CI is that if you repeated this experiment many times, the true mean would fall within the calculated endpoints approximately 95% of the time. If you want to describe the variability of your data, you would use the expression mean ± *SD* (see Lang & Secic, 1997).

SIDEBAR
This example does not imply that you should always remove extreme values from your data set. You should carefully consider any unusual values and determine whether they are valid observations before removing them from your analysis. (It is a good practice to report any data values excluded from an analysis in your write-up and to justify your actions.)

Reporting Results for EXAMPLE 2.1: Quantitative Data With an Unusual Value

The results for the analyses on the IRA data could be reported in the following ways:

Narrative for the Methods Section

"One value in the data for IRA setups was eliminated because the bank was closed for 21 days during the evaluation period. Descriptive statistics were calculated on the remaining 18 values."

Narrative for the Results Section

"IRA setups averaged 13.6 per branch (*SD* = 1.8, *N* = 18)."

or

"The mean (± *SD*) IRA setups was 13.6 (± 1.8)."

If you are reporting the precision of your estimate, you could state the following:

"The mean was 13.6 (95% CI = 12.71 to 14.52) IRA setups per branch."

If you decide that you want to analyze the data *without* removing the extreme value and therefore not make a normality assumption, you could report your findings using the median and interquartile range. For example,

"The number of IRA setups per branch ranged from 5 to 17 setups with a median (interquartile range) of 14 (3)."

Example 2.2

Quantitative Data by Groups

Describing the Problem

A survey was administered to 79 clinic patients to measure their satisfaction with clinic services. Two versions of the survey were randomly assigned to the participants. The following demographic information (by group) is shown in Table 2.3. This table is not created in SPSS, but is created from information gathered from multiple SPSS analyses. The upcoming example will show how to compile the information needed to create this table.

The purpose of this table is to compare the respondents to the two types of surveys on several important demographic variables. The p-values refer to a test of the null hypothesis that the means are equal (see the two-sample t-test examples in Chapter 4: Comparing One or Two Means Using the t-Test). In this table, it appears that the number of years of schooling was significantly higher for those who took the old survey.

Researchers disagree over whether to include the "p-Value" column in tables of this type. The controversy arises in part over the known problem of performing multiple tests within the same experiment. For a discussion of p-values, see Chapter 1.

As described in Chapter 1, when multiple p-values are used in an analysis, it is good practice to use Bonferroni-adjusted significance criteria. In this case, the adjustment would entail using the p-value $0.05/4 = 0.0125$ as the rejection criterion for these tests. Thus, the only significant result in this table would be for the schooling variable (where the reported p-value is 0.003).

Table 2.3 Table Reporting Group Statistics: Baseline Characteristics of Patients in Study by Group

	Mean (*SD*)		
	Old Survey	New Survey	
Characteristic	N = 34	N = 45	*p*-Value
Age	34.3 (11.6)	30.2 (9.21)	0.08
Schooling	12.2 (2.43)	10.5 (2.33)	0.003
Temperature	99.1 (1.24)	99.5 (1.51)	0.27
Minutes	532 (337)	429 (309)	0.16

SPSS Step-By-Step. EXAMPLE 2.2: Quantitative Data by Groups

To calculate descriptive statistics needed to compile the information in Table 2.3 follow these steps in SPSS.

1. Open the data set SURVEY.SAV and select **Analyze/Descriptive Statistics/Explore**. . . .

2. Select *Age, Years of Schooling (Edu), Arrival Temperature (Temp),* and *Minutes in Clinic (Stayminutes)* for the dependent variables and *Survey Version* for the factor list. Click OK to produce output that includes the means and standard deviations. This output is pretty messy and hard to read.

3. To calculate the *p*-values needed for the table, select **Analyze/Compare Means/ Independent-Samples T Test** and select *Age, Years of Schooling (Edu), Arrival Temperature (Temp),* and *Minutes in Clinic (Stayminutes)* as the "Test Variables" and *Survey Version* as the "Grouping Variable." This dialog box is shown in Figure 2.7.

   Click on the "Define groups" button and enter 1 and 2 for the group values as shown in Figure 2.8.

   Click Continue and OK. In the resulting "Independent Samples" table, the *p*-values for each comparison are listed in the "Equal variances assumed" row in the "Sig. 2-tailed" column. For example, the *p*-value for the comparison of mean ages by group, $p = 0.084$ (reported as 0.08 in Table 2.3) is shown in Table 2.4.

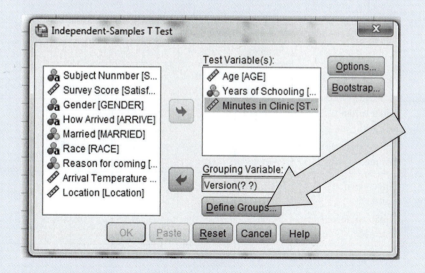

Figure 2.7   Select the Define Groups Button

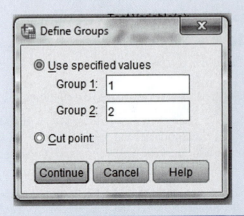

Figure 2.8   Define Groups

More about the *t*-test and this table is discussed in Chapter 4: Comparing One or Two Means Using the *t*-Test.

Table 2.4   Results of *t*-Tests

Independent Samples Test						
		Levene's Test for Equality of Variances				
		F	Sig.	t	df	Sig. (2-tailed)
Age	Equal variances assumed	3.543	.064	1.749	77	.084
	Equal variances not assumed			1.694	61.455	.095
Years of Schooling	Equal variances assumed	2.566	.113	3.045	77	.003
	Equal variances not assumed			3.028	69.606	.003
Minutes in Clinic	Equal variances assumed	.014	.907	1.411	77	.162
	Equal variances not assumed			1.394	67.630	.168

Narrative for the Methods Section

> "The two versions of the survey were randomly assigned to patients as they registered at the clinic."

Narrative for the Results Section

When there are several means to report, it is often clearer to the reader if you report the results in a table such as the one shown in Table 2.3. If you use a Bonferroni-adjusted p-value for your rejection criterion, you should include a statement such as the following:

> "To maintain the $\alpha = .05$ significance level for the table comparisons using a Bonferroni adjustment, a p-value must be less than $p = 0.0125$ (i.e., 0.05/4) to be considered statistically significant."

In either case, the *schooling* difference remains the only significant comparison. We assume that the observed difference of 1.7 years of schooling is a meaningful difference. For more information about using effect size to interpret this difference, see Chapter 4.

Describing Categorical Data

Categorical variables record a characteristic about a subject or object such as race, gender, presence of a disease, or the color of a car model. Think of the word *categories* when you're analyzing categorical data. This data type is sometimes called *qualitative* and is further divided by the terms *nominal* (order not important) and *ordinal* (having order). We will assume categorical data to be nominal unless specified. In this section, two types of descriptive analyses are illustrated for categorical data. They are as follows:

- Frequency tables
- Crosstabulations

Examples illustrate methods for examining categorical data and reporting your results. (Categories can be defined using number or character codes.) Categorical variables include the following:

- Presence of a disease (1 = yes, 0 = no)
- Method of delivery (USPS, UPS, FEDEX, OTHER)
- Marital status (1 = married, 2 = single never married, 3 = single divorced, 4 = single widowed)
- Stage of a disease (1, 2, 3, or 4)

Each of these variables is an observation that places the subject or entity into two or more categories. When we observe summaries of these variables, they are typically given as counts (the number of subjects placed into each category) and/or the corresponding percentages.

Considerations for Examining Categorical Data

Notice in the examples above that some categories have order and some do not. For example, in the marital status variable above, there are four unordered categories, and although these categories are recorded in the data set as numbers (1 to 4), these numbers are simply codes and are not meaningful numerically. They should not be interpreted as implying an ordering of the categories, nor should they be used in arithmetic calculations (e.g., mean, etc.). For the purposes of analysis, these categorical data are reported as counts, frequencies, or percentages of subjects falling into various categories. In the marital status example, the categories have no order and are thus nominal variables. On the other hand, stage of cancer (from 1 to 4), rank in the military, and finish order in a race (first place, second place, etc.) are ordinal categorical variables since these categories have a logical order.

Tips and Caveats

When Should Categorical Variables Be Treated as Quantitative Data?

Sometimes, ordinal data such as responses using a Likert scale (1 = *strongly disagree,* 2 = *disagree,* 3 = *neutral,* 4 = *agree,* 5 = *strongly agree*) are treated as quantitative data. As a general guideline, in order for the mean and other arithmetically obtained quantities (e.g., standard deviation) to make sense, it must be reasonable to assume that the differences between any two categories are equal. For example, if the categories are 1, 2, 3, 4, 5, then it must be reasonable to consider the difference between categories 2 and 3 to be the same as the difference between 4 and 5, and so on. Therefore, we recommend that it is rarely the case that you treat categorical data as quantitative since the assumption of equal distance between categories cannot usually be assumed.

Describing Categorical Data Examples

The following examples illustrate techniques for assessing and describing categorical data using statistics and graphs.

Example 2.3

Quantitative Data With Unusual Values

Describing the Problem

Suppose you are interested in exploring the variables in a data set from the U.S. Department of Energy (2014) containing fuel economy information on 2014 model year automobiles. Your first strategy might be to look for unusually large or small data values by finding the minimum and maximum for each quantitative variable of interest.

SPSS Step-By-Step. EXAMPLE 2.3:
Quantitative Data With Unusual Values

1. Open the data set CARS2014.SAV and select **Analyze/Descriptive Statistics/Descriptives**. . . .

2. Select the variables *Eng_Displ, CityMPG,* and *HwyMPG,* and *Num_Gears*. (See Figure 2.9.)

3. Click OK, and the table in Table 2.5 is displayed.

The results are shown in Table 2.5 for four of the variables. In this output, the minimum value for the *Num_Gears* (*Number of Gears*) variable is 1. This seems odd that a car would have only one gear, but by examining the data, it can be seen that several cars have Continuously Variable Transmission (CVT) which do not have typical gears like most cars. The data are correct, since CVT transmissions are different from conventional transmissions. That information might be handled differently when looking

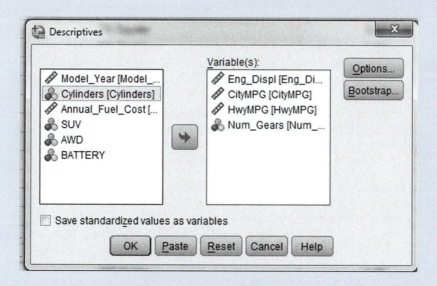

Figure 2.9   Select Variables to Analysis in Descriptives Procedure

Table 2.5   Searching for Unusual Values

Descriptive Statistics

	N	Minimum	Maximum	Mean	Std. Deviation
Eng_Displ	1155	1.00	8.40	3.3497	1.39504
CityMPG	1155	8	53	19.85	5.678
HwyMPG	1155	13	48	27.48	6.360
Num_Gears	1155	1	9	6.17	1.441
Valid N (listwise)	1155				

Source: Reprint Courtesy of International Business Machines Corporation, © International Business Machines Corporation

at the transmission data. In fact, we might want to (at least temporarily) label the cars with CVT transmission as "missing" when calculating statistics involving an analysis concerning the number of transmission gears. If your study deals only with vehicles with conventional geared transmissions, you may want to exclude the CVT cars from your analysis. (Assigning missing values and selecting cases in SPSS is discussed in Appendix A: A Brief Tutorial for Using SPSS for Windows.)

Continuing with the automobile data example, suppose you want to compare *CityMPG* between SUVs and non-SUVs in the 2014 automobile data set (excluding hybrids and CVT transmission vehicles), and you want to investigate whether the normality assumption makes sense for each group. The following shows how to look at these data:

4. To set the *Num_Gears* missing value at 1, make sure you are in the CARS2014 data window and click on the Variable View tab at the bottom left. When the Variable View is displayed, click on the cell for *Num_Gears* in the Missing column. Click on the ellipses (. . .) and enter 1 as a discrete missing value as shown in Figure 2.10 and click OK.

5. As in step 1, select **Analyze/Descriptive Statistics/Descriptives** . . . and OK, and examine the Minimum value for *Num_Gears*. It is now 4 instead of 1, and the number of non-missing cases for that variable is now 1108 instead of 1155 because all cars where *Num_Gears* = 1 have been left out of that calculation as shown in Table 2.6. (Setting this missing value for Num_Gears did not change the means of the other variables.)

6. To examine the data further, create side-by-side boxplots of the car data comparing SUVs and non-SUVs. Select **Graphs/Legacy Dialogs/Boxplot** . . . , select the

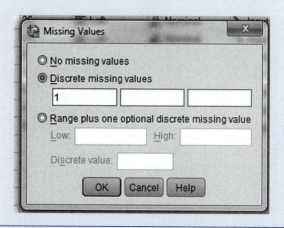

Figure 2.10   Indicate Missing Value

Table 2.6   Revised Analysis of Car Data

Descriptive Statistics

	N	Minimum	Maximum	Mean	Std. Deviation
Eng_Displ	1155	1.00	8.40	3.3497	1.39504
CityMPG	1155	8	53	19.85	5.678
HwyMPG	1155	13	48	27.48	6.360
Num_Gears	1108	4	9	6.39	.990
Valid N (listwise)	1108				

"Simple" option, and choose the radio button for "Summaries for groups of cases." (Other graph options are covered in Chapter 3: Creating and Using Graphs.)

7. Click the Define button. Select *CityMPG* as the "Variable," *SUV* as the "Category Axis," and Carline for "Label Cases by" as shown in Figure 2.11.

8. Click OK to produce the comparative boxplots in Figure 2.12.

The graph in Figure 2.12 shows side-by-side boxplots that indicate that some observations (on the high end of *CityMPG*) are indicated as outliers (marked as an "o") and some as extreme values (marked as an "*"). An outlier is defined (in SPSS) as a value from 1.5 to 3 interquartile ranges (IQRs) beyond the 75th (or below the 25th) percentile, and an extreme value is greater than 3 IQRs beyond the 75th (or below the 25th) percentile. Figure 2.12 shows that there are a number of outliers for non-SUV automobiles,

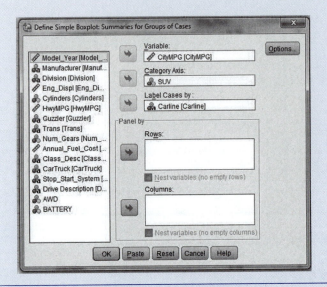

Figure 2.11 Select Variable for (Legacy) Comparative Boxplot

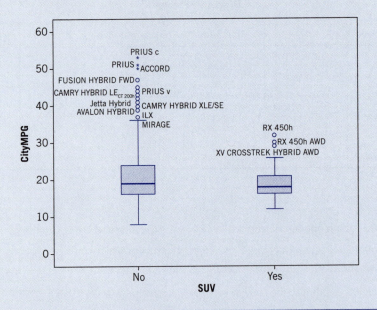

Figure 2.12 Side-By-Side Boxplots Showing Outliers and Extreme Values by Group

but the data for SUVs are less variable, with only a few extreme (high *CityMPG*) values. (Note that the outliers on the chart are hybrid models.)

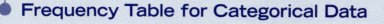

Example 2.4

Frequency Table for Categorical Data

Describing the Problem

In a survey of 79 patients at a clinic, information was collected on how they arrived (car, bus, or walked). You may want to examine the data using a frequency table to report the number and percentage of patients who arrived using each travel method along with a bar chart showing a visualization of these percentages. To display this information, follow the steps in this example:

SPSS Step-By-Step. EXAMPLE 2.4:
Frequency Table for Categorical Data

1. Open the data set SURVEY.SAV and select **Analyze/Descriptive Statistics/ Frequencies**. . . .

2. Select *How Arrived* (*ARRIVED*) as the variable.

3. Click on the Charts button and select **Bar Chart, Percentages, Continue**, and OK. See Figure 2.13.

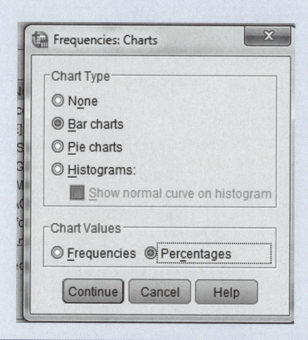

Figure 2.13   Choose Options for Bar Chart

Table 2.7 displays the frequency table produced by SPSS for this data set, and Figure 2.14 shows the associated bar chart. Note that the bar chart information is displayed in percentages rather than counts. We could optionally have produced a similar chart using frequencies (counts).

Table 2.7   Frequency Table for *How Arrived*

How Arrived

		Frequency	Percent	Valid Percent	Cumulative Percent
Valid	BUS	11	13.9	13.9	13.9
	CAR	66	83.5	83.5	97.5
	WALK	2	2.5	2.5	100.0
	Total	79	100.0	100.0	

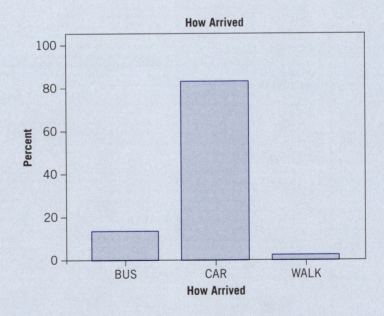

Figure 2.14   Bar Chart for the *How Arrived* Variable

In Table 2.7, the frequency is the number of patients who arrived using each method of transportation. The percentage (and valid percentage, which is the percentage after removing missing values) tells you the percentage of patients arriving by each method. It is clear both from the frequency table and the bar chart that most patients arrived by car.

Reporting Results for Frequency Data

Narrative for the Methods Section

"Arrival methods were examined by finding the number of patients arriving at the clinic using a car, bus, or by walking."

Narrative for the Results Section

"Patients arrived by car 83.5% of the time (66 of 79), 13.9% by bus (11 of 79), and 2.5% by walking (2 of 79). (Round-off error makes the total slightly under 100%.)"

Example 2.5

Crosstabulation of Categorical Variables

Describing the Problem

Using the 2014 automobile data, suppose you want to crosstabulate two variables. Table 2.8 contains a crosstabulation of the variables *SUV* (sport utility vehicle) and *AWD* (all-wheel drive). Specific statistical tests to analyze this type of table are discussed in Chapter 6: Analysis of Categorical Data. In this example, we are only interested in the descriptive information contained in the table.

SPSS Step-By-Step. EXAMPLE 2.5:
Crosstabulation of Categorical Variables

Follow these steps to create the crosstabulation output from the CARS2014 data set:

1. Open the data set CARS2014.SAV and select **Analyze/Descriptive Statistics/ Crosstabs**. . . .

2. From the dialog box, select the variable named *SUV* as the row variable and *AWD* as the column variable as shown in Figure 2.15.

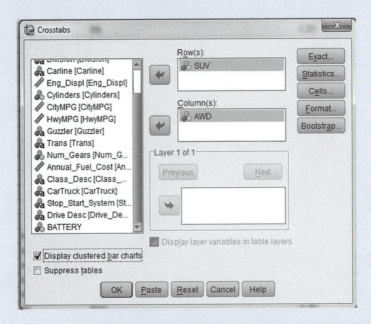

Figure 2.15   Select Variables for Crostabulation Analysis

3. Click on the Cells button and select **Row, Column, and Total Percentages** as shown in Figure 2.16. Click Continue.

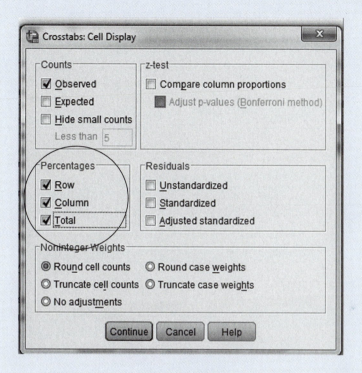

Figure 2.16   Select Cell Options for Crosstabulation Example

4. To display the bar chart, select the "Display clustered bar charts" checkbox (as shown in Figure 2.15).

5. Click OK to display the results as shown in Table 2.8.

Observe that 33.0% (95 of 288) of the SUVs in this data set have all-wheel drive. Also note that 35.1% (95 of 271) of all-wheel-drive vehicles are SUVs and that 8.2% (95 of 1,155) of all vehicles are SUVs with all-wheel drive. A bar chart for these data is shown in Figure 2.17.

This bar chart allows you to visualize the relationship between SUVs and whether they have all-wheel drive. In this chart, it is visually clear that most non-SUVs do not have all-wheel drive, while a larger percentage of the vehicles classified as SUVs have all-wheel drive. You can also see that there are many more non-SUVs than there are SUVs in this data set.

Table 2.8 Output for Crosstabulation Example

SUV * AWD Crosstabulation

			AWD		Total
			No	Yes	
SUV	No	Count	691	176	867
		% within SUV	79.7%	20.3%	100.0%
		% within AWD	78.2%	64.9%	75.1%
		% of Total	59.8%	15.2%	75.1%
	Yes	Count	193	95	288
		% within SUV	67.0%	33.0%	100.0%
		% within AWD	21.8%	35.1%	24.9%
		% of Total	16.7%	8.2%	24.9%
Total		Count	884	271	1155
		% within SUV	76.5%	23.5%	100.0%
		% within AWD	100.0%	100.0%	100.0%
		% of Total	76.5%	23.5%	100.0%

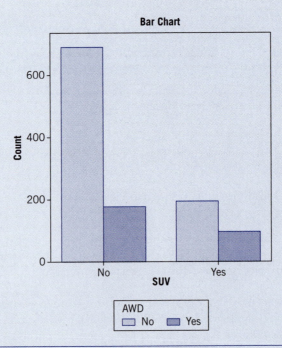

Figure 2.17 Clustered Bart Chart for SUV Data

Reporting Crosstabulation Results

To describe the information in a frequency table or crosstabulation in your report or article, you should always include counts along with percentages (Lang & Secic, 1997). For example, your description (**from the information in the crosstabulation above**) might be as follows:

Narrative for the Methods Section

"The relationship between model type and all-wheel drive was examined using crosstabulation."

Narrative for the Results Section

"This table shows that 33.0% (95 of 288) of SUV models and 20.3% (176 of 867) of non-SUV models have all-wheel drive."

SUMMARY

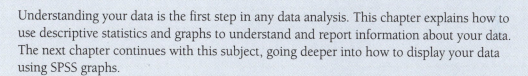

Understanding your data is the first step in any data analysis. This chapter explains how to use descriptive statistics and graphs to understand and report information about your data. The next chapter continues with this subject, going deeper into how to display your data using SPSS graphs.

REFERENCES

American Psychological Association (APA). (2013). *Publication manual of the American Psychological Association* (6th ed.). Washington, DC: Author.

Fay, M. P., & Proschan, M. A. (2010). Wilcoxon-Mann-Whitney or *t*-test? On assumptions for hypothesis tests and multiple interpretations of decision rules. *Statistics Surveys, 4,* 1.

Lang, T. A., & Secic, M. (1997). *How to report statistics in medicine.* Philadelphia, PA: American College of Physicians.

Sawilowsky, S. S. (2005). Misconceptions leading to choosing the t test over the Wilcoxon Mann-Whitney U test for Shift in Location Parameter. *Journal of Modern Applied Statistical Methods, 4*(2), 598–600.

U.S. Department of Energy. (2014). *Model 2014 model year fuel economy data.* Retrieved from http://www.fueleconomy.gov/

Creating and Using Graphs

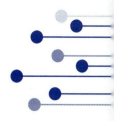

Introduction to SPSS Graphs

Marilyn vos Savant made it into the Guinness Book of World Records as the person with the highest IQ ever recorded. She once said about statistics that they "can be used to support or undercut almost any argument." Another brainy person (Albert Einstein) said, "Everything should be made as simple as possible, but not simpler." Taking these two ideas together, the purpose of displaying data in the form of a graph should be to simplify information and never to exaggerate or deceive.

Graphs are often used in conjunction with statistical procedures to visually explain or support findings from hypothesis testing or descriptive studies. To that end, this chapter explains how to help you use SPSS to display various types of graphs in ways that tell an accurate story of your data. To use graphs effectively (and truthfully), we present the following guidelines.

Guidelines for Creating and Using Graphs

There are (at least) two uses for graphs. First, they can be useful for identifying problems or interesting data points in your data set. Second, when reporting your results, graphs are useful for clarifying findings. Example 2.1 in the previous chapter illustrated the use of graphs to visualize the distribution of data. This chapter concentrates on the use of graphs as a way of describing statistical results. In general, graphs should be used in reports or presentations as an alternative to tables when the table would contain too many entries to be easily understood or when the graph more clearly illustrates your results. Any number of textbooks and journal specifications contain guidelines relating to the use of graphs (see Tufte, 2001). Here are a few general guidelines for using and reporting graphs:

1. Use simple graphs when possible. Avoid three-dimensional graphs since they often distort your message and contain spurious and distracting information.

2. Label all plots and axes clearly.

3. When creating two or more graphs that will be compared in some way, the range of values for each axis on every graph should be the same. Axes should generally begin with zero if that is the natural minimum. Otherwise, use the

minimum value of the measurement as the minimum value for the axis.

4. Axis intervals on plots should be equal.

5. Many statisticians recommend the use of bar charts instead of pie charts. (In *The Visual Display of Quantitative Data*, Edward Tufte [2001] wrote, "The only worse design than a pie chart is several of them" [p. 178]).

6. Stick with standard charts when possible. Avoid custom complex charts that attempt to display several messages at once.

As IBM SPSS evolved over the years, there have been several generations of graphs included in the program. In the Graph menu, you will find the following graphing methods that allow you to create graphs.

- Chart Builder
- Graphboard Template Chooser
- Legacy Dialog (Plots)

These three graphing methods often create exactly the same plots, but there are also differences. There are some plots that are not available under all graphing methods, and for similar plots across graphing methods, there may be options in one method that are not in the others. Each method has a different flavor and origin. Some of these differences will be illustrated in the upcoming examples. However, our intention is not to illustrate the differences or similarities among graphing methods for each type of graph. Our purpose is to provide you with the basics for producing standard graphs that should enable you to figure out how to create the graphs that are not covered here.

In addition, a number of statistical procedures have plots "built in" to the analyses. This chapter concentrates on the options in the Graph menu. All three types of graphing methods are illustrated in Example 3.1 (scatterplot), and following examples will (mostly) use the Chart Builder to illustrate how to create graphs.

Chart Builder

The SPSS Chart Builder is an interactive window that allows you to drag and click on options to build a chart by specifying variables from your data and features of the chart. When you select **Graphs/Chart Builder** the first time, Figure 3.1 is displayed. This message warns you that the SPSS data types for all of your variables must be set up properly (Scale, Ordinal, or Nominal in SPSS terminology) and that any categorical variables should include category labels. You can select the checkbox "Don't show the dialog again" to avoid seeing this box in the future. If needed, set up the measure types (Scale, Ordinal, or Nominal) for variables by clicking on the "Define Variable Properties" or by selecting the Variable View tab on the data screen.

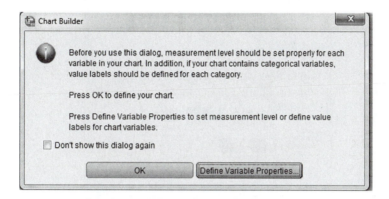

Figure 3.1   Chart Builder Warning Message

When you click OK on the initial Chart Builder Box, the main Chart Builder interactive dialog box appears as shown in Figure 3.2. In upcoming examples, we will illustrate how to select variables, chart types, and options to create the graph you need.

Graphboard Template Chooser

The Graphboard Template Chooser is a second method for creating SPSS charts or graphs. Using this method, you can select from ready-made templates called "Graphboard Visualizations" that contain graphs, charts, and plots, and customize the plots appropriate for your variables. When you select **Graph/Graphboard Template Chooser**, you see the dialog box shown in Figure 3.3. Upcoming examples will illustrate how to use this dialog box.

Legacy Plots

Legacy Dialog plots are, as their name implies, plots that have been around a while and continue to be used in current SPSS versions, although the newer (Chart Builder and Graphboard) options are meant to replace most of these old procedures. However, the older plots are still useful, and some users prefer them to the newfangled options. When you select the **Graphs/Legacy Dialogs** method, sub-menus appear as shown in Figure 3.4.

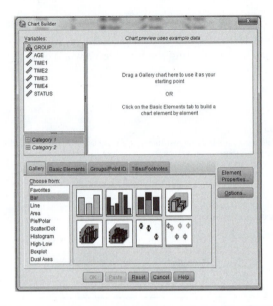

Figure 3.2   Chart Builder Interactive Dialog Box

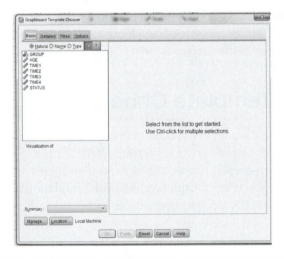

Figure 3.3   Graphboard Template Chooser

Scatterplots

A scatterplot displays the relationship between two scale (quantitative) variables on an x-y coordinate system. It is often used in conjunction with a correlation or regression analysis.

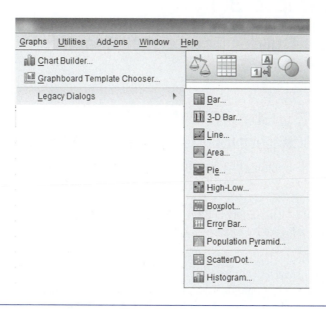

Figure 3.4 Legacy Dialog Plots

Appropriate Applications for a Scatterplot

The following are examples of situations in which a scatterplot might be appropriate to visually display a relationship between variables.

- *Examine the relationship between grades on the midterm Chemistry exam and the final.* You are interested in seeing if people who received high scores on the midterm also get high scores on the final.

- *Does running help SBP?* A number of subjects' Systolic Blood Pressures (SBP) are measured at baseline. Over a few weeks, you observe average time spent on a treadmill and observe differences in SBP. Is the amount of time spent on the treadmill related to differences in SBP?

- *Are opinions about welfare related to age?* You want to visualize this relationship to see if older people are more favorable to a proposed change than younger people.

Design Considerations for a Scatterplot

The two variables of interest in a scatterplot should be scale variables or at least ordinal. If you want to test hypotheses about the existence of a linear relationship between two variables, they should both be scale (quantitative) and normally distributed.

Example 3.1

Chart Builder Scatterplot Example

SPSS Step-By-Step. EXAMPLE 3.1a:
Creating a Scatterplot Using the Chart Builder

In this example, we will examine crime data from Washington, DC for the years from 1978 to 2012.

    1. Open the data DC_CRIME.SAV and select **Graphs/Chart Builder**. If a warning message (as illustrated in Figure 3.1) appears, click OK.

    2. On the Chart Builder Dialog, select **Scatter/Dot** from the list of graph types in the lower left of the dialog. Locate the Simple Scatter option in the list of graph types (the upper left graph icon) and drag that option into the Chart Preview window at the top of the dialog. When you place the Simple Scatter icon in the Chart Preview box, notice that a new section of the dialog appears to the right of the original dialog, labeled "Element Properties." These combined dialog boxes are shown in Figure 3.5.

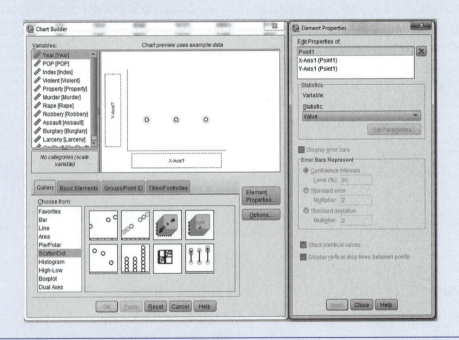

Figure 3.5   Initial Chart Builder Selection for a Simple Scatterplot

3. From the Variables list on the left of the dialog, drag the variable *Year* to the X-axis position at the bottom of the preview graph. Similarly, drag *Assault* to the Y-axis position. The results are shown in Figure 3.6. (The sample plot shown on the screen is not of the actual data at this point.)

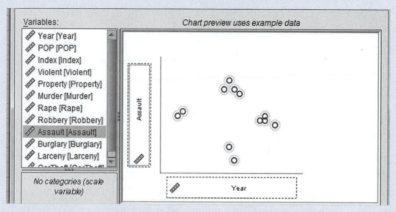

Figure 3.6   Preview of Graph With Year and Assault

4. Click OK. The desired scatterplot is shown in Figure 3.7 where you may observe that Assaults peaked around 1994 and have declined since.

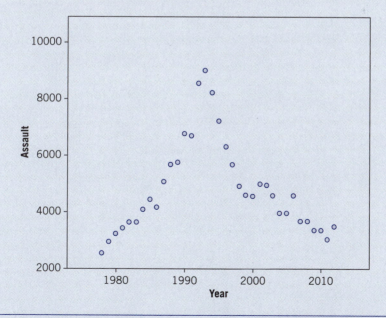

Figure 3.7   Scatterplot of Year by Assault

5. To modify this graph, select **Graph/Chart Builder** again, and the dialog box reappears with all of the information you have previously selected still there. Select the **Title/Footnotes** tab just below the chart viewer and click the Title1 checkbox. A "Content" text box appears to the right where you can enter a title for the chart. Enter "DC Crime Statistics 1978 to 2012" and click Apply and OK. A new version of the chart appears with the title at the top.

6. Other options (tabs) in the Chart Builder dialog allow you to make additional changes. For example, in the Elements Properties dialog (on the right), select Y-axis and change the axis label to "Criminal Assaults." You can select the Basic Elements tab and then Transpose to transpose the x and y axes. There are many more options you can select that are not illustrated here. Once you make any changes and select OK, the new graph appears with those changes made.

Basic chart types supported by Chart Builder include Bar, Line, Area, Pie/Polar, Scatter/Dot, Histogram, Boxplots, and Dual Axes plots. Each of these plots can be edited in a Chart Editor to select other options to modify basic plots. (The Chart Editor is introduced in upcoming examples.)

Graphboard Template Chooser Scatterplot Example

SPSS Step-By-Step. EXAMPLE 3.1b: Creating a Scatterplot Using the Graphboard Template Chooser

1. Using the same data, DC_CRIME.SAV, as in the previous example, select **Graphs/Graphboard Template Chooser**. Click on the Detailed tab at the top left of the dialog and select Scatterplot from the pull-down "Visualization type" options as shown in Figure 3.8.

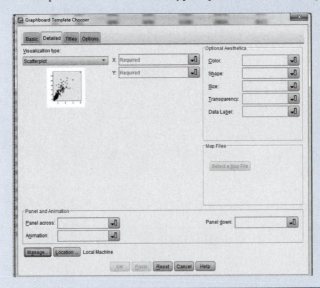

Figure 3.8 Select Type of Plot for Graphboard Template Chooser

2. In the X (Required) option box, select *Year*, and in the Y (Required) option box, select *Assault*.

3. If you click OK, you get the same scatterplot you previously created (Figure 3.7). To illustrate how you can select other options, change the Visualization type to Scatterplot matrix. In the variable selection box, add *Violent, Property, Murder, Rape,* and *Robbery.* Click OK, and a matrix of scatterplots appears, as shown in Figure 3.9.

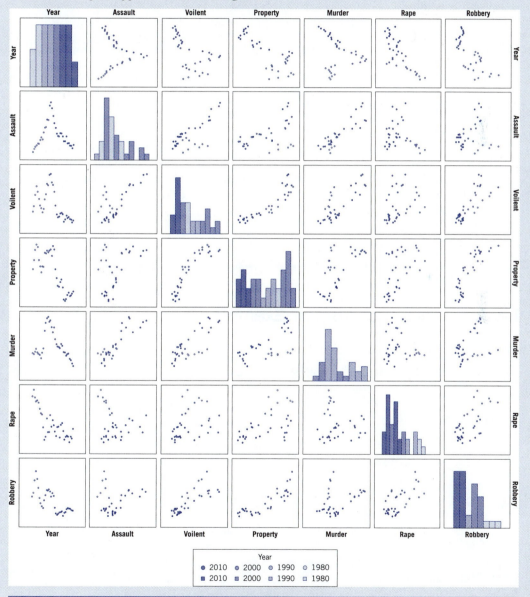

Figure 3.9 Scatterplot Matrix From Graphboard Template Chooser

The histograms on the diagonal for each variable allow you to visualize the distribution of that variable. There are a number of other Graphboard types you can choose in the Template Chooser including the following: Bar, Bar of Counts, Pie, Pie of Counts, 3-D Bar, 3-D Pie, Line, Area, 3-D Area, Path, Ribbon, Surface, Scatterplot, Bubbleplots, 3-D Scatterplot, Scatterplot Matrix, Histogram, Histogram with Normal Distribution, 3-D Histogram, 3-D Density, Dot Plot, 2-D Dot Plot, Boxplot, Heat Map, Parallel, and Maps (Cloropleths).

Instead of showing the same plot over and over again, in the examples here, we use different graphical methods to illustrate different plots. However, not every method can create every plot. For example, a scatterplot matrix similar to the one shown in Figure 3.9 can be designed using the Chart Builder and Legacy Dialog methods, but the option to include the histograms along the dialog is not available in either of these two methods. On the other hand, the grouped scatterplots illustrated in the next example are availale in all three methods. There are too may differences in the capabilities of the three methods to mention in this chapter. If you are unable to create the plot you desire with one method, try the other methods to see if the options you want are available there.

Legacy Dialog Scatterplot Example

SPSS Step-By-Step. EXAMPLE 3.1c: Creating a Scatterplot Using Legacy Dialogs

　　1.　Open the data set named EXAMPLE.SAV and select **Graphs/Legacy Dialogs** . . . and **Scatter/Dot** and you will see the dialog box in Figure 3.10.

　　2.　Select the Simple Scatter icon and click Define. In the resulting dialog box, select *TIME1* as the Y-axis, *AGE* as the X-axis, and *GROUP* as the Set Markers by variable.

　　3.　Click OK to display the graph in Figure 3.11. Notice that the dots appear in three colors keyed to the three categories for the *GROUP* variable.

　　4.　Because it may be difficult to see the group differences by color (if your presentation/ printout is in black and white as it is in this book), edit the chart to change the dots to other shapes. To do this, double-click on the scatterplot to display the Chart Editor. In the Chart Editor, double-click on the scatterplot to display the Chart Properties dialog box shown in Figure 3.12. In this new dialog, click on the Variables tab at the top.

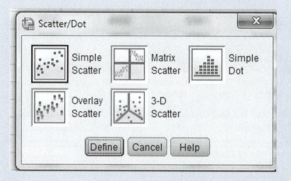

Figure 3.10 Select Type of Scatterplot

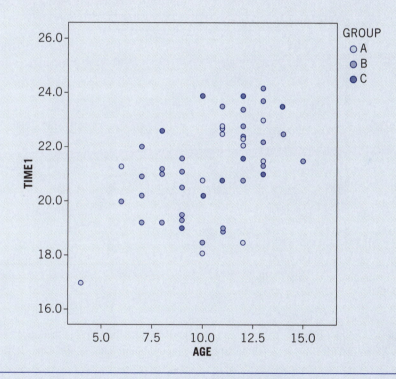

Figure 3.11 Scatterplot With Graphed Data Using Legacy Dialogs

5. In the Variables Tab, click on Style for the Group variable and select the Style: Shape option. Click Apply. A new version of the plot with groups indicated by shaped dots appears. To make the difference more dramatic, click on the Marker tab and change the marker size to 15. Click on Apply, and the plot appears as shown in Figure 3.13.

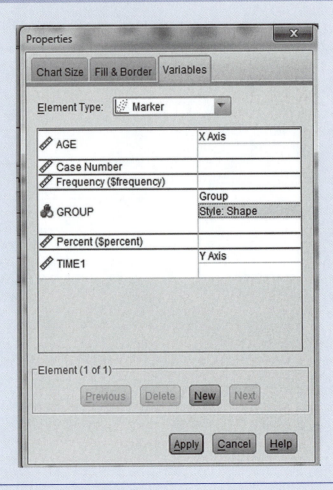

Figure 3.12   Variable Tab in Chart Editor

6.   While still in the Chart Editor, to fit a linear regression line through the scatter of points, select **Elements/Fit Line at Total** to display the regression line. Close the Chart Editor. The resulting graph is shown in in Figure 3.14.

In the upcoming chapter on analysis of covariance, an option to display separate regression lines by groups will be illustrated.

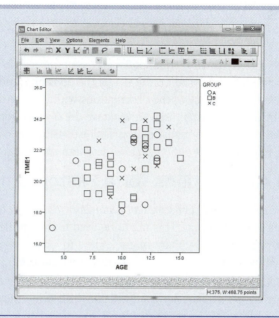

Figure 3.13   Scatterplot With Shaped Dots

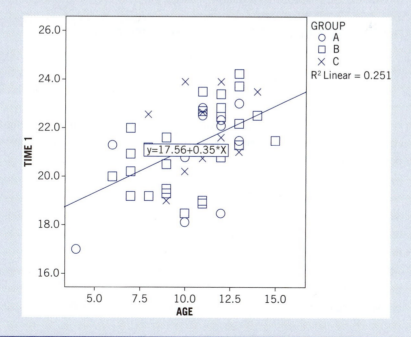

Figure 3.14   Scatterplot With Fitted Regression Line

Histograms

A histogram is composed of bars that illustrate the frequency distribution of a scale (quantitative) variable across (usually) equal divisions (sometimes called bins) of the variable. The width of each bar is based on the size of the divisions, and the height of the bars represents the relative frequency of the observations within those divisions (if the bin widths are equal). A histogram is often used to visualize the distribution of a variable, and in particular to assess the statistical normality of a variable's distribution. A histogram is also a tool for summarizing large amounts of quantitative data into a single graph.

Appropriate Applications for a Histogram

- *Examine the distribution of test scores for a standardized biology test given to all sophomores at a university.* This might be used to determine if there are natural cut-points for assignment of grades and to locate any students with particularly low grades who might need additional tutoring.
- *Visually inspect the distribution of the variable AGE in a data set to determine if the data have an approximate normal distribution.* Knowing the distribution of a variable may impact which statistical test is appropriate for analysis.
- *Display the distribution of salaries for 20,000 employees.* The histogram is a way to visualize large amounts of data in a single graph.

Design Considerations for a Histogram

The display of data as a histogram may be affected by the selection of bin size (width of divisions). Differing bin sizes can change the shape of the histogram. There are several design issues that can lead to misleading interpretations for histograms. These include the following:

- The shape of the histogram is dependent on the bin size, so it is important to choose a bin size that illustrates the distribution of the data. A good starting point is 8 to 12 bins.
- Axes should include a zero base, and there should be a scale on the vertical and horizontal axes.
- 3-D histogram charts may look more interesting, but the volume of taller bars may lead to an incorrect interpretation that they represent more information than is correct.
- All bins (class intervals) should represent the same width. (There is a programming way to create unequal bin sizes in SPSS but be aware that if bin sizes are unequal, the frequency is represented by area and not height.)

When you create a histogram, SPSS chooses bin sizes for you unless you specify a custom bin size. Information on how to select bin size is shown in the following example.

Example 3.2

SPSS Step-By-Step. EXAMPLE 3.2: Creating a Histogram Using the Chart Builder

1. Open the data CARS2014.SAV and select **Graphs/Chart Builder**. If the warning dialog box (Figure 3.1) appears, click OK.

2. Make sure the Gallery tab is selected, and choose Histogram. Drag the Simple Histogram (leftmost icon) into the Chart Preview box as shown in Figure 3.15.

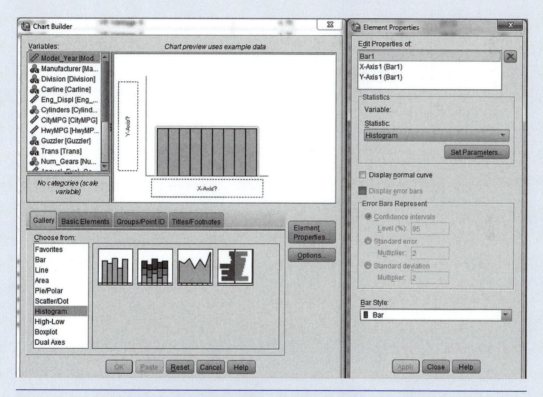

Figure 3.15   Drag the Simple Histogram Icon Into the Chart Preview Box

3. Drag the variable *CityMPG* from the Variables list on the left to the X-axis box in the Chart Preview. Click OK to display the initial histogram shown in Figure 3.16.

4. To modify the graph, double-click on the displayed histogram to enter the Chart Editor. To change the color of the bars, double-click on the bars and the Properties dialog box (on the

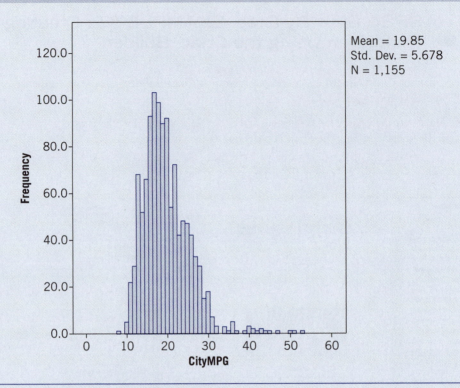

Mean = 19.85
Std. Dev. = 5.678
N = 1,155

Figure 3.16   Histogram of City MPG

right) is displayed with several tab options. In the Properties dialog box, click the Fill & Border icon, and choose a color (such as yellow). In the Pattern pull-down menu, select a crosshatch pattern and click Apply. You will see the chart reflect your changes.

    5.   To display a distribution curve (while still in the Chart Editor), select **Elements/Show Distribution Curve**. In the displayed Properties dialog box, select the Normal radio button and click Close. A normal curve (based on the mean and standard deviation for the current data) is superimposed on the histogram, as shown in Figure 3.17. Note that the histogram bars are crosshatched as previously specified in step 4.

    6.   To change bins in a histogram, double-click on the bars in the Chart Editor to highlight them. In the displayed Properties dialog box, choose the Binning tab. In the X-axis box, select custom, Interval width, and enter 2. Click Apply and Close. Close the Chart Editor and the bins in the histogram will reflect that change as shown in Figure 3.18.

There are many other options in the Chart Editor. We suggest that you use the Chart Editor to put a main title on the histogram and change the axis titles.

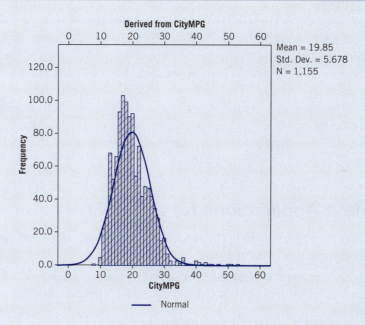

Figure 3.17   Histogram With Crosshatched Bars and a Superimposed Normal Curve

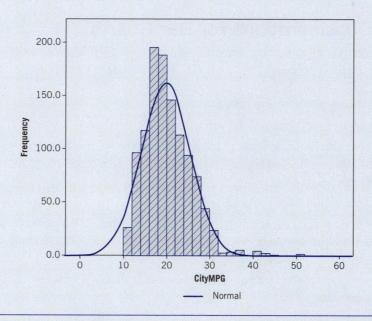

Figure 3.18   Histogram With Custom Bin Size

Bar Charts

A bar chart is not a histogram, although they are often confused. In a bar chart, each bar represents a discrete value (category) and the height of each bar represents the count for that category. The order of the bars is usually not critical. (In a histogram, bars represent the count of items within a range of ordered values.) In the bar chart, bars may also represent means by group, and in this case, may also include error bars. Examples of charts for categorical data are provided in Chapter 6: Analysis of Categorical Data. This section shows how to build a bar chart based on frequencies and another bar chart reporting means with error bars.

Appropriate Applications for a Bar Chart

- *Visualize the number of M&M's in a typical bag of candy by color.* Each bar represents the frequency of a particular color.
- *Visualize the proportion of five different hair colors in a population of 20,000 students.* Each bar represents the proportion (100 * [count/total]) for each hair color.
- *Visualize the relationship of means by group.* Each bar represents a mean value for a group.

Design Considerations for Bar Charts

There are several general design issues that should be considered when creating a bar chart (whether you use SPSS or some other method). These include the following:

- Bar charts should always have a zero base.
- Always include a scale on the vertical axis.
- 3-D bar charts may look more interesting, but the volume of taller bars may lead to an incorrect interpretation that they represent more information than is correct.
- All bars should be of the same width.
- The order of the bars is generally not important when categories represented have no particular order (such as in eye color, or race). A Pareto chart arranges bars from tallest to shortest.
- Bars are typically separated with a blank area between to indicate that the data are categorical.

Example 3.3

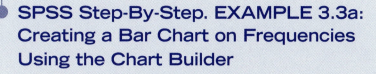

SPSS Step-By-Step. EXAMPLE 3.3a: Creating a Bar Chart on Frequencies Using the Chart Builder

1. Open the data SOMEDATA.SAV and select **Graphs/Chart Builder**. If the warning dialog box (Figure 3.1) appears, click OK.

2. Choose Bar as the chart type and drag the Simple Bar (leftmost) icon into the Chart Preview window. This selects a single bar type.

3. From the variable list, drag *Intervention Group* to the bottom axis in the Chart Preview window. Click OK, and the simple bar chart showing the counts for the three intervention groups is shown in Figure 3.19. As in the histogram example, you could double-click on this chart, enter the Chart Editor, and change the appearance of the chart, such as bar colors, titles, etc.

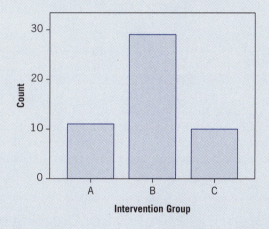

Figure 3.19   Initial Bar Chart

4. To enhance this chart by displaying intervention group by Gender, return to the Chart Builder. Select the Cluster Bar icon (Cluster on X: set color) and drag it into the Chart Preview Window. Drag *Gender* into the "Cluster on X" specification (in the upper right of the Chart Preview). Click OK to display the graph in Figure 3.20. This chart provides a

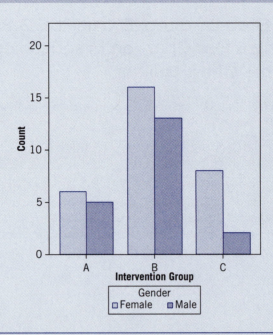

Figure 3.20 Clustered Bar Chart

comparison of gender for each of the three Intervention Groups showing that there are fewer male than females in each group. You could enhance this chart (for example) by double-clicking on it to open the Chart Editor and choosing **Elements/Show Data Labels** to display counts for each bar.

SPSS Step-By-Step. EXAMPLE 3.3b: Creating a Bar Chart Reporting Means Using the Chart Builder

1. Open the data SOMEDATA.SAV and select **Graphs/Chart Builder**. If the warning dialog box (Figure 3.1) appears, click OK.

2. Choose Bar as the chart type and drag the Clustered Bar (second from left) icon into the Chart Preview window.

3. Populate the Chart Viewer with the three variables (*Intervention, Baseline,* and *Gender*) you want used in the plot in the following way: (Note that the X-axis and Cluster on X variables

must be set as nominal or ordinal SPSS Measurement types and the Y-axis variable must be of scale type.)

a) Drag the *Intervention group* variable to the lower (X-axis) position.

b) Drag *Baseline* into the Y-axis (Count) position on the chart. It appears as "Mean Baseline" which indicates that the chart will display mean values for Baseline in the chart.

c) Drag *Gender* into the "Cluster on X: Set Color" position at the top right of the Chart Preview.

4. To include error bars on the graph, click the "Display error bars" (Confidence Intervals Level % 95) in the Element Properties dialog (at the right of the viewer). Click Apply.

5. Click OK in the Chart Builder to create the resulting chart shown in Figure 3.21. This chart displays means (by heights of the bars) by Gender for each intervention along with error bars that indicate the amount of variability in each cluster with a 95% Confidence Interval on the mean.

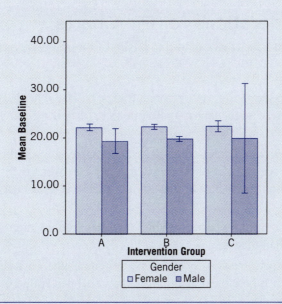

Figure 3.21 Clustered Means Chart With Error Bars

Pie Charts

People have a love-hate relationship with pie charts. Some people like them for their simplicity. Others call them the worst way to display data. Some objections are that pie charts are difficult to compare to other pie charts. Most people can't tell the difference in sizes between similarly sized slices, and it is difficult to determine the number of items in each category. Technically, there are issues in the way people visually interpret areas and degrees in the chart that make it easy to manipulate its meaning (Cleveland, 1985). Nevertheless, they are often used. We'll illustrate how you can create a pie chart using Chart Builder. Slices in pie charts are used to illustrate a proportion of a whole. Many times, the data represented in a bar chart can also be displayed as a pie chart.

Appropriate Applications for a Pie Chart

- *Visualize the proportion of five different hair colors in a population of 20,000 students.* Each pie slice represents the proportion (100 * [count/total]) of each hair color.
- *Visualize the parts of a budget.* Each pie slice represents a proportion (a slice) of an entire budget.

Design Considerations for Pie Charts

There are several design issues that can lead to misleading interpretations for pie charts. These include the following:

- Any time two pie charts are compared, the circle should be the same diameter; otherwise the larger circle appears to carry more weight than a smaller one.
- When pie charts have many slices, it becomes increasingly difficult to compare the sizes of each slice. Pie charts work best when there is one large slice among several and the chart illustrates which category is dominant.
- 3-D pie charts distort wedges making some appear more important (or less important) than they are.
- By selecting specific colors for slices and designing where a slice is located in the chart, it is possible to manipulate the visual perception of the chart's message. (Cleveland, 1985).

Example 3.4

1. Open the data CARS2014.SAV and select **Graphs/Chart Builder**. If the warning dialog box (Figure 3.1) appears, click OK.

2. Select the **Pie/Polar** type graph from the options, and drag the icon into the Chart Preview Box. Select the *Drive Description* variable from the list, and drag it to the "Slice by" box at the bottom of the sample pie chart. Click OK, and the pie chart shown in Figure 3.22 appears.

This chart indicates the proportions of drive types for various vehicles in the CARS2014 data set showing that 2-Wheel Drive, Front is the most common type. You can double-click on the chart to enhance the chart using the Chart Editor. For example, experiment with putting the number of observations for each type in the pie slices by choosing **Elements/Show Data Labels**, and (in the Properties dialog) put the Count option in the Displayed list and remove Percent. Also, double-click on the green pie slice to select it, and choose **Elements/Explode Slice** to separate that slice from the others for the purpose of highlighting that group.

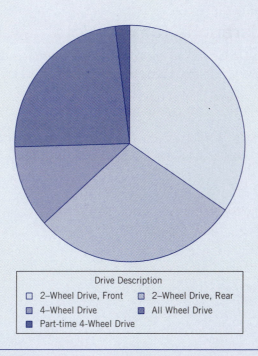

Figure 3.22 Pie Chart of Drive Description

Boxplots

Boxplots (also called box-and-whiskers plots) are a representation of the quartiles of a scale variable with 50% of the data values inside the middle box and 25% of the data (represented by lines, or whiskers) on each side of the box. In general, a boxplot shows the 0th, 25th, 50th, 75th, and 100th percentile of the data (sometimes called the Tukey five-number summary, named after its originator John Tukey). A horizontal line inside the box represents the median.

Appropriate Applications for Boxplots

- *Visualize the distribution of the data.* Assess the approximate normality of data by looking for a symmetric box with a median centered within the box, a box whose length (called the interquartile range, IRQ) is about 25% of the total length (range), and with equal-length whiskers.

- *Locate outliers in a set of data.* Use boxplots to identify data points that are possible outliers. In SPSS, an outlier is defined as a point beyond 1.5*IQR from the top or bottom of the box, and an extreme outlier is 3*IRQ beyond the box.

Design Considerations for Boxplots

Boxplots are a simple way to view a variable's distribution, central tendency, and when displayed by group, allows you to make a visual comparison across groups.

Example 3.5

1. Open the data CARS2014.SAV and select **Graphs/Chart Builder**. If the warning dialog box (Figure 3.1) appears, click OK.

2. Select the boxplot icon from the graph types. Choose the leftmost (Simple Boxplot) icon and drag it into the Chart Preview box.

3. Select (drag) *SUV* to the X-axis and *HwyMPG* into the Y-axis.

4. Select the **Groups/Point ID** tab just below the Chart Preview box, and check the Point ID label checkbox. A new variable box labeled Point Label Variable appears in the Chart Preview. Drag the variable *Carline* into that box.

5. Click OK to display the comparative boxplots shown in Figure 3.23.

These comparative boxplots provide visual evidence that (although there is a lot of overlap) SUVs (SUV = Yes on the plot) tend to get lower highway miles per gallon than non-SUVs (but not always). The boxplots also indicate that several non-SUVs have unusually high miles per gallon. When you examine the labels for these outliers, you see that they are all hybrid vehicles.

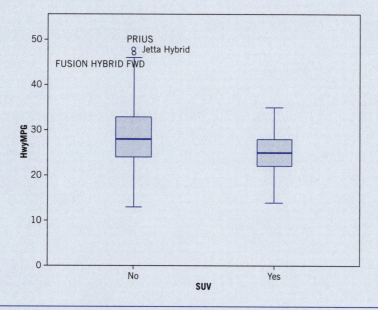

Figure 3.23 Comparative Boxplots Using Cars2014 Data Set

SUMMARY

A number of additional charts and graphs are created throughout the text using the basic three graphing methods illustrated in this chapter:

- Chart Builder
- Graphboard Template Chooser
- Legacy Dialogs

Most charts created by any of these techniques can be edited using the SPSS Chart Editor. All three techniques were illustrated in this chapter, but most examples used in this chapter and throughout the book use the Chart Builder which (we believe) has the most straightforward design mechanism of the three.

REFERENCES

Cleveland, W. S. (1985). *The elements of graphing data*. Monterey, CA: Wadsworth.

Tufte, E. (2001). *The visual display of quantitative information* (2nd ed.). Cheshire: CT: Graphics Press.

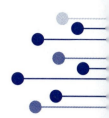

Comparing One or Two Means Using the *t*-Test

The bread and butter of statistical data analysis is the Student's *t*-test.

It was named after a statistician who called himself Student but whose real name was William Gossett. As an employee of Guinness Brewery in Dublin, Ireland, he tackled a number of practical statistical problems related to the operation of the brewery. Since he was discouraged from publishing under his own name, he adopted the Student moniker.

Because of Gossett's work, today's researchers have in their toolbox what is probably the most commonly performed statistical procedure, the *t*-test. The most typical use of this test is to compare means, which is the focus of the discussion in this chapter. Unfortunately, because this test is easy to use, it is also easily misused.

In this chapter, you will learn when, why, and how to appropriately perform a *t*-test and how to present your results. There are three types of *t*-tests discussed in this chapter:

1. One-sample *t*-test, which is used to compare a single mean to a fixed number or "gold standard"

2. Two-sample *t*-test, which is used to compare two population means based on independent samples from two populations or groups

3. Paired *t*-test, which is used to compare two means based on samples that are related in some way

These three types of *t*-tests are discussed along with advice concerning the conditions under which each is appropriate. Examples are given that illustrate how to perform these three types of *t*-tests using SPSS software. The first *t*-test considered is the simplest.

One-Sample *t*-Test

The one-sample *t*-test is used for comparing sample results with a known value. Specifically, in this type of test, a single sample is collected, and the resulting sample mean is compared with a value of interest, sometimes a "gold standard," that is not based on the current sample. For example, this specified value might be one of the following:

- The weight indicated on a can of vegetables
- The advertised breaking strength of a type of steel pipe
- Government specification on the percentage of fruit juice that must be in a drink before it can be advertised as "fruit juice"

The purpose of the one-sample *t*-test is to determine whether there is sufficient evidence to conclude that the mean of the population from which the sample is taken is different from the specified value.

Related to the one-sample *t*-test is a confidence interval on the mean. The confidence interval is usually applied when you are not testing against a specified value of the population mean but instead want to know a range of plausible values of the unknown mean of the population from which the sample was selected.

Appropriate Applications for a One-Sample *t*-Test

The following are examples of situations in which a one-sample *t*-test would be appropriate:

- *Are the soft drink bottles full?* Does the average volume of liquid in filled soft drink bottles match the 12 ounces advertised on the label?
- *Does the diet work?* Is the mean weight loss more than 5 pounds after 3 months for men ages 50 to 60 years, who are given a brochure and training describing a low-carbohydrate diet?
- *Have SAT scores fallen?* Based on a random sample of 200 students, can we conclude that the average SAT score this year is lower than the national average from 3 years ago?

Design Considerations for a One-Sample *t*-Test

The key assumption underlying the one-sample *t*-test is that the population from which the sample is selected is normal. However, this assumption is rarely if ever precisely true in practice, so it is important to know how concerned you should be about apparent nonnormality in your data. The following are rules of thumb (Moore & McCabe, 2012):

- If the sample size is small (less than 15), then you should not use the one-sample *t*-test if the data are clearly skewed or if outliers are present.

- If the sample size is moderate (at least 15), then the one-sample *t*-test can be safely used except when there are severe outliers.
- If the sample size is large (at least 40), then the one-sample *t*-test can be safely used without regard to skewness or outliers.

You will see variations of these rules throughout the literature. In particular, some statisticians will add that the one-sample *t*-test may not be appropriate if the data are skewed (even with a large sample size), or if there are substantial outliers. In these cases, a nonparametric test might be more desirable. See Chapter 8: Nonparametric Analysis Procedures for more information.

Hypotheses for a One-Sample *t*-Test

When performing a one-sample *t*-test, you may or may not have a preconceived assumption about the direction of your findings. Depending on the design of your study, you may decide to perform a one- or two-tailed test.

Two-Tailed *t*-Tests

The basic hypotheses for the one-sample *t*-test are as follows: where μ denotes the mean of the population from which the sample was selected, and μ_0 denotes the hypothesized value of this mean. It should be reiterated that μ_0 is a value that does not depend on the current sample.

H_0: $\mu = \mu_0$ (in words, the population mean is equal to the hypothesized value μ_0).

H_a: $\mu \neq \mu_0$ (the population mean is not equal to μ_0).

One-Tailed t-Tests

If you are only interested in rejecting the null hypothesis if the population mean differs from the hypothesized value in a direction of interest, you may want to use a one-tailed (sometimes called a one-sided) test. If, for example, you want to reject the null hypothesis only if there is sufficient evidence that the mean is larger than the value hypothesized under the null (i.e., μ_0), the hypotheses become the following:

H_0: $\mu = \mu_0$ (the population mean is equal to the hypothesized value μ_0).

H_a: $\mu > \mu_0$ (the population mean is greater than μ_0).

Example 4.1

One-Sample t-Test

Describing the Problem

A certain bolt is designed to be 4 inches in length. The lengths of a random sample of 15 bolts are shown in Figure 4.1.

	length	var	var	var	var	var	var	var	var	var	var
1	4.00										
2	3.95										
3	4.01										
4	3.95										
5	4.00										
6	3.98										
7	3.97										
8	3.97										
9	4.01										
10	3.98										
11	3.99										
12	4.01										
13	4.02										
14	4.02										
15	3.98										

BOLT.SAV [DataSet2] - IBM SPSS Statistics Data Editor

File   Edit   View   Data   Transform   Analyze   Direct Marketing   Graphs   Utilities   Add-ons   Window   Help

Figure 4.1   The Bolt Data

Since the sample size is small ($N = 15$), you should examine the normality of the data before proceeding to the t-test. Refer to Chapter 2: Describing and Examining Data to verify that the data are close to normally distributed by examining a boxplot or Q-Q plot. For this example, we assume that the data are such that an examination convinces us that they are approximately normal.

In this example, the bolts are out of design when they are too short or too long. Therefore, in the one-sample t-test, we test the two-tailed hypotheses:

Null hypothesis (H_0): $\mu = 4$ (the population mean is equal to 4").

Alternative hypothesis (H_a): $\mu \neq 4$ (the population mean is not equal to 4").

To run a one-sample *t*-test on the BOLT data and test this hypothesis, follow these steps:

SPSS Step-By-Step. EXAMPLE 4.1: One Sample *t*-Test

1. Open the data set BOLT.SAV and select **Analyze/Compare Means/One-Sample T Test**. . . .

2. Select *Length* as the test variable and specify 4 as the Test Value as shown in Figure 4.2.

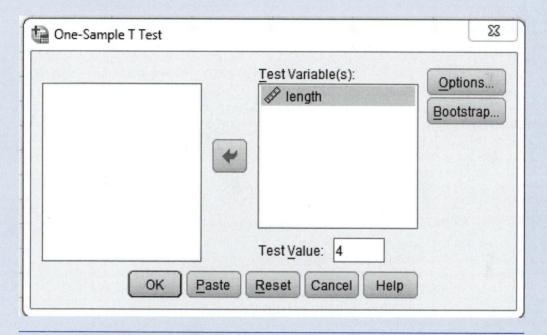

Figure 4.2   Select *Length* as the Test Variable for the *t*-Test

3. Click OK and Table 4.1 is displayed.

Table 4.1   Output for Bolt Data

One-Sample Statistics

	N	Mean	Std. Deviation	Std. Error Mean
length	15	3.9893	.02314	.00597

(Continued)

Table 4.1 (Continued)

One-Sample Test

	t	df	Sig. (2-tailed)	Mean Difference	95% Confidence Interval of the Difference	
					Lower	Upper
length	−1.786	14	.096	−.01067	−.0235	.0021

The output for the one-sample t-test is two tables. The first table, "One-Sample Statistics," provides simple statistics for the bolt data and shows that the sample mean of the lengths is 3.9893" with a standard deviation of 0.02314. (You should report these values to fewer digits as discussed in Chapter 1.) In the "One-Sample Test" output, we see that $t = -1.786$ with a (two-tailed) p-value of 0.096. Thus, at the $\alpha = .05$ level of significance, we do not reject the null, and we do not conclude that there is a problem with the lengths.

We make the following observations concerning the output:

- The "Mean Difference" value of −0.01067 given in the table is $\bar{x} - \mu_0$, (i.e., 3.9893 − 4).
- The confidence interval on the hypothesized difference above is given as [−0.0235, 0.0021]. It should be noted that this is a 95% confidence interval on the difference $\mu - \mu_0$ instead of an interval for μ. Thus, the fact that this interval contains zero indicates that the test would not be rejected at the $\alpha = .05$ level. Note also that this is a confidence interval on the hypothesized difference ($\mu - 4$) and not on μ.

To obtain a confidence interval for the mean μ, you can modify the interval above by adding 4 to the lower and upper endpoints, or you can use the SPSS Explore procedure (**Analyze/Descriptive Statistics/Explore** . . .) to produce the table shown in Table 4.2 and the boxplot shown in Figure 4.3. The 95% confidence interval for the mean is [3.977, 4.002], and this is the interval you would most likely report. The boxplot provides visual evidence that the data for length are acceptably normal.

Reporting the Results

The following examples illustrate how you might report this t-test in a publication format.

Narrative for the Methods Section

"A one-sample Student's t-test was performed to test the hypothesis that the mean bolt length is 4 inches."

Table 4.2   Explore Output Showing the Confidence Interval for μ.

Descriptives

			Statistic	Std. Error
length	Mean		3.9893	.00597
	95% Confidence Interval for Mean	Lower Bound	3.9765	
		Upper Bound	4.0021	
	5% Trimmed Mean		3.9898	
	Median		3.9900	
	Variance		.001	
	Std. Deviation		.02314	
	Minimum		3.95	
	Maximum		4.02	
	Range		.07	
	Interquartile Range		.04	
	Skewness		−.346	.580
	Kurtosis		−.919	1.121

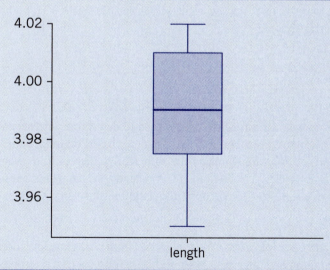

Figure 4.3   A Boxplot of the Bolt Length Data

Narrative for the Results Section

> "The bolt lengths were not significantly different from 4 inches, $t(14) = -1.79$, $p = 0.10$."

Or to be more complete,

> "The mean bolt length (mean = 3.989, $SD = 0.023$, $N = 15$) was not significantly different from the hypothesized value of 4 inches, $t(14) = -1.79$, $p = 0.10$."

A description of the confidence interval would read as follows:

> "A 95% confidence interval on the mean bolt length using a Student's t distribution with 11 degrees of freedom is [3.977, 4.002]. Since this interval contains 4 inches, there is not significant evidence that the mean bolt length is different from 4."

Analogous hypotheses could be specified for the case in which you want to reject H_0 only if there is sufficient evidence that the population mean is less than μ_0. SPSS always reports a two-tailed p-value, so you should modify the reported p-value to fit a one-tailed test by dividing it by 2 if your results are consistent with the direction specified in the alternative hypothesis and an *a priori* decision was made that a one-tailed test was appropriate. For more discussion of the issues of one- and two-tailed tests, see the section "Hypotheses for a Two-Sample t-Test" in this chapter.

Two-Sample *t*-Test

The two-sample (independent groups) t-test is used to determine whether the unknown means of two populations are different from each other based on independent samples from each population. If the two-sample means are sufficiently different from each other, then the population means are declared to be different. A related test, the paired t-test, to be discussed in the next section, is used to compare two population means using samples that are paired in some way.

The samples for a two-sample t-test can be obtained from a single population that has been randomly divided into two subgroups, with each subgroup subjected to one of two treatments (e.g., two medications) or from two separate populations (e.g., male and female). In either case, for the two sample *t*-test to be valid, it is necessary that the two samples are independent (i.e., unrelated to each other).

Appropriate Applications for a Two-Sample *t*-Test

In each of the following examples, the two-sample (independent groups) *t*-test is used to determine whether the population means of the two groups are different.

- *How can my flour make more dough?* Distributors often pay extra to have products placed in prime locations in grocery stores. The manufacturer of a new brand of whole-grain flour wants to determine if placing the product on the top shelf or on the eye-level shelf produces better sales. From 40 grocery stores, he randomly chooses 20 for top-shelf placement and 20 for eye-level placement. After a period of 30 days, he compares average sales from the two placements.

- *What's the smart way to teach economics?* A university is offering two sections of a microeconomics course during the fall semester: (1) meeting once a week with taped lessons provided on a CD or on the Internet and (2) having three sessions a week using standard lectures by the same professor. Students are randomly placed into one of the two sections at the time of registration. Using results from a standardized final exam, the researcher compares mean differences between the learning obtained in the two types of classes.

- *Are males and females different?* It is known that males and females often differ in their reactions to certain drugs. As a part of the development of a new antiseizure medication, a standard dose is given to 20 males and 20 females. Periodic measurements are made to determine the time it takes until a desired level of drug is present in the blood for each subject. The researcher wants to determine whether there is a gender difference in the average speed at which the drug is assimilated into the blood system.

Design Considerations for a Two-Sample *t*-Test

The characteristics of the *t*-tests in the above examples are the following:

A Two-Sample *t*-Test Compares Means

In an experiment designed to use the two-sample *t*-test, you want to compare means from a quantitative variable such as height, weight, amount spent, or grade. In other words, it should make sense to calculate the mean of the observations. This measurement is called your "response" or "outcome" variable. Note: The outcome measure *should not* be a categorical (nominal/discrete) variable such as hair color, gender, or occupational level, even if the data have been numerically coded.

You Are Comparing Independent Samples

The two groups contain subjects (or objects) that are not paired or matched in any way. These subjects typically are obtained in one of two ways:

- Subjects (or items) are selected for an experiment in which all come from the same population and are *randomly* split into two groups (e.g., placebo vs. drug or two different marketing campaigns). Each group is exposed to identical conditions except for a "treatment," which may be a medical treatment, a marketing design factor, exposure to a stimulus, and so on.
- Subjects are randomly selected from two separate populations (e.g., male vs. female) as in the medical example above.

The *t*-Test Assumes Normality

A standard assumption for the *t*-test to be valid when you have small sample sizes is that the outcome variable measurements are normally distributed. That is, when each sample is graphed as a histogram, the shape approximates a bell curve. When the distribution of the data is markedly skewed, the mean is a poor representation of central tendency and thus violates the assumptions of this test.

Are the Variances Equal?

Another consideration that should be addressed before using the *t*-test is whether the population variances can be considered to be equal. The two-sample *t*-test is robust against moderate departures from the normality and variance assumption, but independence of samples must not be violated. For specifics, see the section below titled "Deciding Which Version of the *t*-Test Statistic to Use."

Hypotheses for a Two-Sample *t*-Test

As with any version of the *t*-test, when performing a two-sample *t*-test, you may or may not have a preconceived assumption about the direction of your findings. Depending on the design of your study, you may decide to perform a one- or two-tailed test.

Two-Tailed Tests

In this setting, there are two populations, and we are interested in testing whether the population means (i.e., μ_1 and μ_2) are equal. The hypotheses for the comparison of the means in a two-sample t-test are as follows:

H_0: $\mu_1 = \mu_2$ (the population means of the two groups are the same).

H_a: $\mu_1 \neq \mu_2$ (the population means of the two groups are different).

One-Tailed Tests

If your experiment is designed so that you are only interested in detecting whether one mean is larger than the other, you may choose to perform a one-tailed (sometimes called one-sided) t-test. For example, when you are only interested in detecting whether the population mean of the second group is larger than the population mean of the first group, the hypotheses become the following:

H_0: $\mu_1 = \mu_2$ (the population means of the two groups are the same).

H_a: $\mu_2 > \mu_1$ (the population mean of the second group is larger than the population mean of the first group).

SIDEBAR
If you intend to use a one-tailed test, you should decide this before collecting the data, and the decision should never be based on the fact that you could obtain a more significant result by changing your hypotheses to be one-tailed. Generally, in the case of the two-sample t-test, if there is any possibility that there would be interest in detecting a difference in either direction, the two-tailed test is more appropriate. In fact, you will find that some statisticians believe that it is almost always inappropriate to use a one-tailed t-test.

Since SPSS always reports a two-tailed p-value, you must modify the reported p-value to fit a one-tailed test by dividing it by 2. Thus, if the p-value reported for a two-tailed t-test is 0.06, then the p-value for this one-sided test would be 0.03 if the results are supportive of the alternative hypothesis (i.e., if $\bar{X}_2 > \bar{X}_1$). If the one-sided hypotheses above are tested and $\bar{X}_2 < \bar{X}_1$, then the p-value would actually be greater than 0.50, and the null hypothesis should not be rejected.

Tips and Caveats for a Two-Sample t-Test

Don't Misuse the t-Test

Be careful! Don't be among those who misuse the two-sample t-test. Experimental situations that are sometimes inappropriately analyzed as two-sample t-tests are the following:

- *Comparing paired subjects.* A group of subjects receives one treatment, and then the same subjects later receive another treatment. This is a paired design (not independent samples). Other examples of paired observations would be fruit from upper and lower branches of the same tree, subjects matched on several demographic items, or twins. This type of experiment is appropriately analyzed as a paired test and not as a two-sample test. See the "Paired *t*-Test" section later in this chapter.

- *Comparing to a known value.* Subjects receive a treatment, and the results are compared to a known value (often a "gold standard"). This is a one-sample *t*-test. See the "One-Sample *t*-Test" section.

Preplan One-Tailed *t*-Tests

Only perform a one-tailed test when your experiment is designed with that type of test in mind. As previously mentioned, most statistics programs provide *p*-values for two-tailed tests. Therefore, if your experiment is designed so that you are performing a one-tailed test, the *p*-values should be modified as mentioned above.

Small Sample Sizes Make Normality Difficult to Assess

Although the *t*-test is robust against moderate departures from normality, outliers (unusually large or small numbers) can cause problems with the validity of the *t*-test. As your sample sizes increase, the normality assumption for the two-sample *t*-test becomes less of an issue because of the central limit theorem (i.e., sample means are approximately normal for moderately large sample sizes even when the original populations are nonnormal). Refer back to the guidelines regarding normality and sample size given in the section "Design Considerations for a One-Sample *t*-Test." Studies have shown that the two-sample *t*-test is more robust to nonnormality than the one-sample methods. The two-sample methods perform well for a wide range of distributions as long as both populations have the same shape and sample sizes are equal. Selection of sample sizes that are equal or nearly so is advisable whenever feasible (see Posten, 1978). In fact, if your sample sizes are nearly equal, then the one-sample *t*-test guidelines about sample size requirements regarding normality can be thought of as applying to the sum of the two-sample sizes in a two-sample *t*-test (see Moore & McCabe, 2012). A more conservative approach is to base your decision on the smaller of the two sample sizes, especially when sample sizes are very different. If your sample sizes are small and you have a concern that your data are not normally distributed, an alternative to the two-sample *t*-test is a nonparametric test called the Mann-Whitney test (see Chapter 8: Nonparametric Analysis Procedures). If the data collected are of a variable that has been well researched in the literature and has been shown to be normal, you can generally make the assumption that your sample is from a normally distributed distribution.

Performing Multiple t-Tests Causes Loss of Control of the Experiment-Wise Significance Level

If an experiment involves the strategy of comparing three or more means, the investigator may consider using the familiar t-test to perform all pairwise comparisons. However, this strategy leads to the loss of control over the experiment-wise significance level (i.e., the probability of incorrectly finding at least one significant difference in all possible pairwise comparisons when all means are equal). A more appropriate procedure for comparing more than two means is an analysis of variance (see Chapter 7: Analysis of Variance and Covariance for more information).

Interpreting Graphs Associated With the Two-Sample t-Test

Graphs are useful tools for understanding an analysis. A graph produced by many software programs in association with the t-test is the side-by-side boxplot. This plot aids in the visual assessment of the *normality (symmetry)* of the data as well as the *equal variance assumption*. In addition, the boxplots allow you to visually assess the degree to which the two data sets are separated. The histogram and normal probability plots are also helpful. For additional information on the use of these graphs, see Chapter 2: Describing and Examining Data.

Deciding Which Version of the t-Test Statistic to Use

Most statistical packages compute two versions of the t-statistic, denoted here as t_{EQ} and t_{UNEQ}. The statistic t_{EQ} is based on the assumption that the two population variances are equal, and a pooled estimate of the (equal) population variances is used. Since the population variances are assumed to be equal in this case, the pooled estimate of the common variance is a weighted average of the two sample variances. The statistic t_{UNEQ} does not assume equal variances.

There are two common methods for determining which of the two versions of the t-test to use for an analysis. Both methods make the same assumptions about normality.

1. A simple conservative approach recommended by a number of recent statistics texts (see, e.g., Moore & McCabe, 2012; Watkins, Scheaffer, & Cobb, 2008) is to *always* use the t-test that does not assume equal variances unless you have evidence that the two variances are equal. This is a conservative approach and is based on studies that have shown that tests for equality of variances are often unreliable.

2. The classical approach to deciding which version of the *t*-test to use is to formally test the equal variance assumption using an *F*-test. The results of these tests are typically provided in the output from statistical packages. (SPSS uses Levene's version of the *F*-test.) Typically, the decision criteria for deciding on equality of variances are as follows: If the *p*-value for the *F*-test is less than 0.05, you conclude that the variances are unequal and use the *t*-test based on unequal variances.

If you don't know which of these two approaches to use, we recommend that you use the conservative criterion. That is, always use the "unequal" version of the *t*-test unless there is evidence that the variances are equal. In most cases, both versions of the *t*-test will lead to the same conclusion. Here are several items to consider when deciding which version of the *t*-test to use:

1. Although test statistic t_{UNEQ} does not actually follow a *t*-distribution even when the populations are normal, the *p*-value given in the statistics packages provides a close approximation. The degrees of freedom may not necessarily be an integer.

2. There are a number of professors who follow the classical decision-making procedure that a test for equality of variances (and maybe also for normality) be performed to determine which version of the *t*-test to use. (Some statisticians argue that these pretests inflate the experiment-wise error rate, so it is recommended that the *t*-test *p*-value be adjusted in these cases.) An alternative that would not require a *p*-value adjustment is to rely on past knowledge that the data are normal and variances between groups can be assumed to be equal. Others accept that there is always a "look" at the data distribution before an analysis and no adjustment for this look is necessary. See Sawilowsky (2002) p. 466.

3. If one or more of the sample sizes are small and the data contain significant departures from normality, you should perform a nonparametric test in lieu of the *t*-test. See the section "Tips and Caveats for a Two-Sample *t*-Test" above.

Two-Sample *t*-Test Examples

The following two examples illustrate how to perform a two-sample *t*-test, create appropriate graphs, and interpret the results.

Example 4.2

Two-Sample t-Test With Equal Variances

Describing the Problem

A researcher wants to know whether one fertilizer (Brand 1) causes plants to grow faster than another brand of fertilizer (Brand 2). Starting with seeds, he grows plants in identical conditions and randomly assigns fertilizer "Brand 1" to seven plants and fertilizer "Brand 2" to six plants. The data for this experiment are as follows, where the outcome measurement is the height of the plant after 3 weeks of growth. The data are shown in Table 4.3.

Table 4.3   Fertilizer Data

Fertilizer Brand 1	Fertilizer Brand 2
51.0 cm	54.0 cm
53.3	56.1
55.6	52.1
51.0	56.4
55.5	54.0
53.0	52.9
52.1	

Since either fertilizer could be superior, a two-sided *t*-test is appropriate. The hypotheses for this test are $H_0: \mu_1 = \mu_2$ versus $H_a: \mu_1 \neq \mu_2$ or, in words, the following:

Null hypothesis (H_0): The mean growth heights of the plants using the two different fertilizers are the same.

Alternative hypothesis (H_a): The mean growth heights of the plants using the two fertilizers are different.

Arranging the Data for Analysis

Setting up data for this type of analysis is not intuitive and requires some special formatting. To perform the analysis for the fertilizer data using most statistical software programs (including

SPSS), you must set up the data using two variables: a classification or group code and an observed (outcome/response) variable. Thus, the way the data are listed in Table 4.3 (although it may make sense in your workbook or spreadsheet) is *not* how a statistical software program requires the data to be set up to perform a two-sample *t*-test. Instead, the data should be set up using the following format:

- *Select a grouping code to represent the two fertilizer types.* This code could be numeric (i.e., 1, 2) or text (i.e., A, B or BRAND1, BRAND2). For this example, use the grouping code named *Type*, where 1 represents Brand1 and 2 represents Brand2.
- *Name the outcome variable.* The outcome (response) variable is the observed height and is designated with the variable named *Height*.
- *The grouping codes specify which observation belongs to which type of fertilizer.* Thus, to set up the data for most statistics programs, place one observation per line, with each data line containing two variables: a fertilizer code (*Type*) and the corresponding response variable (*Height*).

Figure 4.4 illustrates how the data should be set up for most statistics programs, where it should be noted that there is one item (plant) per row.

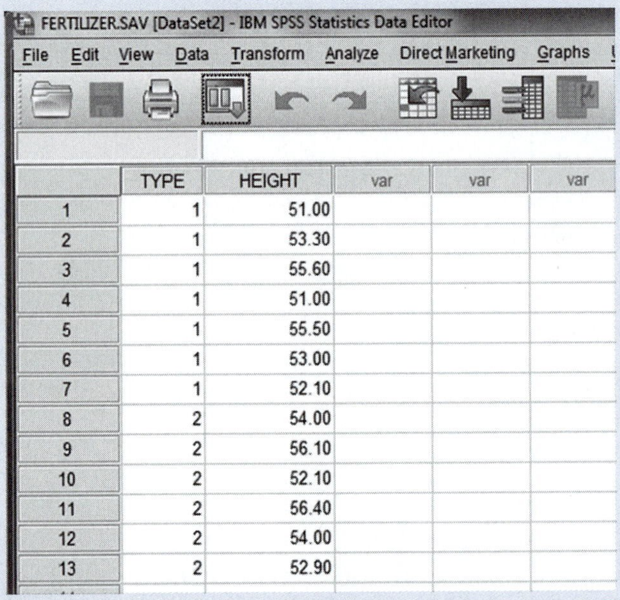

	TYPE	HEIGHT	var	var	var
1	1	51.00			
2	1	53.30			
3	1	55.60			
4	1	51.00			
5	1	55.50			
6	1	53.00			
7	1	52.10			
8	2	54.00			
9	2	56.10			
10	2	52.10			
11	2	56.40			
12	2	54.00			
13	2	52.90			

Figure 4.4 SPSS Editor Showing Fertilizer Data

The values 1 and 2 in the "type" column represent the two brands of fertilizer and the "height" variable is the outcome height measurement on the plants. (The codes 1 and 2 in this data set were arbitrarily selected. You could have used 0 and 1 or any other set of binary codes.)

Before performing the *t*-test you should check to see whether your data meet the assumptions of normality and equality of variances. A visual way to check those assumptions is with a boxplot, as discussed in Chapter 2 (Graphs/Legacy dialogs/Boxplot/Summaries for Groups or Cases with *Height* as the variable and Type as the Category Axis.) The comparative boxplots for these data is shown in Figure 4.5.

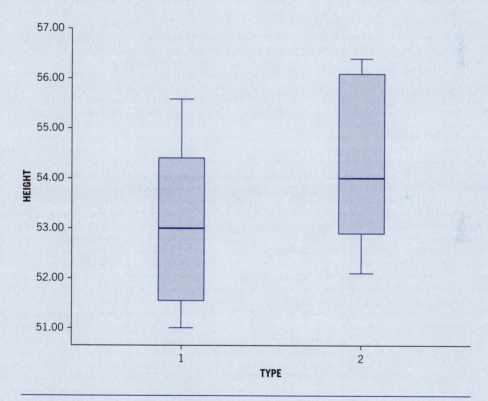

Figure 4.5   Boxplots for the Fertilizer Study

From the listing of the data and boxplots, notice that the sample sizes are small, with only seven observations in Group 1 and six observations in Group 2. Also note that the distributions of both groups are relatively symmetric and the variances appear to be fairly similar. There is no evidence of any sizable outliers.

Do not interpret the large overlap in the boxes as providing conclusive evidence that the means are not different. Although it will turn out that there is no difference in this example, when sample sizes are large, you may see considerable overlap in the boxes even when there is a significant *p*-value for the *t*-test. (This would indicate that there is evidence that means are different even though there is sizable overlap between the populations.)

With this information in hand, proceed to perform a *t*-test:

SPSS Step-By-Step. Two-Sample *t*-Test With Equal Variances

To run the two-sample *t*-test on the FERTILIZER.SAV data, follow these steps:

1. Open the data set FERTILIZER.SAV and select **Analyze/Compare Means/ Independent Samples T Test**. . . .

2. Select *Height* as the Test Variable and *Type* as the Grouping Variable.

3. Click on the Define Groups button and define the group values as 1 and 2 as shown in Figure 4.6.

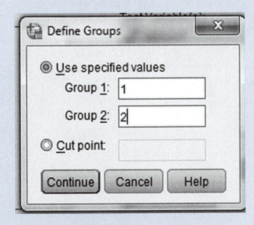

Figure 4.6 Specify Group Values for Two-Sample *t*-Test

4. Click Continue and OK and the tables shown in Table 4.4 are displayed.

5. To display the boxplot in Figure 4.5 select **Graphs/Legacy Dialog/Boxplot** and choose Simple Boxplot and then Define. Select *Height* as the Variable and *Type* as the Category Axis.

The resulting output is shown in Table 4.4. The "Group Statistics" table shows that the standard deviations (variances) for the two groups are similar, as was visually seen in the boxplot. (Remember that the variance is the square of the standard deviation.)

Table 4.4 Two-Sample *t*-Test Output for Fertilizer Data

Group Statistics

	TYPE	N	Mean	Std. Deviation	Std. Error Mean
HEIGHT	1	7	53.0714	1.90938	.72168
	2	6	54.2500	1.70968	.69797

Independent Samples Test

		Levene's Test for Equality of Variances		t-test for Equality of Means					95% Confidence Interval of the Difference	
		F	Sig	t	df	Sig. (2-tailed)	Mean Difference	Std.Error Difference	Lower	Upper
HEIGHT	Equal variances assumed	.075	.790	−1.163	11	.269	−1.17857	1.01329	−3.40881	1.05166
	Equal variances not assumed			−1.174	10.963	.265	−1.17857	1.00398	−3.38922	1.03208

From the "Independent Samples Test" in Table 4.4, first notice the results of the *F*-test (Levene's test) for evaluating the equality of variance. The *p*-value 0.79 indicates that the variances are not significantly different. You now have two pieces of information that indicate the variances are similar (the boxplot and Levene's test).

Therefore, if you are comfortable with this information, the appropriate *t*-test is the one that assumes equal variances. However, if you choose to go with the conservative approach, you would use the "Equal variances not assumed" *t*-test. In this case, your final decision for the significance of the *t*-test would not be different.

The following information discusses methods of interpreting the output from the "Independent Samples Test" table.

- *Making a decision based on the p-value.* The *p*-value for the equal variances *t*-test is $p = 0.269$. Since this *p*-value is greater than 0.05, the decision would be that there is no significant variance difference between the two groups. (Do not reject the null hypothesis.) Thus, there is not enough evidence to conclude that the mean heights are different. If you use the approach in which equal variances are not assumed, the *p*-value is $p = 0.265$, which is almost identical to the "equal variance" *p*-value. Thus, your decision would be the same.
- *Making a decision based on the confidence interval.* The 95% confidence intervals for the *difference in means* are given in the last two columns of Table 4.4. The interval associated with the assumption of equal variances is [–3.41 to 1.05], while the confidence interval when equal variances are not assumed is [–3.39 to 1.03]. Since these intervals include 0 (zero), we again conclude that there is no significant difference between the means using either assumption regarding the variances. Thus, you would make the same decisions discussed in the *p*-value section above. The confidence interval gives more information than a simple *p*-value. Each interval above indicates that plausible values of the mean difference lie between about –3.4 and 1.0. Depending on the nature of your experiment, the information about the range of the possible mean differences may be useful in your decision-making process.

Reporting the Results of a (Nonsignificant) Two-Sample *t*-Test

The following sample write-ups illustrate how you might report this two-sample *t*-test in publication format. For purposes of illustration, we use the "equal variance" *t*-test for the remainder of this example:

Narrative for the Methods Section

"A two-sample Student's *t*-test using a pooled estimate of the variance was performed to test the hypothesis that the resulting mean heights of the plants for the two types of fertilizer were equal."

Narrative for the Results Section

"The mean heights of plants using the two brands of fertilizer were not significantly different, $t(11) = -1.17, p = 0.27$."

Or, to be more complete,

"The mean height of plants using fertilizer Brand 1 ($M = 53.07, SD = 1.91, N = 7$) was not significantly different from that using fertilizer Brand 2 ($M = 54.25, SD = 1.71, N = 6$), $t(11) = -1.17, p = 0.27$."

A description of the confidence interval would read as follows:

"A 95% confidence interval on the difference between the two population means using a Student's t distribution with 11 degrees of freedom is [−3.41, 1.05], which indicates that there is not significant evidence that the fertilizers produce different mean growth heights."

Example 4.3

Two-Sample t-Test With Variance Issues

Describing the Problem

Seventy-six subjects were given an untimed test measuring the dexterity required for a particular job skill as a part of a research project at a job placement center for inner-city youth. The sample consisted of 17 males and 59 females. Time to complete the test was recorded (in minutes). The researcher wants to know whether the test is gender neutral. As a part of that analysis, she wonders if the average time to complete the test will be the same for both male and female participants.

Since the researcher is simply interested in determining whether there is a difference in the average times for males and females, a two-sided t-test is appropriate. The hypotheses for this test could be written (in words) as follows:

> *Null hypothesis* (H_0): The mean times to finish the skills test are the same for both genders.

> *Alternative hypothesis* (H_a): The mean times to finish the skills test differ for the two genders.

The data for this analysis are entered into a data set in a format similar to the previous example, using one line per subject, with a group variable (*Gender*) containing two values (M and F) and a variable containing the response variable (*Time*). As in Example 4.2, it is a good practice to look at a plot of the data (as discussed in Chapter 2). For this example, boxplots for the grouped data of the JOB.SAV data set are shown in Figure 4.7. (**Graphs/Chart Builder/Boxplot** [Simple] with *Time* as the X-axis and *Gender* as the Y-axis.)

The side-by-side boxplots show that the data are fairly symmetric and thus consistent with approximate normality. The dots labeled "33," "59," "58," and "24" show that there are several "moderate outliers" although none appear too extreme. The difference in sizes of the boxes illustrates that the equality of variances may be questionable. With this information in mind, we proceed with the t-test:

SPSS Step-By-Step: EXAMPLE 4.3:
Two-Sample t-Test With Variance Issues

To create the output in SPSS for this example, follow these steps:

1. Using the data set JOB.SAV, select **Analyze/Compare Means/Independent Samples T Test**. . . .

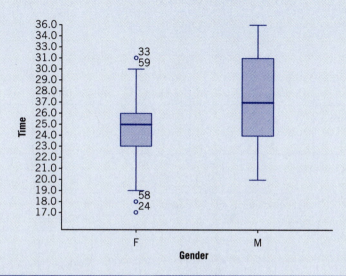

Figure 4.7 Side-By-Side Boxplots for Job Placement Data

2. Select *Time* as the test variable and *Gender* as the grouping variable.

3. Click on the Define Groups button and define the group values as M and F. (This is similar to the boxplots in Figure 4.5, but with M and F as the groups.)

4. Click Continue and then OK, and the output shown in Table 4.5 appears.

Table 4.5 shows the results of performing the two-sample *t*-test. From the "Group Statistics" table, note that there are 59 females and 17 males in the sample. Also note that the standard deviation for males is substantially larger than for females.

In the "Independent Sample Test" table, the test for equality of variances labeled "Levene's Test" yields a significant *p*-value (Sig.) of $p = 0.013$. This indicates that, according to this criterion, the variances cannot be considered equal. This result indicates that you should use the "Equal variances not assumed" *t*-test. Using the conservative approach mentioned earlier, you would also choose to use the unequal variances *t*-test.

- *Making a decision based on the p-value.* Because equal variances are not assumed, you should use the set of statistics labeled "equal variances not assumed" in the "*t*-test for equality of means" section of the "Independent Samples Test." The *p*-value for this

Table 4.5 Two-Sample *t*-Test Results for Job Placement Data

Group Statistics

	Gender	N	Mean	Std. Deviation	Std. Error Mean
Time	M	17	27.529	4.7318	1.1476
	F	59	24.627	2.8881	.3760

Independent Samples Test

		Levene's Test for Equality of Variances		t-test for Equality of Means						
									95% Confidence Interval of the Difference	
		F	Sig	t	df	Sig. (2-tailed)	Mean Difference	Std. Error Difference	Lower	Upper
Time	Equal variances assumed	6.450	.013	3.126	74	.003	2.9023	.9285	1.0521	4.7525
	Equal variances not assumed			2.403	19.557	.026	2.9023	1.2077	.3795	5.4251

version of the *t*-test is $p = 0.026$. Since this *p*-value is less than 0.05, the decision would be that there is a significant difference between the two group means. (Reject the null hypothesis.) Thus, there is evidence to conclude that the mean times to complete the test differ by gender. (Regardless of the statistical results, the researcher should evaluate whether an average difference of 2.9 minutes [27.529 minus 24.627] is important in terms of the goals of the research.)

- *Making a decision based on the confidence interval.* To analyze these data using confidence intervals, refer to the section of Table 4.5 labeled "95% confidence interval of the difference" on the second line of statistics labeled "equal variance not assumed." The interval for the difference in means (male minus female) is [0.3795, 5.4251]. Since the interval does not include 0 (zero), the conclusion is that (at the 0.05 level of significance) you should reject the null hypothesis and conclude that there is a statistically significant difference in the population means. Also, since the confidence interval contains only positive values for the (male minus female) difference in the means, there is evidence that males take longer on average to perform the task.

Calculating Effect Size for a Two-Sample *t*-Test

Although not part of SPSS output, sometimes it is useful to report an effect size for a two-sample *t*-test. This measure quantifies the difference between the two groups and helps you decide whether a statistical significance is also a meaningful difference. A common measure of the effect size is called Cohen's *d*. For a *t*-test where the *t*-statistic is already calculated, you have the information from the SPSS output needed to calculate Cohen's, which is given by

$$d = \frac{t(n_1 + n_2)}{\sqrt{df(n_1 n_2)}}$$

Thus, for the comparison of plant heights by fertilizer brand, you would calculate

$$d = -1.17(6 + 7) / [\sqrt{(11)(6*7)}] = -.707$$

The interpretation for this number (regardless of any statistical significance indicated by a *p*-value) is based on Cohen (1988) where

- *d* from 0.2 to 0.5 is considered a small effect,
- *d* from 0.5 to 0.8 is considered a moderate effect, and
- *d* of 0.8 and above is considered a large effect.

Ignoring the negative (which is changed if you take the groups in the opposite order), the size of the observed difference would be considered to be moderate.

Paired *t*-Test

The paired *t*-test (also called a dependent samples *t*-test) is appropriate for data in which the two samples are correlated or related in some way. This type of analysis is appropriate for the three separate data collection scenarios:

- Pairs consist of before and after measurements on a single group of subjects or patients.
- Two measurements on the same subject or entity (right and left eye, for example) are paired.
- Subjects in one group (e.g., those receiving a treatment) are paired or matched on a one-to-one basis with subjects in a second group (e.g., control subjects). (Sometimes this is done using biological twins.)

In all cases, the data to be analyzed are the differences within pairs (e.g., the right eye measurement minus the left eye measurement). The difference scores are then analyzed as a one-sample *t*-test.

Associated Confidence Interval

The confidence interval associated with a paired *t*-test is the same as the confidence interval for a one-sample *t*-test using the difference scores. The resulting confidence interval is usually examined to determine whether it includes zero.

Appropriate Applications for a Paired *t*-Test

The following are examples of paired data that would properly be analyzed using a paired *t*-test.

- *Does the diet work?* A developer of a new diet is interested in showing that it is effective. He randomly chooses 15 subjects to go on the diet for 1 month. He weighs each patient before and after the 1-month period to see whether there is evidence of a weight loss at the end of the month.

- *Is a new teaching method better than standard methods?* An educator wants to test a new method for improving reading comprehension. Twenty students are assigned to a section that will use the new method. Each of these 20 students is matched (age, race, gender, initial reading level) with a student with similar reading ability who will spend the semester in a class using the standard teaching methods. At the end of the semester, the students in both sections will be given a common reading comprehension exam, and the average reading comprehension differences between the matched pairs is compared.

- *Do new eye drops work better than standard drops?* A pharmaceutical company wants to test a new formulation of eye drops with its standard drops for reducing redness. Fifty subjects who have similar problems with eye redness in each eye are randomly selected for the study. For each subject, an eye is randomly selected to be treated with the new drops, and the other eye is treated with the standard drops. At the end of the treatment schedule, the redness in each eye is measured using a quantitative scale.

Design Considerations for a Paired *t*-Test

Pairing Observations May Increase the Ability to Detect Differences

A paired *t*-test is recommended when variability between groups may be sufficiently large to mask any mean differences that might exist between the groups. Pairing is a method for obtaining a more direct measurement on the difference being examined. For example, in the diet example above, one method of assessing the performance of the diet would be to select 30 subjects and randomly assign 15 to go on the diet and 15 to eat regularly for the next month (i.e., the control group). At the end of the month, the weights of the subjects on the diet could be compared with those in the control group to determine whether there is evidence of a difference in average weights. Clearly, this is not a desirable design since the variability of weights of subjects within the two groups will likely mask any differences that might be produced by one month on the diet. A better design would be to select 15 subjects (or even better, 30 subjects) and measure the weights of these subjects before and after the month on the diet. The 15 differences between the before and after weights for the subjects provide much more focused measurements of the effect of the diet than would independent samples.

Paired *t*-Test Analysis Is Performed on the Difference Scores

The data to be analyzed in a paired *t*-test are the differences between pairs (e.g., the before minus after weight for each subject in a diet study or differences between matched pairs in the study of teaching methods). The difference scores are then analyzed using a one-sample *t*-test.

The Paired *t*-Test Assumes Normality of the Differences

The basic assumption for the paired *t*-test to be valid when you have small sample sizes is that the difference scores are normally distributed and that the observed differences represent a random sample from the population of differences. (See the section on testing for normality, "Describing Quantitative Data," in Chapter 2.) Also, using difference scores can be misleading in cases where there are ceiling or floor limits to the individual values, when there is a substantial "regression to the mean" for observations, or when initial values are not representative of the sample (particularly in longitudinal data).

Hypotheses for a Paired *t*-Test

The hypotheses to be tested in a paired *t*-test are similar to those used in a two-sample *t*-test. In the case of paired data, μ_1 and μ_2 refer to the population means of the before and after measurements on a single group of subjects or to the first and second pair in the case of matched subjects. The null hypotheses may be stated as H_0: $\mu_1 = \mu_2$. However, in the case of paired data, it is common practice to make use of the fact that the difference between the two population means (i.e., $\mu_1 - \mu_2$) is equal to the population mean of the difference scores, denoted μ_d. In this case, the hypotheses are written as follows:

H_0: $\mu_d = 0$ (the population mean of the differences is zero).

H_a: $\mu_d \neq 0$ (the population mean of the differences is not zero).

Example 4.4

Paired t-Test

Consider the diet example described above. The data for this example include two variables reporting before and after weights for 15 randomly selected subjects who participated in a test of a new diet for a 1-month period. Figure 4.8 illustrates the data format, where it can be seen that the before and after weights for a subject are entered on the same row. In this case, we want to determine whether there is evidence that the diet works. That is, if we calculate differences as d_i = "before" weight minus "after" weight, then we should test the following hypotheses:

H_0: $\mu_d = 0$ (the mean of the differences is zero; i.e., the diet is ineffective).

H_a: $\mu_d > 0$ (the mean of the differences is positive; i.e., the diet is effective).

DIET.SAV [DataSet1] - IBM SPSS Statistics Data Editor

File   Edit   View   Data   Transform   Analyze   Direct Marketing   Graphs   Utilities   Add-ons   Window   Help

	subject	before	after	var	var	var	var	var
1	1	210	204					
2	2	207	205					
3	3	183	182					
4	4	195	196					
5	5	187	177					
6	6	201	193					
7	7	158	152					
8	8	180	182					
9	9	173	165					
10	10	198	186					
11	11	225	218					
12	12	243	237					
13	13	168	174					
14	14	177	178					
15	15	196	199					

Figure 4.8   SPSS Editor Showing DIET.SAV Data

The following example illustrates how to perform this test in either of two ways: first using data pairs, then using the differences.

SPSS Step-By-Step. EXAMPLE 4.4: Paired *t*-Test

Using the data pairs (as shown in Figure 4.9)

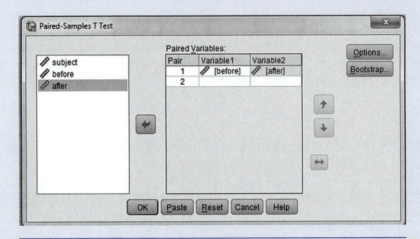

Figure 4.9   Select Variables for Paired *t*-Test

1. Open the data set DIET.SAV and select **Analyze/Compare Means/Paired-Samples T Test**. . . .

2. Select the two variables for which you want the difference to be taken. In this case, choose *Before* as Pair 1 Variable 1 and *After* as Pair 1 Variable 2 as shown in in Figure 4.9.

3. Click OK and Table 4.6 is displayed.

In this output, the sample mean of the difference scores is 3.533, with a standard deviation of the differences given by 5.330. The calculated *t*-statistic (with 14 *df*) is given by 2.567, which has a *p*-value of 0.022. When interpreting these results, notice that the mean of the *"before minus after"* differences is positive, which is supportive of the alternative hypothesis that $\mu_d > 0$. Since this experiment from its inception was only interested in detecting a weight loss, it can be viewed as a one-sided test. Thus, for a one-sided hypothesis test, the reported *p*-value should be one half of the *p*-value given in the computer output (i.e., $p = 0.011$). That is, at the $\alpha = .05$ level, we reject H_0 and conclude that the weight loss diet is effective. The output also includes a 95% confidence interval on the mean difference.

It should be noted that this confidence interval is two-sided. In this case, the fact that the interval [0.58, 6.49] contains only positive values suggests that $\mu_d > 0$ (i.e., that the diet is effective).

Table 4.6 Results for a Paired *t*-Test (Selected Output)

Paired Samples Statistics

		Mean	N	Std. Deviation	Std. Error Mean
Pair 1	before	193.40	15	22.232	5.740
	after	189.87	15	21.250	5.487

Paired Samples Test

		Paired Differences							
					95% Confidence Interval of the Difference				Sig.
		Mean	Std. Deviation	Std. Error Mean	Lower	Upper	t	df	(2-tailed)
Pair 1	before - after	3.533	5.330	1.376	.582	6.485	2.567	14	.022

Programming Notes: It should be noted that the order of the difference, i.e., in this case "*Before – After*," is determined by your placement of the variable names in the dialog box shown in Figure 4.9. SPSS will calculate differences as Variable1 – Variable 2.

It should be noted that the default order of the difference (i.e., in this case, "*Before – After*") is determined by the order in which the variables are entered into the database. That is, using the paired *t*-test option and the data in the data set DIET.SAV, SPSS will by default calculate the difference "*Before – After*." Calculation of the difference "*After – Before*" can be obtained by directly calculating the difference and performing a one-sample *t*-test on the difference scores, as illustrated in the next example.

Using the Difference Scores

A second way to perform this analysis is using difference scores. The same results as those obtained in Table 4.6 can be obtained by directly computing the "*Before – After*" differences and performing a one-sample *t*-test on the differences. (See the section "Creating a new variable using computation" in Appendix B.) After creating a new variable named *Difference*, you can perform the analysis shown in the following example:

SPSS Step-By-Step. EXAMPLE 4.5:
Paired *t*-Test Using Difference Scores

To perform the one-sample *t*-test on the new variable called *Difference* that exists in the data set DIET_WITH_DIFFERENCE.SAV, follow these steps:

1. Open the data set DIET_WITH_DIFFERNCE.SAV and select **Analyze/Compare Means/One-Sample T Test**. . . .

2. Select *Difference* as the test variable and specify 0 as the Test Value. Click OK and Table 4.7 is displayed.

Table 4.7   Paired *t*-Test Results Obtained Using a Calculated Difference Variable

One-Sample Statistics

	N	Mean	Std. Deviation	Std. Error Mean
Difference	15	3.5333	5.33006	1.37622

One-Sample Test

			Test Value = 0			
					95% Confidence Interval of the Difference	
	t	df	Sig. (2-tailed)	Mean Difference	Lower	Upper
Difference	2.567	14	.022	3.53333	.5816	6.4850

3. One way to display the boxplot of the difference scores in the DIET_WITH_DIFFERENCES.SAV data set is to select **Analyze/Descriptive Statistics/Explore** . . . , add *Difference* to the Dependent List, click on the Plots radio button at the bottom left of the dialog box, and click OK. The boxplot shown in Figure 4.10 is displayed.

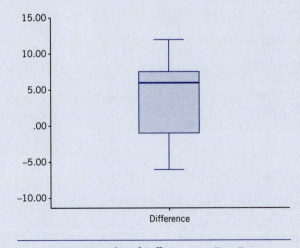

Figure 4.10   Boxplot of Differences in Diet Data

The reported mean difference is 3.53333 (and the *p*-value for the test is $p = 0.022$). These results are consistent with those obtained earlier. If it were desirable, you could have calculated the differences using the formula "*After – Before*." In this case, the mean difference would be −3.53 and the *t*-value would be −2.567, but the *p*-value would remain the same.

> Note than in this version of the test (where you are testing the precalculated difference), you could choose some other value to test. For example, if this diet advertised that you'd lose at least 10 pounds, you could enter that as the test value. In the paired *t*-test version, the hypothesis tested is that the difference is zero.

Reporting the Results for EXAMPLE 4.4: Paired *t*-Test

The following sample write-ups illustrate how you might report this paired *t*-test in publication format.

Narrative for the Methods Section

> "A paired *t*-test was performed to ascertain whether the diet was effective."

Narrative for the Results Section

> "There is evidence that the mean weight loss is positive, that is, that the diet is effective in producing weight loss, $t(14) = 2.567$, one-tailed $p = 0.01$."

Or, more completely,

> "The mean weight loss ($M = 3.53$, $SD = 5.33$, $N = 15$) was significantly greater than zero, $t(14) = 2.567$, one-tailed $p = 0.01$, providing evidence that the diet is effective in producing weight loss after one month."

Calculating Effect Size for a Paired *t*-Test

To calculate the Cohen's *d* effect size measure from the SPSS output for a paired *t*-test, you can use this formula.

$$d = \text{Mean difference/Standard Deviation of the difference} = M/SD$$

For this example, calculate

$$d = 3.53/5.33 = 0.662$$

The interpretation for this number is based on Cohen (1988) where

> *d* from 0.2 to 0.5 is considered a small effect

> *d* from 0.5 to 0.8 is considered a moderate effect

> *d* of 0.8 and above is considered a large effect

Thus, the observed difference would be considered moderate.

SUMMARY

The *t*-test is one of the most widely used statistical procedures. It comes in three basic varieties: the single-sample *t*-test, the two-sample *t*-test, and the paired *t*-test. This chapter presents a concise, but not exhaustive, description of how to perform, interpret, and report the results of *t*-tests. The next chapter is about correlation and regression analysis.

REFERENCES

Cohen, J. (1988). *Statistical power analysis for the behavioral sciences* (2nd ed.). Mahwah, NJ: Lawrence Erlbaum Associates.

Moore, D., & McCabe, G. (2012). *Introduction to the practice of statistics* (7th ed.). New York, NY: Freeman.

Posten, H. O. (1978). The robustness of the two-sample *t*-test over the Pearson system. *Journal of Statistical Computation and Simulation*, 6, 195–311.

Sawilowsky, S. S. (2002). Fermat, Schubert, Einstein, and Behrens-Fisher: The probable difference between two means when $\sigma_1^2 \neq \sigma_2^2$. *Journal of Modern Applied Statistical Methods*, 1(2), 461–472.

Watkins, A., Scheaffer, R., & Cobb, G. (2008). *Statistics in action: Understanding a world of data*. Emeryville, CA: Key College Publishing.

Correlation and Regression

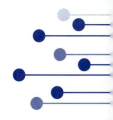

Have you ever noticed that, on the average, the more money people earn, the more expensive the car they drive? I drive a 9-year-old Honda. Does that tell you anything? You might refer to the association between income and type of car using the term *correlation*. In statistical terms, a correlation is a mathematical measure of the strength of association between two quantitative variables—in this case, between income and value of the car.

A closely related cousin of correlation analysis is regression analysis. In a classic study, the statistician Karl Pearson compiled the heights of 1,078 fathers and sons where the son had reached full height. As would be expected, a scatterplot of the data shows that taller fathers tend to have taller sons while shorter fathers tend to have shorter sons, as shown in Figure 5.1. A correlation analysis involves measuring the extent to which the points in the scatterplot tend to swarm about a line. Suppose, however, that you want to know how well you can predict the height of a son if you know the height of his father. Using the data, you can come up with a regression line (equation) for performing the prediction. In regression analysis, we are interested in using the relationship between the two variables to predict the value of one of the variables given a value of the other variable.

This chapter describes when and how to use correlation and regression analyses. Specifically, these topics are covered:

- *Correlation*: examining the linear association between two variables
- *Simple linear regression*: examining the relationship between a single predictor and a response variable
- *Multiple linear regression*: examining the relationship between two or more predictor variables with a response variable

Chapter 9 will deal with a specialized type of regression called logistic regression.

Correlation Analysis

A statistic that is often used to measure the strength of a linear association between two variables is the correlation coefficient. Specifically, the correlation covered in this chapter

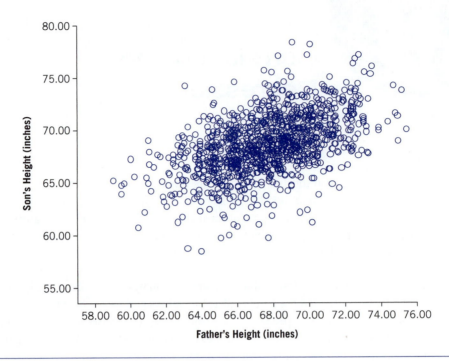

Figure 5.1   Pearson's Scatterplot of Heights of Fathers and Sons

is called Pearson's correlation coefficient (yes—it's the same Pearson who measured the fathers and sons). In this section, we refer to Pearson's correlation coefficient as simply the "correlation coefficient." The theoretical correlation coefficient is often expressed using the Greek letter *rho* (ρ) while its estimate from a set of data is usually denoted by r.

Unless otherwise specified, when we say "correlation coefficient," we mean the estimate (r) calculated from the data. The correlation coefficient is always between -1 and $+1$, where -1 indicates that the points in the scatterplot of the two variables all lie on a line that has negative slope (a perfect negative correlation), and a correlation coefficient of $+1$ indicates that the points all lie on a line that has positive slope (a perfect positive correlation). In general, a positive correlation between two variables indicates that as one of the variables increases, the other variable also tends to increase. If the correlation coefficient is negative, then as one variable increases, the other variable tends to decrease and vice versa. (Neither of these conditions implies causality.)

A correlation coefficient close to $+1$ (or -1) indicates a strong linear relationship (i.e., that the points in the scatterplot are closely packed around a line). However, the closer a correlation coefficient gets to 0, the weaker the linear relationship and the more scattered the swarm of points in the graph. Most statistics packages quote a *t*-statistic along with the correlation coefficient for purposes of testing whether the correlation coefficient is significantly different from zero. A scatterplot is a very useful tool for viewing the relationship and determining whether a relationship is indeed linear in nature.

Appropriate Applications for Correlation Analysis

The correlation coefficient might be used to determine whether there is a linear relationship between the following pairs of variables:

- *What is the relationship between grades in English rhetoric and introductory statistics?* A sample of first-year students is selected at a certain university, and their scores in English rhetoric and introductory statistics are compared.

- *How do Internet sales relate to advertising costs?* The monthly amount spent on Google ads and monthly amount received in orders from an Internet store site are compared.

- *Fatigue versus performance.* Managers track the number of overtime hours worked and the daily cost of mistakes made at a chemical production facility.

Design Considerations for Correlation Analysis

1. *The correlation coefficient measures the strength of a linear relationship between the two variables.* That is, the relationship between the two variables measures how closely the two points in a scatterplot (*X-Y* plot) of the two variables cluster about a straight line. If two variables are related but the relationship is not linear, then the correlation coefficient may not be able to detect a relationship.

2. *Observations should be quantitative (numeric) variables.* The correlation coefficient is not appropriate for qualitative (categorical) variables, even if they are numerically coded. In addition, tests of significance of the correlation coefficient assume that the two variables are approximately normally distributed.

3. *The pairs of data are independently collected.* Whereas, for example, in a one-sample *t*-test, we make the assumption that the observations represent a random sample from some population, in correlation analysis, we assume that observed pairs of data represent a random sample from some bivariate population.

Hypotheses for Correlation Analysis

The usual hypotheses for testing the statistical significance of a Pearson's correlation coefficient are the following:

H_0: $\rho = 0$ (there is no linear relationship between the two variables).

H_a: $\rho \neq 0$ (there is a linear relationship between the two variables).

These hypotheses can also be one-sided when appropriate. This null hypothesis is tested in statistical programs using a test statistic based on Student's t. (SPSS doesn't actually give the t value—just the associated p-value for the two-sided test.) If the p-value for the test is sufficiently small, then you reject the null hypothesis and conclude that ρ is not 0. A researcher will then have to make a professional judgment to determine whether the observed association has "practical" significance. A correlation coefficient of $r = 0.25$ may be statistically significant (i.e., we have statistical evidence that it is nonzero), but it may be of no practical importance if that level of association is not of interest to the researcher. Effect size (discussed below) addresses this issue.

Tips and Caveats for Correlation Analysis

One-Sided Tests

The two-sided p-values for tests about a correlation reported by most statistics programs can be divided by two for one-sided tests if the calculated correlation coefficient has the same sign as that specified in the alternative hypothesis.

Variables Don't Have to Be on the Same Scale

The correlation coefficient is unitless. For example, you can correlate height (inches) with weight (pounds). In addition, given a set of data on heights and weights, it does not matter whether you measure height in inches, centimeters, feet, and so on and weight in pounds, kilograms, and so on. In all cases, the resulting correlation coefficient will be the same.

Correlation Does Not Imply Cause and Effect

A conclusion of cause and effect is often improperly inferred based on the finding of a significant correlation. It is important to understand that correlation does not imply causation. Causation is difficult to imply (let alone prove) and is a task fraught with many problems.

The Effect Size Provides a Description of a Correlation's Strength

The effect size for a correlation measures the strength of the relationship. For correlation, r serves as the numeric measure of the effect size whose strength can be interpreted according to criteria developed by Cohen (1988):

- When *r* is greater than 0.10 and less than 0.30, the effect size is "small."

- When *r* is greater than 0.30 and less than 0.50, the effect size is "medium."

- When *r* is greater than 0.50 the effect size is "large."

Effect sizes smaller than 0.10 would be considered trivial. These terms (small, medium, and large) associated with the size of the correlation are intended to provide you with a specific word you can use to describe the strength of the correlation in a write-up.

Correlations Provide an Incomplete Picture of the Relationship

Suppose, for example, that you have found that for first-year students at a certain university, there is a very strong positive correlation between grades (from 0–100) in rhetoric and statistics. Simply stated, this finding would lead one to believe that rhetoric and statistics grades are very similar (i.e., that a student's score in rhetoric will be very close to his or her score in statistics). However, you should realize that you would get a strong positive correlation if the statistics grade for each student tended to be about 20 points lower than his or her rhetoric grade. (We're not claiming that this is the case—it's just a hypothetical example!) For this reason, when reporting a correlation between two variables, it is good practice to not simply report a correlation but also to report the mean and standard deviation of each of the variables. In addition, a scatterplot provides useful information that should be given in addition to the simple reporting of a correlation. (See the example in Freedman, Pisani, and Purves, 2007, Ch. 9.).

Examine Relationship With a Scatterplot and Watch for Outliers

Always confirm the linear nature of the correlation with a scatterplot (*X-Y* plot) because it is possible for a correlation coefficient to appear important when examination of the data themselves suggest otherwise. Figure 5.2 shows several examples of scatterplots, all of which have a computed correlation coefficient of about 0.72. The upper left scatterplot has the typical appearance of points swarming about a line with a correlation of about 0.72. In the upper right scatter diagram, the apparent linear correlation is nearly entirely due to the extreme value or outlier in the upper right-hand corner of the plot. Without that value, there is no apparent relationship between the two variables. This is an example of what is sometimes referred to as the lollipop effect. (Can you see the lollipop?) In the middle left scatterplot, there seems to be a strong linear relationship between the two variables (much stronger than 0.72). However, notice that there is one data value in the lower right-hand corner of the plot that does not fit this correlation structure. This data value dramatically

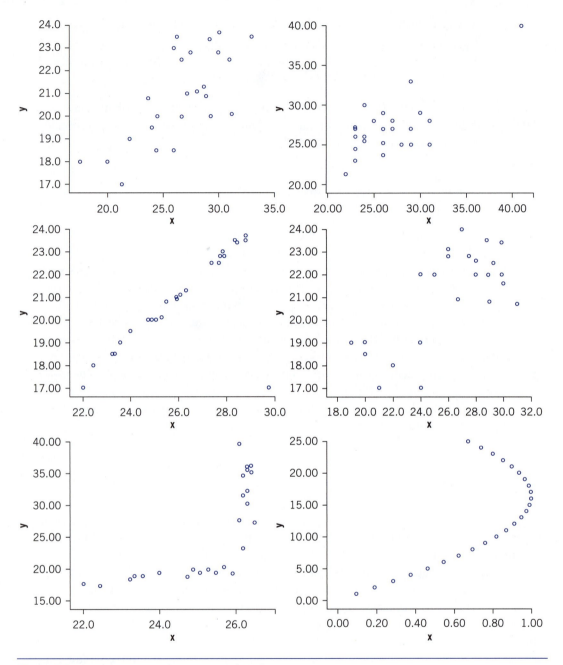

Figure 5.2 Example Scatterplots Associated With $r = .72$

reduces the computed correlation coefficient. Note that this unusual point would not be picked up as an outlier by looking at the univariate (one variable at a time) techniques in

Chapter 2 because it is within an acceptable range of both variables. As always, whenever you see unusual or extreme values in your data set, you should investigate whether these values are "real." Even if the outlying values in the upper right or middle left scatterplots are real, their effect on the correlation and resulting test of significance should be noted. In the middle right scatterplot, there appear to be two groupings of data. These groups may correspond to subpopulations, and it should be noted that there appears to be little or no linear relationship between the two variables within each group. In the lower left scatterplot, the points follow a line with a very small slope for x between 22 and 26 and follow a different and much steeper linear pattern for x greater than 26. In the lower right scatterplot, the variables appear to be very strongly (maybe functionally) related, but the relationship is nonlinear.

Don't Extrapolate

Don't assume that linear relationships observed over certain ranges of the variables will continue to exist if the ranges are extended. Consider the case in which two variables have a strong linear relationship over a certain range of variables. If the range on one or both of the variables is expanded, then the linear relationship observed previously may or may not continue to exist. Over an expanded range, the relationship may become nonlinear or may disappear altogether. See, for example, the bottom left graph in Figure 5.2. This is related to the advice against extrapolation that we will give related to linear regression analysis.

If Variables Are Not Normally Distributed

If you cannot assume normality of the X or Y variable, then you should use Spearman's correlation to measure agreement between the two variables. See Chapter 8: Nonparametric Analysis Procedures for information on this topic.

> To produce the scatterplot of Father and Son's heights shown in Figure 5.1, use the same procedure outlined in steps 1 to 4 above with the data set named PEARSON.SAV.

Example 5.1

Correlation Analysis

Describing the Problem

Data collected on 50 different children include the child's age and the times to complete four different hand-eye coordination tasks (labeled *Time1* to *Time4*). The researcher is interested in understanding the extent to which performances on these tasks are associated with the child's age and with one another. In a preliminary analysis, we want to measure the correlation between *Age* and *Time1*. The following example illustrates how to do this in SPSS.

SPSS Step-By-Step. EXAMPLE 5.1: Correlations

To calculate the correlation coefficient between Age and Time1 and plot the corresponding scatterplot, follow these steps:

1. Open the data set CORRELATION.SAV and select **Analyze/Correlate/ Bivariate**. . . .

2. Select *Age* and *Time1* as variables. Make sure the Pearson checkbox is selected and click OK.

3. To display a scatterplot of the variables, select **Graphs/Chart Builder** and select the Scatter/Dot chart type and drag the Simple Scatter icon into the Chart Preview Box.

4. Select *Time1* as the Y-axis and *Age* as the X-axis variables and click OK. The scatterplot shown in in Figure 5.3 is displayed.

The correlation coefficient for these two variables is $r = 0.501$ with $p < 0.001$. The scatterplot shown in Figure 5.3 confirms that there is a moderate increase in *Time1* as *Age* increases. This scatterplot is similar in appearance to the father-son data in Figure 5.1, and in both cases, the correlation is approximately $r = 0.5$. Recall that the effect size classification, $r = 0.501$ is right on the border between a medium and large effect size.

Because there are five quantitative variables involved (i.e., *Age, Time1* . . . *Time4*), it might be useful to examine them all at once. Follow these steps to examine the relationship between these variables:

1. To create a matrix of correlation coefficients for the variables *Age, Time1, Time2, Time3,* and *Time4,* follow these additional steps: Select **Analyze/Correlate/Bivariate**. . . . Select *Age, Time1, Time2, Time3,* and *Time4* as variables. Make sure the Pearson checkbox is selected and click OK. This creates the output shown in Table 5.1.

2. To display a scatterplot matrix of the same variables, select **Graphs/Chart Builder** and select the **Scatter/Dot** chart type and drag the Scatterplot Matrix icon (bottom row, second from right) into the Chart Preview box. Drag *Age, Time1, Time2, Time3,* and *Time4* into the variable box at the bottom of the sample chart. Click OK. The output shown in Figure 5.4 is displayed.

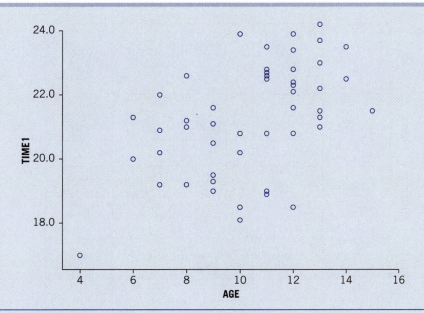

Figure 5.3 Scatterplot of TIME1 by Age

Table 5.1 Matrix of Correlation Coefficients

Correlations

		AGE	TIME1	TIME2	TIME3	TIME4
AGE	Pearson Correlation	1	.501**	.381**	.450**	.488**
	Sig. (2-tailed)		.000	.006	.001	.000
	N	50	50	50	50	50
TIME1	Pearson Correlation	.501**	1	.764**	.686**	.826**
	Sig. (2-tailed)	.000		.000	.000	.000
	N	50	50	50	50	50
TIME2	Pearson Correlation	.381**	.764**	1	.834**	.573**
	Sig. (2-tailed)	.006	.000		.000	.000
	N	50	50	50	50	50
TIME3	Pearson Correlation	.450**	.686**	.834**	1	.649**
	Sig. (2-tailed)	.001	.000	.000		.000
	N	50	50	50	50	50
TIME4	Pearson Correlation	.488**	.826**	.573**	.649**	1
	Sig. (2-tailed)	.000	.000	.000	.000	
	N	50	50	50	50	50

** Correlation is significant at the 0.01 level (2-tailed).

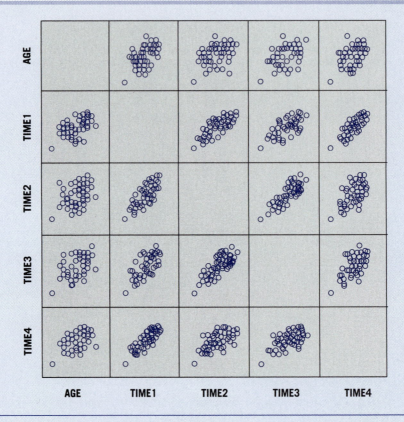

Figure 5.4 Scatterplot Matrix for Example 5.1 Data

In the matrix of correlation coefficients (Table 5.1), the top number in each cell is r, the calculated sample correlation coefficient between the two variables under consideration. The second number in each cell is the p-value, and the third number is the sample size (i.e., the number of valid pairs that were observed.) In this case, all correlations are statistically significant because all p-values are less than 0.05. The matrix is symmetric about the diagonal because, for example, the correlation coefficient between *Age* and *Time1* (0.501) in the first row and second column is the same as the correlation coefficient between *Time1* and *Age* in the second row and first column. Note also that, for example, there is a perfect correlation (i.e., $r = 1$) between *Age* and itself in the first diagonal element. The correlation coefficients range from $r = 0.381$ to $r = 0.834$ (ignoring the diagonal).

Figure 5.4 shows the matrix of scatterplots for these variables and provides a useful visualization corresponding to the results shown in Table 5.1.

Reporting the Results for a Pearson's Correlation

The following example illustrates how you could report the results of a correlation analysis using the variables *Age* and *Time1*. Note that the degrees of freedom for the *t*-test of the correlation hypothesis is $N - 2$ (number of cases minus 2).

Narrative for the Methods Section

"An evaluation of the linear relationship between the child's age and the score on the *Time1* hand-eye coordination exercise was measured using Pearson's correlation."

Narrative for the Results Section

"An analysis using Pearson's correlation coefficient indicated that there is a significant linear relationship between *Age* and performance on *Time1*, $r(48) = 0.50$, $p < 0.001$. For these data, the mean (*SD*) for *Age* was 10.46 (2.43) and for *Time1* was 21.27 (1.72)."

To incorporate the effect size (large) into the narrative, use "An analysis using Pearson's correlation coefficient indicated that there is a large and significant linear relationship. . . ."

Simple Linear Regression

Simple linear regression (SLR) is a statistical tool used to examine the relationship between one predictor (independent) variable and a single quantitative response (dependent) variable. Simple linear regression analysis produces a regression equation that can be used for prediction. A typical experiment involves observing a sample of paired observations in which the independent variable (*X*) may have been fixed at a variety of values of interest and the dependent variable has been observed. These observations are used to create an equation that can be used to predict the dependent variable given a value of the independent variable.

Appropriate Applications for Simple Linear Regression

- *How good is a new medical test?* A new (less expensive) medical test is developed to potentially replace a conventional (more expensive) test. A regression equation is developed to determine how well the new test (independent variable) predicts the results of the conventional test (dependent variable).

- *Systolic blood pressure and smoking.* A medical researcher wants to understand the relationship between weight (independent variable) and systolic blood pressure (dependent variable) in males older than 40 years of age who smoke. A regression equation is obtained to determine how well the blood pressure reading can be predicted from weight for males older than age 40 who smoke.

- *Should I spend more on advertising?* The owner of a Web site wants to know if the weekly costs of advertising (independent variable) on a cable channel are related to the number of visits to his site (dependent variable). In the data collection stage, the advertising costs are allowed to vary from week to week. A regression equation is obtained from this training sample to determine how well number of visits to the site can be predicted from advertising costs.

Design Considerations for Simple Linear Regression

There Is a Theoretical Regression Line

The regression line calculated from the data is a sample-based version of a theoretical line describing the relationship between the independent variable (X) and the dependent variable (Y). The theoretical line has the form

$$Y = \alpha + \beta X + \varepsilon$$

where α is the y-intercept, β is the slope, and ε is an error term with zero mean and constant variance. Notice that $\beta = 0$ indicates that there is no linear relationship between X and Y.

The Observed Regression Equation Is Calculated From the Data Based on the Least Squares Principle

The regression line that is obtained for predicting the dependent variable (Y) from the independent variable (X) is given by

$$\hat{Y} = a + bX,$$

and it is the line for which the sum-of-squared vertical differences from the points in the X-Y scatterplot to the line is a minimum. In practice, $\hat{Y}$ is the prediction of the dependent variable given that the independent variable takes on the value X. We say that the values a and b are the least squares estimates of α and β, respectively. That is, the least squares estimates are those for which the sum-of-squared differences between the observed Y values and the predicted Y values are minimized. To be more specific, the least squares estimates are the values of a and b for which the sum of the quantities $(Y_i - a - bX_i)^2$, $i = 1, \ldots, N$ is minimized.

Several Assumptions Are Involved

These include the following:

1. *Normality.* The population of Y values for each X is normally distributed.

2. *Equal variances.* The populations in Assumption 1 all have the same variance.

3. *Independence.* The dependent variables used in the computation of the regression equation are independent. This typically means that each observed X-Y pair of observations must be from a separate subject or entity.

You will often see the assumptions above stated in terms of the error term ε. Simple linear regression is robust to moderate departures from these assumptions, but you should be aware of them and should examine your data to understand the nature of your data and how well these assumptions are met.

Hypotheses for a Simple Linear Regression Analysis

To evaluate how well a set of data fits a simple linear regression model, a statistical test is performed regarding the slope (β) of the theoretical regression line. The hypotheses are as follows:

H_0: $\beta = 0$ (the slope is zero; there is no linear relationship between the variables).

H_a: $\beta \neq 0$ (the slope is not zero; there is a linear relationship between the variables).

The null hypothesis indicates that there is no linear relationship between the two variables. One-sided tests (specifying that the slope is positive or negative) can also be performed.

SIDEBAR

The statistical test for the hypothesis that the slope is zero in a simple linear regression is mathematically equivalent to the test in correlation analysis that $\rho = 0$.

A low p-value for this test (less than 0.05) would lead you to conclude that there is a linear relationship between the two variables and that knowledge of X would be useful in the prediction of Y.

Tips and Caveats for Simple Linear Regression

Don't Extrapolate

Once a regression line is obtained and it is concluded that there is indeed a significant linear relationship upon which to base the predictions, you can use the line for predicting Y values for a given value X. However, the linear relationship that is established applies only to the range of X values used in developing the regression line. Based on the analysis leading to the regression equation, you have no way of knowing whether the observed linear relationship exists beyond the range of the observed X values. For example, consider the data shown in the bottom left scatterplot in Figure 5.2. Suppose you have access to only the data for which $X \le 26$ and you find the regression line for predicting Y from X. It can be seen that this line will do a good job of predicting Y for X between 22 and 26. However, if you use this line to predict the value of Y when $X = 26.4$, it is clear that the predicted Y will be much lower than the actual Y because the nature of the relationship between X and Y changed at about $X = 26$. The regression line you obtained applies only to the range of X values used in its computation. Using the regression equation to predict Y when $X = 27$ would obviously give very lousy estimates. Thus, using a regression equation to predict Y for any value of X that is outside the range of X values observed is called extrapolation. Don't do it!

Analyze Residual Plots

Residuals are calculated as $e = Y - \hat{Y}$ for each pair of observations in the data set, where $\hat{Y}$ is the prediction obtained from the regression line and Y is the original data value. Note that for each X-Y pair in the data set, a residual is computed, and a scatterplot of these residuals is often plotted with the independent variable on the horizontal axis and the residuals on the vertical axis. If the assumptions are met, then this scatterplot should appear as random points centered at zero. It may also be useful to plot the residuals using run-order as the horizontal axis. (Run-order is the order in which the observations were observed.)

Examination of residual plots can help you determine whether the assumptions are met. For example, if the residuals follow some sort of nonlinear curve, then this may be an indication that a linear regression is not appropriate. If the spread of the points around the center line tends to change across the range of the independent variable, this may be an indication that the assumption of equal variances is not appropriate. If a pattern appears in a run-order residual plot, you should determine if there was some type of change over time (e.g., fatigue) that influenced the data values.

Sometimes, standardized residuals (residuals divided by their standard error) are plotted. In this case, the basic patterns to be examined are the same, but the standardizing makes it easier to identify outliers. If a standardized residual is larger than 2 or 3 in absolute value, it may indicate an outlier or at least a data point of some interest. For more discussion of residual analysis, see Kleinbaum, Kupper, Nizam, and Rosenberg (2013), and for more on outlier detection, see Rousseeuw and Annick (2005).

Transformations

If the residuals do not appear to be random in the residual plot, you may consider applying a transformation to one or both of the variables to help eliminate the problem. Common transformations include the logarithm and the square root. Depending on the type of nonlinearity observed, you may want to apply this transformation to the independent variable, the dependent variable, or both. Information on how to transform data to create new variables in SPSS is given in Appendix A: A Brief Tutorial for Using IBM SPSS for Windows. A good reference for learning more about transformations is Kleinbaum et al. (2013).

Additional Tips

Other tips and caveats similar to those in correlation analysis include the following:

- Variables need not be on the same scale.
- A p-value less than 0.05 indicates only that there is *some* predictive value when using X to predict Y.
- The finding of a significant predictive relationship does not imply cause and effect.
- The two-sided p-values associated with the test for slope given by most statistics programs can be divided by two for one-sided tests if the slope estimate has the same sign as that specified in the alternative hypothesis.
- Relationships should be examined using scatterplots.

Interval Estimates

There are several interval estimates used in simple linear regression.

- *Confidence interval for* β. You can obtain confidence intervals on the parameter β related to the hypothesis test mentioned above. If the resulting

95% confidence interval contains zero, then there is not sufficient evidence to conclude that the theoretical slope is nonzero (i.e., there is not significant evidence of a linear relationship).

- *Confidence interval for mean of* Y *for given value of* X. This is really a collection of confidence intervals, one for each value of the independent variable. The upper and lower limits of these confidence intervals are typically drawn as curves across the range of observed values of X (see Figure 5.5).

- *Prediction interval for future value of* Y *given* X. This interval is technically not a confidence interval. The interpretation of a 95% prediction interval for Y given X is as follows. Suppose we randomly select a new data pair for which the independent variable takes on the value X. We are 95% sure that the corresponding value of Y will fall in this prediction interval. This interval is similar to the confidence interval on the mean value of Y for a given value X but is somewhat wider.

$$Predicted\ Task = 1.599 + 0.083(52) = 5.915$$

Example 5.2

Simple Linear Regression

Describing the Problem

A random sample of 14 students is selected from an elementary school, and each student is measured on a creativity score (*Create*) using a new testing instrument and on a task score (*Task*) using a standard instrument. The *Task* score is the mean time taken to perform several hand-eye coordination tasks. Because the test for the creativity test is much cheaper, it is of interest to know whether you can substitute it for the more expensive *Task* score. That is, can you create a regression equation that will effectively predict a *Task* score (the dependent variable) from the *Create* score (the independent variable)?

Figure 5.5 shows a scatterplot of the two variables along with the regression line and the confidence intervals for the mean of Y given X. In the plot, we use the standard practice of plotting the independent variable (*Create*) on the X-axis and the dependent variable (*Task*) on the Y-axis. By observing the scatterplot (try to ignore the line and interval estimates for now), you can verify that there is a positive correlation between the two variables, and it appears that knowing *Create* should help in predicting *Task*. It is also clear that knowing *Create* does not in any way perfectly predict *Task*.

This example illustrates how to perform the regression analysis:

SPSS Step-By-Step. EXAMPLE 5.2:
Simple Linear Regression

1. Open the file REGSIMP.SAV and select **Analyze/Regression/Linear**. . . .

2. Select *Task* as the dependent variable and *Create* as the independent variable and click OK. Two of the output tables, the Model Summary and Coefficients tables for the analysis, are shown in Table 5.2.

Table 5.2 Results of Simple Linear Regression Analysis

Model Summary

Model	R	R Square	Adjusted R Square	Std. Error of the Estimate
1	.744[a]	.553	.516	1.2328

a. Predictors: (Constant), create

Coefficients[a]

Model		Unstandardized Coefficients		Standardized Coefficients	t	Sig.
		B	Std. Error	Beta		
1	(Constant)	1.599	1.008		1.586	.139
	create	.083	.022	.744	3.856	.002

a. Dependent Variable: task

The Model Summary table (Table 5.2) provides information about the correlation between *Task* and *Create* where $r = 0.744$ indicating that there is a positive relationship between the two variables (as one increases in value, so does the other). The "create" line in the Coefficients table gives the results of the two-sided hypothesis test that the theoretical slope of the regression line for predicting *Task* from *Create* is 0. In this case, $p = 0.002$ indicates that you should reject the null hypothesis and conclude that there is a statistically significant linear relationship between the two variables, and therefore that *Create* should be useful in predicting *Task*.

The sample regression equation displayed on the plot was created from the "Unstandardized Coefficients" in the Coefficients table. Thus, the regression equation for predicting *Task* from *Create* is

$$\text{Predicted } Task = 1.599 + 0.083(Create),$$

or said in words, you predict the *Task* value by multiplying *Create* by 0.083 and adding 1.599.

> Note that the *p*-value associated with the "Constant" term is for testing H_0: $\alpha = 0$ (i.e., that the theoretical y-intercept is zero). In most cases, this will not be of interest to you. That is, usually the only *p*-value of interest will be the one associated with the independent variable (i.e., the one used for testing whether the slope is significantly different from zero).

3. Using the REGSIMP.SAV data set, to produce a scatterplot of the data with a fitted regression line, select **Graphs/Legacy Dialogs/Scatter/Dot**. Select **Simple Scatter** and click **Define**. Drag the variable *Task* to the Y-axis and *Create* to the X-axis and click OK.

4. To draw the regression line on the plot, once the scatterplot appears, double-click on it to enter the SPSS Chart Editor:

   - From the Chart Editor menu, select **Elements/Fit Line at Total**.
   - Click the Fit Line tab and select Linear as the Fit Method. (If you do not want the label showing the regression equation on the line, unclick the option "Attach label to line.")
   - In the Confidence Interval box, select Mean (leave percentage at 95). (This draws the 95% confidence interval for the mean of Y given X on the scatterplot.)
   - Click Apply and Close.

5. Close the chart editor (File/Close). The plot in Figure 5.5 is displayed.

Figure 5.5 shows the scatterplot along with the regression line which seems to provide reasonable estimates for *Task* for each value of *Create*. For another student who has a *Create* score of 52, you would predict a *Task* score using the equation

$$\text{Predicted Task} = 1.599 + 0.083(52) = 5.915$$

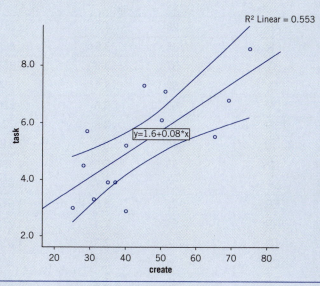

Figure 5.5   Scatterplot for Simple Linear Regression Example

which is visually consistent with the regression line in Figure 5.5 at $X = 52$. A visual inspection of the scatterplot indicates, however, that although the relationship is (strongly) statistically significant, the scatter of points around the regression (prediction) line is not extremely tight. Therefore, although statistically significant, these results may or may not lead you to conclude that the *Create* test results can be adequately predicted using *Task*. This is a decision that you will have to make based on your professional knowledge of the subject matter. For example, you must determine whether you are willing to accept the size of possible errors in estimates of *Task* obtained from the regression line. Examining Figure 5.5 you can see that some values of *Task* are as much as 2 units away from the fitted regression line. If making this magnitude of a predictive error is life threatening or costly in some other way, you may feel that the predictive capability of the equation, although statistically significant, is not strong enough to be adopted for actual use.

Another way to determine if this regression is a good fit to the data is with a residual plot. The following steps show how to create this plot:

6. To obtain a residual plot, select **Analyze/Regression/Linear** . . . selecting the dependent (*Task*) and independent (*Create*) variables as before and then do the following:

7. Click the Save button and select unstandardized residuals (top right of the Save dialog box).

8. Click Continue and OK. (Note: This has placed a new variable *Unstandardized Residual [RES_1]* in the data file as shown in Figure 5.6.)

	subject	create	task	RES_1
1	AE	28	4.5	.57915
2	FR	35	3.9	-.60136
3	HT	37	3.9	-.76722
4	IO	50	6.1	.35468
5	DP	69	6.8	-.52099
6	YR	75	8.6	.78143
7	QD	40	2.9	-2.01601
8	SW	65	5.5	-1.48927
9	DF	29	5.7	1.69622
10	ER	25	3.0	-.67206
11	RR	51	7.1	1.27175
12	TG	45	7.3	1.96934
13	EF	31	3.3	-.86964
14	TJ	40	5.2	.28399

Figure 5.6   Data With Residual Column Added

9. Select the **Graphs/Chart Builder**. Select the **Scatter/Dot** chart type and drag the Simple Scatterplot icon into the Chart Preview box. Drag the *Create* variable to the X-axis and the *Unstandardized Residual (RES_1)* variable to the Y-axis and click OK. A preliminary chart appears in the Output window.

10. To place a horizontal line at $Y = 0$, double-click on the new scatterplot to enter the SPSS Chart Editor. From the Chart Editor menu, select **Options/Y Axis Reference Line**. Indicate Y axis position as 0. Click Apply and Close. Close the chart editor (**File/Close**). The resulting residual plot is shown in Figure 5.7.

This residual plot suggests that the underlying assumptions are met because it shows a random scatter of points above and below the zero line. With so few points, it is difficult to determine whether there is any pattern of concern.

Reporting the Results for a Simple Linear Regression

The following example illustrates how you could report the results of a simple linear regression analysis using the variable *Create* to predict the variable *Task*.

Narrative for the Methods Section

"An evaluation of how the new *Create* score predicts the standard *Task* score was examined using simple linear regression."

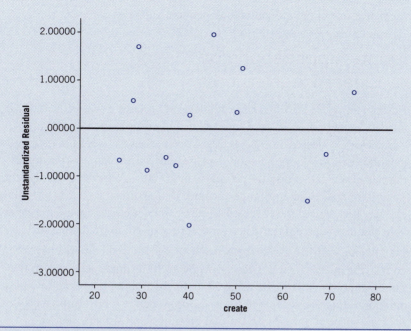

Figure 5.7 Residual Plot for Simple Linear Regression Example

Narrative for the Results Section

The simple linear regression analysis indicates a statistically significant linear relationship where the new *Create* exam scores are used to predict the *Task* exam scores, $\beta = 0.083$, $t(12) = 3.056$ $p = .002$ with $R^2 = 0.553$. To incorporate the effect size (large based on r) in to the narrative, use "The simple linear regression analysis indicates a large and significant linear relationship. . . ."

Multiple Linear Regression

Multiple linear regression is an extension of simple linear regression in which there is a single dependent (response) variable (Y) and k independent (predictor) variables X_i, $i = 1, \ldots,$ k. In multiple linear regression, the dependent variable is a quantitative variable while the independent variables may be quantitative or indicator (0, 1) variables. The usual purpose of a multiple regression analysis is to create a regression equation for predicting the dependent variable from a group of independent variables. Desired outcomes of such an analysis may include the following:

1. Screen independent variables to determine which ones are good predictors and thus find the most effective (and efficient) prediction model.

2. Obtain estimates of individual coefficients in the model to understand the predictive role of the individual independent variables used.

Appropriate Applications of Multiple Linear Regression

- *How can the selling price of a house be predicted?* A large city is broken down into 50 "neighborhoods," and for each neighborhood, the following variables are collected: average selling price per square foot of houses in the neighborhood (AST), population density, yearly crime rate, proportion of nonbusiness acres, proportion of lots over 25,000 square feet, average square footage for residential dwellings, distance to downtown, and average family income. It is desired to see how well AST can be predicted using the other variables and which of the other variables are useful in predicting AST.

- *Does tutoring help?* To assess the effectiveness of tutorial help in a psychology course, the instructor wants to know how well the grade achieved on the final exam can be predicted using all or a subset of the following variables: amount of time spent on Web tutorials, time spent in small tutorial classes, the time spent in one-on-one tutorial meetings, and student gender.

- *Can emergency room costs be predicted by observing initial injury measures?* Administrators at a hospital want to know how well the cost of a visit to the emergency room can be predicted using all or a subset of the following variables: evidence of intoxication, AIS score (injury severity), gender, type of injury (blunt, burn, or penetrating), GCS (Glasgow Coma Scale) score, and initial systolic blood pressure.

Design Considerations for Multiple Linear Regression

A Theoretical Multiple Regression Equation Exists That Describes the Relationship Between the Dependent Variable and the Independent Variables

As in the case of simple linear regression, the multiple regression equation calculated from the data is a sample-based version of a theoretical equation describing the relationship between the k independent variables and the dependent variable Y. The theoretical equation is of the form

$$Y = \alpha + \beta_1 X_1 + \beta_2 X_2 + \ldots + \beta_k X_k + \varepsilon$$

where α is the intercept term and β_i is the regression coefficient corresponding to the ith independent variable. Also, as in simple linear regression, ε is an error term with zero mean and constant variance. Note that if $\beta_i = 0$, then in this setting, the ith independent variable is not useful in predicting the dependent variable.

The Observed Multiple Regression Equation Is Calculated From the Data Based on the Least Squares Principle

The multiple regression equation that is obtained from the data for predicting the dependent variable from the k independent variables is given by

$$\hat{Y} = a + b_1 X_1 + b_2 X_2 + \ldots + b_k X_k$$

As in the case of simple linear regression, the coefficients a, $b_1, b_2, \ldots$, and b_k are least squares estimates of the corresponding coefficients in the theoretical model. That is, as in the case of simple linear regression, the least squares estimates a and $b_1, \ldots, b_k$ are the values for which the sum-of-squared differences between the observed y values and the predicted y values are minimized.

Several Assumptions Are Involved

These include the following:

1. *Normality*. The population of Y values for each combination of independent variables is normally distributed.

2. *Equal variances*. The populations in Assumption 1 all have the same variance.

3. *Independence*. The dependent variables used in the computation of the regression equation are not correlated. This typically means that each observed y value must be from a separate subject or entity.

Hypotheses for Multiple Linear Regression

In multiple regression analysis, the usual procedure for determining whether the ith independent variable contributes to the prediction of the dependent variable is to test the following hypotheses:

$H_0: \beta_i = 0$

$H_a: \beta_i \neq 0$

SIDEBAR

Most statistics programs also give the *t*-statistic and associated *p*-value for testing the null hypothesis H_0: $\alpha = 0$. As in the case of simple linear regression, you will usually not be interested in testing whether the *y*-intercept is zero.

for $i = 1, \ldots, k$. Each of these tests is performed using a *t*-test. There will be k of these tests (one for each independent variable), and most statistical packages report the corresponding *t*-statistics and *p*-values. Note that if there were no linear relationship whatsoever between the dependent variable and the independent variables, then all of the β_is would be zero. Most programs also report an *F*-test in an analysis of variance output that provides a single test of the following hypotheses:

H_0: $\beta_1 = \beta_2 = \ldots = \beta_k = 0$ (there is no linear relationship between the dependent variable and the collection of independent variables).

H_a: At least one of the β_is is nonzero (there is a linear relationship between the dependent variable and at least one of the independent variables).

The analysis-of-variance framework breaks up the total variability in the dependent variable (as measured by the total sum of squares) by that which can be explained by the regression using $X_1, X_2, \ldots, X_k$ (the regression sum of squares) and that which cannot be explained by the regression (the error sum of squares). It is good practice to check the *p*-value associated with this overall *F*-test as the first step in the testing procedure. Then, if this *p*-value is less than 0.05, you would reject the null hypothesis of no linear relationship and proceed to examine the results of the *t*-tests. However, if the *p*-value for the *F*-test is greater than 0.05, then you have no evidence of any relationship between the dependent variable and any of the independent variables, so you should not examine the individual *t*-tests. Any findings of significance at this point would be questionable.

R-Square

Another measure that assesses the performance of the multiple regression is the R^2 (R-squared) statistic. This statistic reports the strength of the relationship between the set of independent variables and the dependent variable. R^2 ranges from 0 (meaning no linear relationship) to 1.0 (meaning perfect linear relationship). R^2 is the ratio of the regression sum of squares divided by the total sum of squares and measures the proportion of the variation in the dependent variable that is accounted for by the regression. For example, an R^2 of 0.89 would typically be described by reporting that 89% of the variability in the dependent variable is accounted for by the regression.

Model Selection Procedures for Multiple Linear Regression

It is often the case when working with multiple linear regression that there are a number of candidate independent variables, and the goal is to create a model that contains some group of these variables that most efficiently predict the dependent variable. Based on the discussion above concerning testing hypotheses in a multiple regression, it is tempting to conclude that the best way to proceed is to enter all of the independent variables of possible interest into the multiple regression equation and choose the ones for which the corresponding p-values are less than 0.05. However, this may not produce desirable results, often because of collinearity among the independent variables.

Collinearity occurs when independent variables are themselves highly correlated or when one independent variable is nearly a linear combination of two or more independent variables. The presence of collinearity among the independent variables can cause problems in interpretation of the resulting multiple regression equations. If there are strong interrelationships among the independent variables, then coefficient estimates cannot be trusted to be meaningful. For example, if an independent variable is by itself positively related to the dependent variable, then you would expect the coefficient associated with this variable to be positive. The presence of collinearity can sometimes reverse the sign of the coefficient leading to confusing interpretations.

Suppose, for example, that you have two independent variables that are each positively correlated with the dependent variable and also strongly positively correlated with each other. Because the two variables are highly positively correlated with each other, they are introducing very similar information into the regression equation for predicting the dependent variable, and it will often be the case that only one of these independent variables is needed. However, if these two variables are simultaneously placed into the regression equation, this may result in confusing results such as one variable having a positive coefficient and the other a negative coefficient, one or both variables appearing to be insignificant, and so on.

One method to assess the relationships among possible predictors is to create a matrix of correlations (and scatterplots) as illustrated earlier in this chapter. Using that information, you can often identify which variables might exhibit collinearity.

One solution may be to create new variables that are themselves linear combinations of the existing independent variables.

Below is a list of techniques that can be used for deciding which of a group of candidate independent variables should be used in a final model. The first three methods are called automated variables selection procedures since they use criteria computed within the program to "decide" on a "best" set of variables for the model based on the available data.

1. *Forward selection.* This procedure enters variables in a stepwise manner using an entry criterion for selecting the next variable to be entered. At each step,

an associated *p*-value is checked to determine whether the selected variable contributes enough to be included.

2. *Backward elimination*. All independent variables are initially entered into the equation. At each step, there is a removal criterion for selecting the next variable to be removed from the model and an associated *p*-value to determine whether the selected variable should be removed.

3. *Stepwise entry*. This procedure adds independent variables one at a time as in forward selection. However, at each step, a backward elimination procedure is used to see whether any variables should be removed.

4. *Best subset regression*. This strategy reports the multiple regression based on a subset of a specified number, say, *m*, of independent variables for which R^2 (or some other criterion) is maximized among all possible subsets of *m* independent variables. Note: This option is not available in SPSS but is available in statistics programs such as SAS (SAS Institute, 2011) and WINKS (TexasSoft, 2012).

5. *Hierarchical selection*. We recommend that researchers use a hierarchical (nonautomated) selection procedure in which the researcher first decides, because of his or her intimate knowledge of the subject, which variables should be included as predictor variables. For example, if part of your concern is if gender is predictive of a measure involving cystic fibrosis, you should include gender as a predictor in the model regardless of any of the other techniques. Once you have included important research variables as predictors in the model, you can supplement the list of predictors using the other (automated) techniques listed above.

A few other issues that should be considered when selecting variables:

- *Include only variables that make sense*. Variables selected for inclusion in a prediction model should make sense in the context of the analysis. If it is not clear why a variable should be predictive, it may be best to not include it in your model, even if the selection criterion chooses it.

- *Force important variables into a model*. You may sometimes want to force variables of obvious importance to be included in a final model even if the selection procedures do not choose it. (This relates to the hierarchical approach listed in the selection procedure 5 above.)

- *Be wary of variable selection results*. It is interesting to note that the various selection procedures described above may lead to different final models. It is good practice to use several of these techniques and to compare the final models. (The stepwise and forward selection procedures are similar. If one of these is being used, then also try backward elimination.) Some researchers argue that backward elimination procedures are preferable to the forward selection and stepwise procedures. Among other issues, it has been shown that in forward selection and stepwise approaches, the R^2 values are biased high, and the resulting p-values do not have proper meaning. These problems are not as severe in backward elimination methods (see Mantel, 1970). Our advice is that you should not let any automated variable selection procedure be the sole criterion by which your final model is chosen. (See selection procedure 5 above.)

We do not recommend using automated techniques as your sole method of selecting a set of predictive variables. We recommend that researchers use some version of a hierarchical selection (option is below), which can be supplemented by additional automated techniques.

Tips and Caveats for Multiple Linear Regression

Besides the tips and caveats described in the previous simple linear regression section above, here are some additional considerations:

Using Indicator Variables

Your independent variables may include a categorical variable with two or more categories. Examples might be race, location of hospital, brand of milling machine, and so on. To include these variables in the equation, indicator variables must be used. For example, if you have a variable called *Race* that includes the categories White, African American, Hispanic, and Other (four categories), you would need to create three indicator variables (i.e., the variables take on the values 0 and 1) to account for these categories. These new variables might be named *White, AA,* and *Hispanic* and can be constructed as follows: If a subject is "White," the variables take on the following values: *White* = 1, *AA* = 0, and *Hispanic* = 0. If a subject is African American, the variables take on the following values: *White* = 0, *AA* = 1, *Hispanic* = 0, and so forth. Note that if the subject is "Other," the variables take on the following values: *White* = 0, *AA* = 0, and *Hispanic* = 0. Thus, these three indicator variables uniquely account for all four categories using 0, 1 indicator variables. In this case, all three variables (*White, AA,* and *Hispanic*) would be used as independent variables in the multiple regression equation. Thus, a general rule is that the number of independent variables required to account for a categorical variable is the number of categories minus one.

Don't Extrapolate

As with simple linear regression, predictions obtained using the multiple regression equation should be used only for independent variables that are (as a group) within the range of independent variables used in the computation of the regression equation.

Too Many Predictors?

The number of independent variables that should be used in your final model is limited by the number of observations. A rule of thumb used by some researchers is to limit the number of independent variables to one independent variable for every 10 observations. Thus, if you have 50 observations, this rough guide would suggest that you should limit your final regression model to a maximum of about five independent variables.

Model Interpretation and Evaluation for Multiple Linear Regression

Model evaluation is performed using graphs and statistical tests. Some commonly used procedures for assessing the performance of a multiple regression model are discussed here. These include the following:

- *Compare competing R^2 values*. Compare the R^2 values of competing models to see if there is one that results in a larger R^2 value than the others. However, you should be aware that if you start with a multiple regression with three variables and add a fourth variable to this list, then the R^2 value will nearly always increase and will never decrease. Thus, a simple increase in R^2 is not sufficient evidence for deciding to include an additional variable. Comparison of R^2 values thus makes the most sense when you are comparing candidate models with the same number of independent variables.

- *Analyze residual plots*. Plots of residuals similar to those discussed in the section on simple linear regression are also useful in multiple regression. In multiple regression, the residuals are calculated as the difference between an actual Y value and its corresponding predicted value. As in the simple linear regression case, these plots should show a random behavior with no real pattern. As in simple linear regression, if a standardized residual is larger than 2 or 3, it may indicate an outlier or at least a data point of some interest. In multiple regression, you can plot separate residual plots for each of the independent variables on the horizontal axis. It is also common practice to plot residuals versus the predicted Y values or against run-order. See Kutner, Nachtsheim, and Neter (2004) for a discussion of residual analysis in multiple regression.

Effect Size

A measure of effect size for multiple regression is Cohen's (1988) f^2 calculated as

$$f^2 = \frac{R^2}{1 - R^2}$$

which is interpreted as

- When f^2 is greater than 0.02 and less than 0.15, the effect size is "small."
- When f^2 is greater than 0.15 and less than 0.35, the effect size is "medium."
- When f^2 is greater than 0.35, the effect size is "large."

For an $R^2 = .798$, $f^2 = 3.95$, or a large effect.

Example 5.3

Multiple Linear Regression Analysis

Describing the Problem

An employer wants to be able to predict how well applicants will do on the job once they are hired. He devises four tests (*Test1* to *Test4*) that are designed to measure the skills required for the job. Current employees are selected at random from a group of current workers and given the four tests. These workers are then evaluated by a supervisor, who gives each employee a job proficiency score (*Jobscore*). From the "training data," we wish to develop a multiple regression equation for predicting *Jobscore* from all or a subset of the four test scores.

The following example illustrates an approach to this analysis:

SPSS Step-By-Step. EXAMPLE 5.3: Multiple Linear Regression Analysis

Before doing any multivariate regression, it is helpful to first examine a matrix of scatterplots of all the variables involved. These first few steps produce a scatterplot matrix of the data:

1. Open the data set JOBSCORE.SAV and select **Graphs/Chart Builder**. Select the **Scatter/Dot** icon and drag the Scatterplot Matrix icon into the Chart Preview box.

2. Drag the variables *Test1, Test2, Test3, Test4,* and *Jobscore* into the variables box at the bottom of the sample plot and click OK. Figure 5.8 shows the resulting matrix of scatterplots.

From the matrix of scatterplots in Figure 5.8, you can see there appears to be a linear relationship between *Jobscore* and *Test1*. The association between *Jobscore* and the other variables is unclear. Also, the potential predictor variables do not appear to be highly correlated with each other.

In order to select the best collection of independent variables to be used in the final predictive model, we investigate the use of variable selection methods. These automated methods are not foolproof, and as mentioned previously, you should not rely on one method to find the best set of predictors. To perform the variable selection procedure using the stepwise approach, continue with this example:

3. Using the JOBSCORE.SAV select **Analyze/Regression/Linear** and select *Jobscore* as the dependent variable and *Test1* through *Test4* as the independent variables.

4. Click the Method button and select Stepwise as the entry criterion and click OK. (Click the Options button and observe that you could change the entry and removal criteria and other options in this dialog box. Do not make any changes. Click Continue to exit this dialog box.)

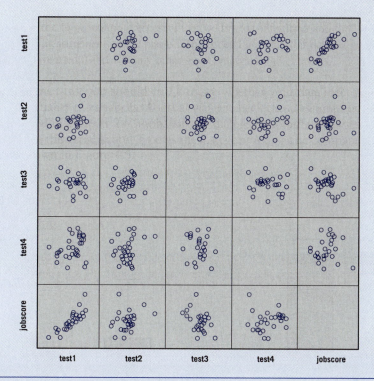

Figure 5.8 Matrix of Scatterplots for JOBSCORE Data

5. From this initial analysis, notice that the variable *Test1* and then *Test3* are entered into the equation and *Test2* and *Test4* are excluded, as shown in Table 5.3.

Table 5.3 Output From Stepwise Model Selection

Coefficients[a]

Model		Unstandardized Coefficients B	Std. Error	Standardized Coefficients Beta	t	Sig.
1	(Constant)	−87.136	26.383		−3.303	.003
	test1	2.575	.317	.861	8.124	.000
2	(Constant)	−11.922	38.641		−.309	.761
	test1	2.406	.295	.805	8.168	.000
	test3	−.768	.311	−.244	−2.475	.022

a. Dependent Variable: jobscore

When applying the stepwise procedure, the variables *Test1* and *Test3* are entered into the model using the default SPSS stopping rules. They are as follows: An entry *p*-value less than 0.05 is required in order for a variable to be added to the model at a given step, while a *p*-value greater than 0.10 is required for a variable to be removed from the model. The results of this stepwise procedure are shown in Table 5.3 where it can be seen that (not surprisingly) *Test1* was selected as the first variable to be entered, *Test3* was entered into the model next. No further variables satisfied the entry criterion.

Continue with the analysis by examining a second selection method: backward elimination:

6. Using the same JOBSCORE.SAV data select **Analyze/Regression/Linear** . . . and this time indicate Backward as the Entry criteria. Examine the results shown in Table 5.4.

Notice that this method selects *Test1*, *Test3*, and *Test4* to be included in the model. Although this method is used on the same data (with the same stopping rule for removal), the final model is different. This is an indication that the automated techniques can give differing answers. Given that there is no previous expectation that any particular test will be predictive, we next describe how to choose between the two possible models.

Table 5.4 Output From Backward Model Selection

Coefficients[a]

Model		Unstandardized Coefficients		Standardized Coefficients	t	Sig.
		B	Std. Error	Beta		
1	(Constant)	28.150	42.787		.658	.518
	test1	2.404	.288	.804	8.336	.000
	test2	.308	.216	.138	1.425	.169
	test3	−.874	.292	−.277	-2.995	.007
	test4	−.778	.351	−.209	-2.218	.038
2	(Constant)	32.723	43.702		.749	.462
	test1	2.513	.285	.840	8.820	.000
	test3	−.808	.295	−.256	−2.738	.012
	test4	−.650	.347	−.175	−1.871	.075

a. Dependent Variable: jobscore

Comparing Competing Models

Two possible models were identified. Both models have a strong model fit ($p < 0.001$), according to the ANOVA F-tests. However, we want to choose between these two competing models.

Sometimes competing models are compared by looking at their R^2 values. In this example, the two-variable model has $R^2 = .798$ and the three-variable $R^2 = .827$. One of the problems with comparing these models using R^2 values is that simply from mathematical considerations, R^2 should be larger for the model with *Test1, Test3,* and *Test4* than for the model with *Test1* and *Test3* even if *Test4* is not providing significantly important new information. In fact, the p-value (In the Sig. column of Table 5.4) is 0.075 which indicates that *Test4* is only marginally predictive. If you decide that the three-variable model is not substantially better, then you might choose the two-variable model based on the desire for parsimony (i.e., selection of the model with the fewest variables if there is no important difference in the models). Other criteria such as Mallows C_p and AIC are designed for directly comparing models with different numbers of independent variables. See Kutner, Nachtsheim, and Neter (2004).

Another way to assess the fit is to examine the contribution for each individual variable in the proposed model. In Table 5.3, the "Sig." column reports the p-value associated with a test that the associated β coefficient is zero for each of the predictors currently in the model. For the two predictors *Test1* and *Test3* in Model 2 of the table, these p-values are both less than 0.05. If either of these p-values were large, it would suggest that the variable was not providing important information to the equation and should possibly be dropped.

When faced with several model candidates, you must decide which one not only best fits the data but also which one makes the most sense in the context of your research and which one uses the fewest variables to create an acceptable model. For example, if each test costs $25 to administer and there are potentially 1,000 candidates, eliminating a single unneeded test would save $25,000.

Based on these considerations, let's use the model with the two independent variables (*Test1* and *Test3*). From model 2 in Table 5.3 we see that corresponding regression equation for predicting *Jobscore* is given by

$$\text{Predicted Jobscore} = -11.922 + 2.406 \text{ Test1} - 0.768 \text{ Test3}.$$

Thus, using this equation will provide a measure of prediction for how new employees will perform on the job.

Residual Analysis

To assess how well a chosen model fits the data, you should perform a residual analysis. Continuing with Example 5.3, we illustrate how to perform the analysis and interpret the results.

7. Using the same JOBSCORE.SAV data in the previous steps, select **Analyze/ Regression/Linear** with *Jobscore* as the dependent variable and *Test1* and *Test3* as the independent variables. Select Enter as the Entry Criterion.

8. Click the Save button and select both the unstandardized predicted values and unstandardized residuals and click Continue and OK. Note: This places new variables: *Unstandardized Predicted Value (Pre_1)* and *Unstandardized Residual (Res_1)* in the data file. Click Continue.

9. To select casewise diagnostic analysis, check the Statistics button and select Casewise diagnostics. Click Continue and OK. The added variables are shown in Figure 5.9.

10. To produce a residual plot using the JOBSCORE.SAV data, select **Graphs/Chart Builder**. Select the **Scatter/Dot** chart type and drag the Simple Scatterplot icon into the Chart Preview box. Drag the *Unstandardized Predicted Value* variable to the X-axis and the *Unstandardized Residual* variable to the Y-axis. Click OK.

11. Double-click on the resulting graph to enter the SPSS Chart Editor. Add a reference line at 0 by selecting **Options/Y Axis Reference Line**. Click Apply and Close in the Properties box.

	subject	test1	test2	test3	test4	jobscore	PRE_1	RES_1
1	1	75	100	90	78	107	99.38021	7.32763
2	2	51	85	88	71	58	43.16962	14.75536
3	3	99	96	94	85	145	154.05393	-9.30843
4	4	92	106	84	67	153	144.89523	7.92132
5	5	90	89	83	69	120	140.85137	-20.36521
6	6	67	77	83	65	64	85.51007	-21.97392
7	7	109	67	71	50	291	195.78926	95.62800
8	8	94	112	105	107	140	133.57048	6.52227
9	9	105	176	99	96	167	164.64864	2.48919
10	10	74	102	88	63	98	98.51092	-.52153
11	11	84	69	37	78	173	161.76230	11.19740
12	12	83	111	48	99	153	150.90342	2.14245
13	13	83	50	91	68	112	117.86092	-5.44853
14	14	71	107	111	48	99	73.61860	25.02462

Figure 5.9   JOBSCORE Data With Added Residual Variables

12. To change the numbers on the axes to have fewer decimal points, select **Edit/Select X Axis**. In the Properties dialog box, select the Number Format tab and change Decimal Places to 1. Click Apply and Close. Do the same procedure for the Y Axis.

13. Close the Chart Editor. The resulting graph is shown in Figure 5.10.

The residual plot in Figure 5.10 plots the unstandardized residuals plotted against the (unstandardized) predicted *Jobscore* variable. Notice that the points are spread randomly around the zero line with one of the points for a predicted *Jobscore* with a value of about 200 somewhat out of place. Additionally, there is the appearance of a possible increase in variability as the predicted *Jobscore* increases.

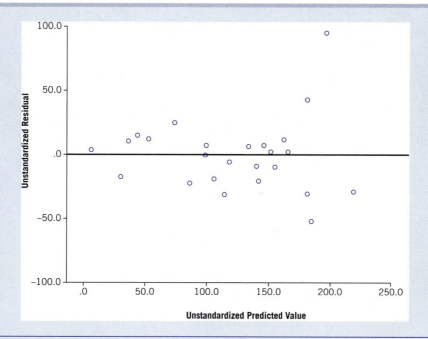

Figure 5.10　Residual Plot for JOBSCORE.SAV Data

The "Casewise Diagnostics" table in the output (Table 5.4) indicates that the record with the large residual (i.e., with a residual of approximately 100) is a potential outlier since it has a standardized residual greater than 3. The program identifies this as case number 7. You should investigate this case to see if there is something unusual about this subject. Perhaps it is a superstar employee whose performance would be difficult to predict using the developed model. You might consider rerunning the analysis without this unusual value to see how that might influence your model.

Table 5.4　Casewise Diagnostics

Casewise Diagnostics[a]

Case Number	Std. Residual	Jobscore	Predicted Value	Residual
7	3.203	291	195.79	95.628

a. Dependent Variable: jobscore

Reporting the Results for a Multiple Linear Regression

The following illustrates how you could report the results of a simple linear regression analysis using the *Test* variables to predict the variable *Jobscore*.

Narrative for the Methods Section

"Using a stepwise procedure for variable selection in a multiple linear regression, we determined that the variables Test1 and Test3 were the best predictors for Jobscore."

Narrative for the Results Section

"The multiple linear regression analysis found Test1 ($p < .001$) and Test3 ($p < .022$) to be significant predictors of Jobscore with $R^2 = 0.798$, $F(2,22) = 43.16$, $p < .001$. Cohen's f^2 for this analysis is 3.95 indicating a large effect."

SUMMARY

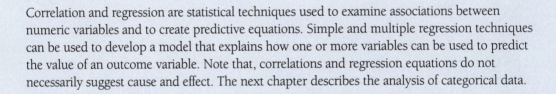

Correlation and regression are statistical techniques used to examine associations between numeric variables and to create predictive equations. Simple and multiple regression techniques can be used to develop a model that explains how one or more variables can be used to predict the value of an outcome variable. Note that, correlations and regression equations do not necessarily suggest cause and effect. The next chapter describes the analysis of categorical data.

REFERENCES

Cohen, J. (1988). *Statistical power analysis for the behavioral sciences* (2nd ed.). Mahwah, NJ: Lawrence Erlbaum Associates.

Freedman, D., Pisani, R., & Purves, R. (2007). *Statistics* (4th ed.). New York, NY: W. W. Norton & Company.

Kleinbaum, D. G., Kupper, L. L., Nizam, A., & Rosenberg E. D. (2013). *Applied regression analysis and other multivariate methods* (5th ed.). Belmont, CA: Centage Learning.

Kutner, M. H., Nachtsheim, C., Neter J. (2004). *Applied linear statistical models* (4th ed.). Burr Ridge, IL: McGraw-Hill Irwin.

Mantel, N. (1970). Why stepdown procedures in variable selection. *Technometrics, 12*, 621–625.

Rousseeuw, P. J., & Annick M. L. (2003). *Robust regression and outlier detection. Vol. 589*. Hoboken, NJ: John Wiley & Sons.

SAS Institute Inc. (2011). *SAS/STAT software: Reference, Version 9.3*. Cary, NC: SAS Institute.

TexasSoft. (2012). *WINKS Statistical Software Users Guide, Version 7*. Cedar Hill, TX: TexasSoft.

CHAPTER 6

Analysis of Categorical Data

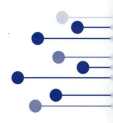

People like to clump things into categories. Virtually every research project involves categorizing some of its observations into neat, little distinct bins: male or female; marital status; broken or not broken; small, medium, or large; race of patient; with or without a tonsillectomy; and so on. When we collect data by categories, we record counts—how many observations fall into a particular bin. Categorical variables are usually classified as being of two basic types: nominal and ordinal. Nominal variables involve categories that have no particular order such as hair color, race, or clinic site, while the categories associated with an ordinal variable have some inherent ordering (categories of socioeconomic status, etc.). Unless otherwise stated, the procedures discussed here can be used on any type of categorical data. There are some specific procedures for ordinal data, and they will be briefly discussed later in the chapter.

Statisticians have devised a number of ways to analyze and explain categorical data. This chapter explains each of the following methods:

- *A contingency table analysis* is used to examine the relationship between two categorical variables.
- *McNemar's test* is designed for the analysis of paired dichotomous, categorical variables to detect disagreement or change.
- *The Mantel-Haenszel test* is used to determine whether there is a relationship between two dichotomous variables controlling for or within levels of a third variable.
- *Interrater reliability (kappa)* tests whether two raters looking at the same occurrence (or condition) give consistent ratings.
- *A goodness-of-fit test* measures whether an observed group of counts matches a theoretical pattern.
- A number of other categorical data measures are also briefly discussed.

Sometimes researchers collect data that is quantitative, such as age or weight, and then categorize it into bins to create ordinal data, or categorize data into only two groups to create a dichotomous (Yes, No) variable. Care must be taken with this technique since you lose some information about the data in the categorization. See Royston, Altman, and Sauerbrei (2006).

To get the most out of the information in this chapter, when analyzing a set of data, you should first verify that your variables are categorical and then try to match the hypotheses you are testing with the ones described in this chapter. If it is not clear that the hypotheses you are testing match any of these given here, we recommend that you consult a statistician.

Contingency Table Analysis ($r \times c$)

Contingency table analysis is a common method for analyzing the association between two categorical variables. Consider a categorical variable that has r possible response categories and another categorical variable with c possible categories. In this case, there are $r \times c$ possible combinations of responses for these two variables. The $r \times c$ crosstabulation or contingency table has r rows and c columns consisting of $r \times c$ cells containing the observed counts (frequencies) for each of the $r \times c$ combinations. This type of analysis is called a contingency table analysis which uses a chi-square statistic to compare the observed counts with those that would be expected if there were no association between the two variables.

Appropriate Applications of Contingency Table Analysis

The following are examples of situations in which a chi-square contingency table analysis would be appropriate.

- *Criminal behavior and alcohol drinking*. A study compares types of crime and whether the criminal is a drinker or abstainer.
- *Is there a gender preference*? An analysis is undertaken to determine whether there is a gender preference between candidates running for state governor.
- *Job training and dropout rates*. Reviewers want to know whether worker dropout rates are different for participants in two different job-training programs.

- *Analysis of questionnaire response rates.* A marketing research company wants to know whether there is a difference in response rates among small, medium, and large companies that were sent a questionnaire.

Design Considerations for a Contingency Table Analysis

Two Sampling Strategies

Two separate sampling strategies lead to the chi-square contingency table analysis discussed here.

1. *Test of independence.* A single random sample of observations is selected from the population of interest, and the data are categorized on the basis of the two variables of interest. For example, in the marketing research example above, this sampling strategy would indicate that a single random sample of companies is selected, and each selected company is categorized by size (small, medium, or large) and whether that company returned the survey.

2. *Test for homogeneity.* Separate random samples are taken from each of two or more populations to determine whether the responses related to a single categorical variable are consistent across populations. In the marketing research example above, this sampling strategy would consider there to be three populations of companies (based on size), and you would select a sample from each of these populations. You then test to determine whether the response rates differ among the three company types.

The two-way table is set up the same way regardless of the sampling strategy, and the chi-square test is conducted in exactly the same way. The only real difference in the analysis is in the statement of the hypotheses and conclusions.

Expected Cell Size Considerations

The validity of the chi-square test depends on both the sample size and the number of cells. Several rules of thumb have been suggested to indicate whether the chi-square approximation is satisfactory. One such rule suggested by Cochran (1954) says that the approximation is adequate if no expected cell frequencies are less than one and no more than 20% are less than five.

Combining Categories

When there are many categories in a variable which cause there to be low expected frequencies in a number of cells, it may be necessary to combine similar or adjacent categories to make expected values in cells large enough to make the test valid. See the section that follows later in this chapter on Mantel-Haenszel comparisons for information on one way to examine information within categories.

Hypotheses for a Contingency Table Analysis

The statement of the hypotheses depends on whether you used a test of independence or a test for homogeneity.

Test of Independence

In this case, you have two variables and are interested in testing whether there is an association between the two variables. Specifically, the hypotheses to be tested are the following:

H_0: There is no association between the two variables.

H_a: The two variables are associated.

Test for Homogeneity

In this setting, you have a categorical variable collected separately from two or more populations. The hypotheses are as follows:

H_0: The distribution of the categorical variable is the same across the populations.

H_a: The distribution of the categorical variable differs across the populations.

Tips and Caveats for a Contingency Table Analysis

Use Counts—Do Not Use Percentages

It may be tempting to use percentages in the table and calculate the chi-square test from these percentages instead of the raw observed frequencies. This is incorrect—don't do it!

No One-Sided Tests

Notice that the alternative hypotheses above do not assume any "direction." Thus, there are no one- and two-sided versions of these tests. Chi-square tests are inherently nondirectional ("sort of two-sided") in the sense that the chi-square test is simply testing whether the observed frequencies and expected frequencies agree without regard to whether particular observed frequencies are above or below the corresponding expected frequencies.

Each Subject Is Counted Only Once

If you have n total observations (i.e., the total of the counts is n), then these n observations should be independent. For example, suppose you have a categorical variable *Travel* in which subjects are asked what means they use to commute to work. It would not be correct to allow a subject to check multiple responses (e.g., car and commuter train) and then include all of these responses for this subject in the table (i.e., count the subject more than once). On such a variable, it is usually better to allow only one response per variable. If you want to allow for multiple responses such as this, then as you are tallying your results, you would need to come up with a new category, "car and commuter train." This procedure can lead to a large number of cells and small expected cell frequencies.

Using Ordinal Categories

Sometimes categories are ordered, such as small, medium, and large. If order is an important component in your research question, a chi-square analysis may not be appropriate. If both variables are ordered categorical (ordinal), you should consider a Spearman's correlation analysis. (See Chapter 8: Nonparametric Analysis Procedures.) If one variable is categorical and one is ordinal, consider performing a Mann-Whitney or Kruskal-Wallis analysis. (See Chapter 8: Nonparametric Analysis Procedures.)

SIDEBAR
IBM SPSS has an optional module called Exact Tests. These tests analyze contingency tables using a more accurate and computing intensive process based on finding exact table probabilities. In the case of a 2 x 2 (two rows and two column) table, the exact analysis (Fisher's) output is included in the standard output. To get this type of result for larger tables, you must purchase the SPSS Exact Tests module separately.

Explain Significant Findings

The simple finding of a significant result in a contingency table analysis does not explain in what way the results are significant. It may be important for you to examine the observed and expected frequencies and explain your findings in terms of which of the differences between observed and expected counts are the most striking.

Contingency Table Examples

The following two examples of contingency table analysis illustrate a variety of the issues involved in this type of analysis.

Example 6.1

$r \times c$ Contingency Table Analysis

Describing the Problem

In 1909, Karl Pearson conducted a now classic study involving the relationship between criminal behavior and the drinking of alcoholic beverages. He studied 1,426 criminals, and the data in Table 6.1 show the drinking patterns in various crime categories. (The term *coining* in the table is a term for counterfeiting that is no longer in common usage.) This table is made up of counts in 6 x 2 = 12 cells, and, for example, 300 subjects studied were abstainers who had been convicted of stealing.

Table 6.1 Pearson's Crime Analysis Data

Crime	Drinker	Abstainer	Total
Arson	50	43	93
Rape	88	62	150
Violence	155	110	265
Stealing	379	300	679
Coining	18	14	32
Fraud	63	144	207
Total	753	673	1426

The hypotheses of interest are as follows:

H_0: There is no association between type of crime and drinking status.

H_a: There is an association between type of crime and drinking status.

The following example illustrates how to perform an analysis on these data.

SPSS Step-By-Step. EXAMPLE 6.1: $r \times c$ Contingency Table Analysis With Data Stored in Count Form

While most data sets in SPSS are stored casewise, you can store count data such as that shown in Table 6.1. These data are available (in count form) in file CRIME.SAV. In order to create this data set, follow these steps:

1. Open the data set CRIME.SAV. The contents of CRIME.SAV are shown in Figure 6.1.

2. Note that this data set includes the variables *Crime, Drinker,* and *Count*. In the Variable View, notice that the *Crime* categories are 1 for arson, 2 for rape, 3 for violence, 4 for stealing, 5 for coining, and 6 for fraud. For *Drinker*, the value 1 indicates drinker and 2 indicates abstainer. The *Count* variable indicates, for example, that there were 43 persons who were arsonists (*Crime* = 1) and abstainers (*Drinker* = 2). Also note that the variables *Crime* and *Drinker* are classified as Nominal in the Measure column within Variable View.

3. Select **Data/Weight Cases** . . . and select the "weight case by" option with *Count* as the Frequency variable used. Click OK.

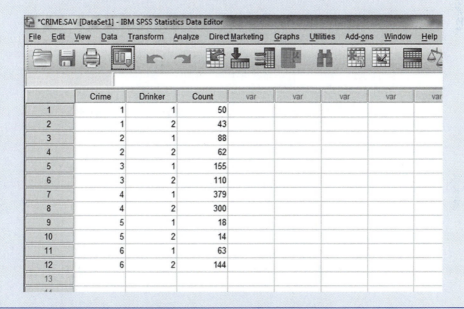

Figure 6.1 CRIME.SAV Count Form Data Set

Once you have specified this information, you are ready to perform the analysis. Follow these steps:

4. Select **Analyze/Descriptive Statistics/Crosstabs**. . . .

5. Choose *Crime* as the row variable and *Drinker* as the column variable.

6. Select the checkbox labeled "Display Clustered Bar Charts."

7. Click the Statistics button and select Chi-Square and Continue.

8. Click the Cells button and select Expected in the Counts box and select Row in the Percentages section and Continue.
9. Click OK, and SPSS creates the output shown in Table 6.2.

Table 6.2 Output for Crime Data

Crime * Drinker Crosstabulation

			Drinker		Total
			Drinker	Non Drinker	
Crime	Arson	Count	50	43	93
		Expected Count	49.1	43.9	93.0
		% within Crime	53.8%	46.2%	100.0%
	Rape	Count	88	62	150
		Expected Count	79.2	70.8	150.0
		% within Crime	58.7%	41.3%	100.0%
	Violence	Count	155	110	265
		Expected Count	139.9	125.1	265.0
		% within Crime	58.5%	41.5%	100.0%
	Stealing	Count	379	300	679
		Expected Count	358.5	320.5	679.0
		% within Crime	55.8%	44.2%	100.0%
	Coining	Count	18	14	32
		Expected Count	16.9	15.1	32.0
		% within Crime	56.3%	43.8%	100.0%
	Fraud	Count	63	144	207
		Expected Count	109.3	97.7	207.0
		% within Crime	30.4%	69.6%	100.0%
	Total	Count	753	673	1426
		Expected Count	753.0	673.0	1426.0
		% within Crime	52.8%	47.2%	100.0%

Table 6.2 shows output for these data where we see not only the cell frequencies shown in Table 6.1 but also the expected cell frequencies (under the null hypothesis of no association) and the row percentages. That is, for each cell, the table gives the percentage of the row total that this cell count represents. For example, there were 93 arsonists, and 50 of these said they were drinkers. The row percentage in this case tells us that 50 is 53.8% of 93. From the bottom of the table, it can be seen that slightly more than half (i.e., 753 out of 1,426 or 52.8%) of the subjects were drinkers.

If this pattern turns out to be consistent among all crime categories (i.e., if about 52.8% were drinkers in each crime category), then this would be evidence against an association between type of crime and drinking status, and we would thus not expect to reject the null hypothesis.

However, examination of the table reveals the interesting result that while every other crime category has a few more drinkers than abstainers, the crime category of "Fraud" shows a strong preponderance of abstainers. Note that if there were no association between the two variables, then we would expect, for example, that about 52.8% of the 93 arson subjects (i.e., 49.1) would be drinkers and that about 47.2% of these 93 subjects (i.e., 43.9) would be abstainers. In the case of arson, for example, the observed frequencies are quite similar to these "expected" frequencies. In contrast, for the criminals involved in fraud, the observed frequencies are very different from the expected frequencies. Notice that while the expected count for abstainers involved in fraud is 97.7, the observed count is 144—clearly a large and unanticipated difference if there is no association between crime and drinking status.

In Table 6.3, we show the statistical results related to the analysis of these data. The value of the chi-square statistic is 49.731, with 5 degrees of freedom and $p = 0.000$ (this would be reported as $p < 0.001$), and thus we reject the null hypothesis of no association and conclude that there is a relationship between crime and drinking status. As previously mentioned, this relationship is primarily due to the unusual fact that about 70% of the criminals convicted of fraud were abstainers. (One wonders if there was some "fraud" involved in these criminals' answers to this question.) It can also be seen that the expected frequencies are relatively close to the observed frequencies for each cell except in the cells for fraud. The bar chart in Figure 6.2 provides a visual confirmation that the pattern for fraud crimes is different than the other crimes. All three pieces of information lead you to conclude that the crime of fraud is more common to abstainers and that the other crimes are more common to drinkers.

Before proceeding, it should be noted that the likelihood ratio statistic given in Table 6.3 is an alternative to the Pearson chi-square. While these two test statistics usually give similar results (as they did in this example), it is common to use Pearson's chi-square.

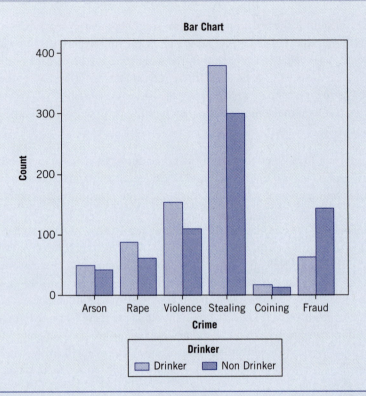

Figure 6.2   Bar Chart for Crime Versus Drinking Analysis

Table 6.3   Chi-Square Tests for Crime Data

Chi-Square Tests

	Value	df	Asymp. Sig. (2-sided)
Pearson Chi-Square	49.731[a]	5	.000
Likelihood Ratio	50.517	5	.000
Linear-By-Linear Association	26.320	1	.000
N of Valid Cases	1426		

a. 0 cells (0.0%) have expected count less than 5. The minimum expected count is 15.10.

Program Comments

In this example, we instructed SPSS to display the table showing the observed and expected frequencies under the Cells option. We can also ask for the row, column, and total percentages. For example, if total percentages were selected, then the percentage of each observed frequency of the total sample size would be displayed in each cell.

Reporting the Results of a Contingency Table Analysis

The following illustrates how you might report this chi-square test in a publication format.

Narrative for the Methods Section

> "A chi-square test was performed to test the null hypothesis of no association between type of crime and incidence of drinking."

Narrative for the Results Section

> "An association between drinking preference and type of crime committed was found χ^2 (5, $N = 1,426$) = 49.7, $p < 0.001$."

Or, to be more complete,

> "An association between drinking preference and type of crime committed was found, χ^2 (5, $N = 1,426$) = 49.7, $p < 0.001$. Examination of the cell frequencies showed that about 70% (144 out of 207) of the criminals convicted of fraud were abstainers, while the percentage of abstainers in all of the other crime categories was less than 50%."

Example 6.2

2 × 2 Contingency Table Analysis

A number of experiments involve binary outcomes (i.e., 1 and 0, yes and no). Typically, these occur when you are observing the presence or absence of a characteristic such as a disease, flaw, mechanical breakdown, death, failure, and so on. The analysis of the relationship between two bivariate categorical variables results in a 2 × 2 crosstabulation of counts. Although the 2 × 2 table is simply a special case of the general $r \times c$ table, the SPSS output for the 2 × 2 tables is more extensive.

Consider an experiment in which the relationship between exposure to a particular reagent (a substance present in a commercial floor cleanser) and the occurrence of a type of reaction (mild skin rash) was studied. Two groups of subjects were studied: One group of 20 patients was exposed to the reagent, and the other group was not. The 40 subjects were examined for the presence of the reaction. The summarized data are shown in Table 6.4. To perform an analysis on this table, follow these step-by-step instructions:

Table 6.4 Exposure/Reaction Data

	Reaction	No Reaction	Marginal Total
Exposed	13	7	20
Not Exposed	4	16	20
Marginal Total	17	23	40

SPSS Step-By-Step. EXAMPLE 6.2: 2 × 2 Contingency Table Analysis With Data Stored Casewise

The data in this example are in file EXPOSURE22.SAV as 40 casewise observations on the two variables *Exposure* (0 = exposed, 1 = not exposed) and *Reaction* (0 = reaction, 1 = no reaction). This data file was created using *Exposure* and *Reaction* as numeric variables with the labels given above. A portion of the data is shown in Figure 6.3.

1. Open the data set EXPOSURE22.SAV and select **Analyze/Descriptive Statistics/Crosstabs**. . . .

2. Choose *Exposure* as the Row variable and *Reaction* as the column variable.

3. Click the Statistics button and select Chi Square and Continue.

4. Click the Cells button and select Expected in the Counts box and select Row in the Percentages section and Continue.

5. Select the Clustered Bar Charts option and click OK.

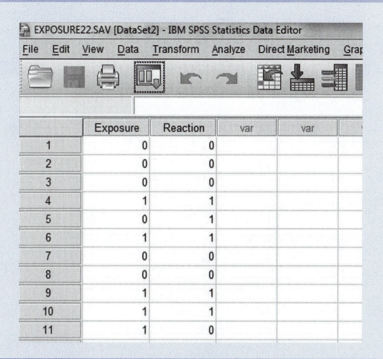

Figure 6.3 First 11 Cases of EXPOSURE22.SAV

The output includes Table 6.5 where the observed and expected frequencies are shown along with row percentages. Table 6.6 shows typical statistical output for a 2 x 2 table.

These results report a Pearson chi-square of 8.286 with 1 degree of freedom and $p = 0.004$. It should be noted that in the 2×2 setting, use of the rule of thumb that no more than 20% of the expected values are less than 5 requires that none of the four expected values should be less than 5. Footnote b reports this fact for these data.

The continuity correction statistic (Yates's correction) is an adjustment of the chi-square test for 2 x 2 tables used by some statisticians to improve the chi-square approximation. This correction has a more dramatic effect when expected values are relatively small. The continuity correction reduces the size of the chi-square value and thus increases the p-value. In this case, the corrected chi-square value is 6.547 with $p = 0.011$. When there are small expected values in the 2×2 table, many statisticians recommend reporting the results of Fisher's exact test. This test is based on all possible 2×2 tables that have the observed marginal frequencies (i.e., 20 in each of the exposed and nonexposed groups, with 17 having a reaction and 23 not experiencing the reaction).

The probabilities of obtaining each of the possible tables when the null hypothesis is true are obtained. Then the p-value is calculated as the sum of

Table 6.5 Output for 2 × 2 Exposure/Reaction Data

Exposure * Reaction Crosstabulation

			Reaction		
			Reaction	No Reaction	Total
Exposure	Exposed	Count	13	7	20
		Expected Count	8.5	11.5	20.0
		% within Exposure	65.0%	35.0%	100.0%
	Not Exposed	Count	4	16	20
		Expected Count	8.5	11.5	20.0
		% within Exposure	20.0%	80.0%	100.0%
Total		Count	17	23	40
		Expected Count	17.0	23.0	40.0
		% within Exposure	42.5%	57.5%	100.0%

Table 6.6 Statistical Output for 2 × 2 Exposure/Reaction Data

Chi-Square Tests

	Value	df	Asymp. Sig. (2-sided)	Exact Sig. (2-sided)	Exact Sig. (1-sided)
Pearson Chi-Square	8.286[a]	1	.004		
Continuity Correction[b]	6.547	1	.011		
Likelihood Ratio	8.634	1	.003		
Fisher's Exact Test				.010	.005
Linear-By-Linear Association	8.079	1	.004		
N of Valid Cases	40				

a. 0 cells (0.0%) have expected count less than 5. The minimum expected count is 8.50.

b. Computed only for a 2x2 table.

these probabilities from all tables that are as rare, or rarer than, the one observed if the hypothesis is true. For these data, the resulting p-value for Fisher's two-sided test is $p = 0.010$. There is no actual test statistic to quote when using Fisher's exact test, and there is a one-sided version if that is desired. All of the results are consistent in leading to rejection of the null hypothesis at the $\alpha = 0.05$ level and thus to the conclusion that there is a relationship between the reagent and reaction. In this case, the exposed subjects had a significantly higher rate of response to the reagent (65% or 13 of 20) than did nonexposed subjects (20% or 4 of 20).

Reporting the Results of a 2 × 2 Contingency Table Analysis

The following illustrates how you might report this chi-square test in a publication format.

Narrative for the Methods Section

"A chi-square test was performed to test the hypothesis of no association between exposure and reaction."

Narrative for the Results Section

"A higher proportion of the exposed group showed a reaction to the reagent, $\chi^2 (1, N = 40) = 8.29, p = 0.004$."

Or, to be more complete,

"A higher proportion of the exposed group (65% or 13 of 20) showed a reaction to the reagent than did the nonexposed group (20% or 4 of 20), $\chi^2 (1, N = 40) = 8.29, p = 0.004$."

Analyzing Risk Ratios in a 2 × 2 Table

Another way to analyze a 2 × 2 table is by examining measures of risk. In a medical setting, for example, a 2 × 2 table is often constructed where one variable represents exposure (to some risk factor) and the other represents an outcome (presence or absence of disease). In this case, the researcher is interested in calculating measures of risk. The odds ratio (OR) is used as a measure of risk in a retrospective (case control) study. A case control study is one in which the researcher takes a sample of subjects based on their outcome and looks back in history to see whether they had been exposed. If the study is a prospective (cohort) study, where subjects are selected by presence or absence of exposure and observed over time to see if they come down with the disease, the appropriate measure of risk is the relative risk (RR). In fact, OR is an estimate of RR and is used when you cannot calculate RR. If the outcome is rare, the values of the odds ratio and relative risk are approximately equal.

Table 6.7 Standard Risk Analysis Table

Outcome			
Risk Factor	**Present**	**Absent**	**Total**
Exposed	a	b	$a + b$
Not Exposed	c	d	$c + d$
Total	$a + c$	$b + d$	$N = a + b + c + d$

A standard format for risk analysis data is given in Table 6.7. Note that subjects with the outcome of interest are counted in the first column, and those exposed to the risk factor are given in the first row so that "a" represents the number of subjects who were exposed to the risk factor and had the outcome of interest.

For a retrospective study, the appropriate measure of risk is the odds ratio. In this case, the observed odds of having the outcome when exposed is a/b, while the corresponding odds when not exposed is c/d. Thus, the odds ratio is estimated to be $(a/b)/(c/d) = ad/bc$. So, for example, if the odds ratio is 3, then this means that the odds of having the outcome of interest are three times larger in the exposed group than in the nonexposed group. Similarly, in a prospective study, we use the relative risk. In this case, it makes sense to say that the estimated risk of having the outcome of interest is $a/(a + b)$ for the exposed group and $c/(c + d)$ for the nonexposed group. Thus, the estimated relative risk is $\dfrac{a/(a+b)}{c/(c+d)}$, and if, for example, the relative risk is 3, this indicates that the observed risk of having the outcome of interest is three times greater in the exposed group than in the nonexposed group.

In many retrospective analyses, we are interested in assessing whether the odds ratio is (statistically) different from 1. If the OR is shown to be greater than 1, for example, it provides evidence that a risk (measured by the size of OR) exists relative to the reference group. An OR that is not significantly different from 1 provides no evidence that a risk exists. If the OR is significantly less than 1, it implies that exposure to the factor provides a benefit relative to the reference group.

Appropriate Applications for Retrospective (Case Control) Studies

The following are examples of retrospective (case control) studies in which the odds ratio is the appropriate measure of risk.

- *Survival and lung cancer*. In order to investigate smoking and lung cancer, a group of patients who have lung cancer (cases) are compared to a control group without lung cancer. Each of the subjects in these two groups is then classified as being a smoker (i.e., the exposure) or a nonsmoker.

- *Vaccination and autism*. In order to assess whether having received the measles, mumps, and rubella vaccine increases the risk of developing autism, a group of autistic children and a control group of nonautistic children are compared on the basis of whether they have previously received the vaccine.

Appropriate Applications for Prospective (Cohort) Studies

- *History of concussions*. A group of football players with a history of concussion is compared over a 2-year period with a control group of football players with no history of concussion to see whether those with such history are more likely to experience another concussion during that period.

- *Cholesterol and heart attacks*. Samples of 500 subjects with high cholesterol and 500 subjects without high cholesterol are followed for the next 10 years to determine whether subjects in the high-cholesterol group were more likely to have a heart attack during that period.

In Example 6.3 we reexamine the data analyzed in Example 6.2 from the perspective of a risk analysis.

Program Comments

For SPSS to calculate the correct values for the odds ratio, you will need to set up your SPSS data set in a specific way so that the resulting 2 x 2 output table appears in the standard display format shown in Table 6.7. In this table, notice that subjects at risk are in the first row and subjects not at risk are in the second row of the table. Similarly, those who experience the outcome of interest are placed in column 1. For SPSS to produce this table, you must designate row and column positions alphabetically or in numerical order. That is, in the current example, the risk factor is coded so that 0 = exposed and 1 = not exposed. You could also code them as 1 = exposed and 2 = not exposed. Both of these coding strategies put the exposed subjects in the first row of the table. If, for example, you used the opposite strategy where 0 = not exposed and 1 = exposed, that would place those having the exposure in the second row. This would cause the OR to be calculated as 0.135 (which is the inverse of the OR = 7.429). This coding conundrum is unfortunate since most people intuitively code their data with 1 meaning exposure and 0 meaning no exposure. However, to make the results come out correctly in SPSS, you should use the guidelines listed above.

Example 6.3

Analyzing Risk Ratios for the Exposure/Reaction Data

Consider again the data in Tables 6.4 and 6.5 related to the exposure to a reagent and the occurrence of a particular reaction. In the previous discussion of these data, we intentionally did not specify whether the data were collected for purposes of a prospective or retrospective study. In the following, we discuss both types of analyses.

Analysis as a Retrospective (Case Control) Study

We assume here that 17 subjects experiencing the reaction were selected for study along with 23 subjects who did not experience such a reaction (see Table 6.4). We then look back to determine which of these subjects experienced the particular exposure in question.

To calculate the odds ratio for this analysis, follow these steps:

SPSS Step-By-Step. EXAMPLE 6.3:
Risk Analysis Associated With a 2 × 2
Contingency Table Analysis (Data Stored Casewise)

1. Open the data set EXPOSURE22.SAV and select **Analyze/Descriptive Statistics/Crosstabs**. . . .

2. Choose *Exposure* as the Row variable and *Reaction* as the column variable.

3. Click the Statistics button and select the Risk checkbox and Continue.

4. Click OK.

The resulting output includes Table 6.8.

The calculated odds ratio (odds ratio for exposure) of 7.429 estimates that the odds of having the reaction when exposed is 7.429 times greater than the odds when not exposed. Since the 95% confidence interval of the true odds ratio—that is, [1.778, 31.040]—stays greater than 1, then you can interpret this result as being statistically significant (i.e., you can conclude that the odds of having the reaction when exposed is higher than the odds when not exposed).

Analysis as a Prospective (Cohort) Study

In this setting, using the same data and analysis, we assume that 20 subjects who experienced the particular exposure and 20 who did not were chosen for the study. These subjects were then followed

Table 6.8   Risk Analysis Results

Risk Estimate

	Value	95% Confidence Interval	
		Lower	Upper
Odds Ratio for Exposure (Exposed/Not Exposed)	7.429	1.778	31.040
For Cohort Reaction = Reaction	3.250	1.278	8.267
For Cohort Reaction = No Reaction	.438	.232	.827
N of Valid Cases	40		

over time to see whether they had the reaction. In this case, the appropriate measure of risk is relative risk, and the value of 3.25, labeled as "For cohort Reaction = Reaction," indicates that the observed risk of having the reaction is 3.25 times greater for the exposed group than for the nonexposed group. The corresponding 95% confidence interval on the true relative risk is [1.278, 8.267], which again stays greater than 1 and thus indicates a significant result.

Reporting the Results of a Risk Analysis

The following illustrates how you might report risk analysis results in a publication format.

Narrative for the Methods Section of a Retrospective (Case Control) Study

"To examine the relative risk of having the reaction when exposed, we calculated an odds ratio."

Narrative for the Results Section of a Retrospective (Case Control) Study

"The odds of having the reaction were 7.43 times greater for subjects in the exposed group than for subjects not exposed to the reagent (OR = 7.4, 95% CI = 1.8, 31.0). Thus, the odds ratio is significantly greater than 1, suggesting that the true odds of having the reaction are greater for the exposed group."

Narrative for the Methods Section of a Prospective (Cohort) Study

"To examine the relative risk of having the reaction when exposed, we calculated relative risk."

SIDEBAR
A savvy researcher will use the confidence interval not only to assess significance but to also determine what practical meaning this risk would entail if the true value were at the lower or upper end of the interval. Also, it is helpful to interpret confidence intervals in the context of results from other published studies.

McNemar's Test

In the section on contingency table analysis, we saw that a test for independence can be used to test whether there is a relationship between dichotomous categorical variables such as political party preference (Republican or Democrat) and voting intention (plan to vote or do not plan to vote). Also, in Example 6.2, researchers were interested in determining whether there was a relationship between exposure to a risk factor and occurrence of a reaction. While in these cases, it is of interest to determine whether the variables are independent, in some cases, the categorical variables are paired in such a way that a test for independence is meaningless. McNemar's test is designed for the analysis of paired dichotomous, categorical variables in much the same way that the paired t-test is designed for paired quantitative data.

Appropriate Applications of McNemar's Test

The following are examples of dichotomous categorical data that are paired and for which McNemar's test is appropriate.

- *How does a new scanning procedure compare with the ECG?* An electrocardiogram (ECG) and a new scanning procedure are used to detect whether heart disease is present in a sample of patients with known heart disease. Researchers want to analyze the disagreement between the two measures.

- *Is there a change in political party preference?* A sample of possible voters is polled to determine whether their preferences for the two major political party candidates for president changed before and after a televised debate.

- *Advertising and consumer impressions.* Consumers are selected for a study designed to determine how their impressions of a particular product (favorable or unfavorable) changed before and after viewing an advertisement.

In each case above, the pairing occurs because the two variables represent two readings of the same characteristic (e.g., detection of heart disease, presidential preference, etc.). You already have reason to expect that the readings will agree to some extent, and thus testing for independence using a contingency table approach is not really appropriate. What you want to measure is disagreement or change. That is, in what way do the two heart scan procedures differ, how has the debate or the advertisement changed the opinions of the subjects, and so forth?

Hypotheses for McNemar's Test

In situations for which McNemar's test is appropriate, the interest focuses on the subjects for which change occurred. Following up on the third bulleted example above, suppose an advertiser wants to know whether an advertisement has an effect on the impression consumers have of a product. A group of people are selected, and their feelings about the product before and after viewing the advertisement are recorded as favorable or unfavorable. Thus, there are four categories of "before versus after" responses:

1. Favorable both before and after viewing the advertisement

2. Favorable before and unfavorable after viewing the advertisement

3. Unfavorable before and favorable after viewing the advertisement

4. Unfavorable both before and after viewing the advertisement

We are interested in determining whether the advertisement changed attitudes toward the product. That is, we concentrate on the subjects in categories 2 and 3. Was it more common for a subject to be in category 2 than in category 3 or vice versa? The hypotheses of interest would be the following:

H_0: The probability of a subject having a favorable response to the product before viewing the advertisement and an unfavorable response afterward is equal to the probability of having an unfavorable response to the product before viewing the advertisement and a favorable response afterward.

H_a: The probability of a subject having a favorable response to the product before viewing the advertisement and an unfavorable response afterward is not equal to the probability of having an unfavorable response to the product before viewing the advertisement and a favorable response afterward.

Clearly, the goal of the advertisement would be to improve people's attitudes toward the product; that is, there should be more people in category 3 than category 2. The corresponding one-sided hypotheses reflecting this goal are as follows:

H_0: The probability of a subject having a favorable response to the product before viewing the advertisement and an unfavorable response afterward is equal to the probability of having an unfavorable response to the product before viewing the advertisement and a favorable response afterward.

Example 6.4

McNemar's Test

Continuing with the advertising effectiveness illustration from the list of example analyses, suppose 20 subjects were asked to express their opinions before and after viewing the advertisement. Follow these steps to perform this McNemar's analysis:

SPSS Step-By-Step. EXAMPLE 6.4:
McNemar's Test for Advertising Effectiveness

1. Open the data set MCNEMAR.SAV. Note that the data contain two (nominal) variables labeled *Before* and *After* in casewise form. The data are all dichotomous where 0 indicates nonfavorable and 1 indicates favorable.

2. Select **Analyze/Descriptives Statistics/Crosstabs**. . . .

3. Select *Before* as the Row variable and *After* as the Column variable.

4. Click on the Statistics Button, select McNemar and Continue.

5. Click OK and the results in Tables 6.9 and 6.10 are shown.

A crosstabulation of the responses is shown in Table 6.9, where it can be seen that 13 (9 + 4 on the diagonal) of the 20 subjects did not change their opinions of the product after viewing the advertisement. The important issue concerns how the other 7 (5 + 2) subjects responded. That is, did those who changed their minds tend to change from favorable before to unfavorable after or from unfavorable before to favorable after (clearly the advertiser's preference)? In the table, we see that two subjects changed from a favorable opinion before the advertisement to an unfavorable opinion afterward, while five improved their opinion after the advertisement.

Table 6.9   2 × 2 Table for Advertising Effectiveness Data

before * after Crosstabulation

Count		After		
		Unfavorable	Favorable	Total
Before	Unfavorable	4	5	9
	Favorable	2	9	11
Total		6	14	20

Suppose for the moment that the advertiser is simply interested in knowing whether the advertisement changes the perception of the viewer in either direction. In this case, we would test the first set of hypotheses given previously. The results for this analysis are shown in Table 6.10.

For this analysis, the test yields a *p*-value of 0.453. Since this *p*-value is large, the null hypothesis of equal probabilities is not rejected. That is, there is not enough evidence to say that those who will change their reactions after the advertisement will do so in one direction more than the other.

Table 6.10 McNemar's Test Results for Advertising Effectiveness Data

Chi-Square Tests

	Value	Exact Sig. (2-Sided)
McNemar Test		.453[a]
N of Valid Cases	20	

a. Binomial distribution used.

As mentioned earlier, it is probably the case that the advertiser wants to show that there is a stronger tendency for subjects to improve their opinion after the advertisement; that is, it is more likely to be in category 3 than category 2. In this case, you would want to test the second set of hypotheses given previously (i.e., the one-sided hypotheses). The data support the alternative of interest since five people who changed were in category 3 and only two were in category 2. Thus, for this one-sided hypothesis, the *p*-value in the table should be cut in half, but even with this reduction, the results are still not significant. (This nonsignificant result could have resulted from a sample size too small to detect a meaningful difference. See the discussion of the power of a test in Chapter 1.)

Reporting the Results of McNemar's Test

The following illustrates how you might report these McNemar test results in a publication format in the setting in which the alternative specifies an improved impression after viewing the advertisement.

Narrative for the Methods Section

> "McNemar's test was used to test the null hypothesis that the probability of changing from favorable before to unfavorable after viewing the advertisement is equal to the probability of changing from unfavorable before to favorable after viewing the advertisement."

Narrative for the Results Section

> "Using McNemar's test, no significant tendency was found for subjects who changed their opinion to be more likely to have a favorable opinion of the product after viewing the advertisement ($p = 0.23$)."

H_a: The probability of a subject having a favorable response to the product before viewing the advertisement and an unfavorable response afterward is less than the probability of having an unfavorable response to the product before viewing the advertisement and a favorable response afterward.

Mantel-Haenszel Meta-Analysis Comparison

The Mantel-Haenszel method is often used (particularly in meta-analysis) to pool the results from several 2×2 contingency tables. It is also useful for the analysis of two dichotomous variables while adjusting for a third variable to determine whether there is a relationship between the two variables, controlling for levels of the third variable.

Appropriate Applications of the Mantel-Haenszel Procedure

- *Disease Incidence*. Case control data for a disease are collected in several cities, forming a 2×2 table for each city. You could use a Mantel-Haenszel analysis to obtain a pooled estimate of the odds ratio across cities.
- *Pooling Results From Previous Studies*. Several published studies have analyzed the same categorical variables summarized in 2×2 tables. In meta-analysis, the information from the studies is pooled to provide more definitive findings than could be obtained from a single study. Mantel-Haenszel analysis can be used to pool this type of information. For more on meta-analysis, see Cooper, Hedges, and Valentine (2009).

Hypotheses Tests Used in Mantel-Haenszel Analysis

The hypotheses tested in the Mantel-Haenszel analysis are as follows:

H_0: There is no relationship between the two variables of interest when controlling for a third variable.

H_a: There is a relationship between the two variables of interest when controlling for a third variable.

Design Considerations for a Mantel-Haenszel Test

A Mantel-Haenszel analysis looks at several 2×2 tables from the same bivariate variables, each representing some strata or group (e.g., information from different departments at a university, etc.) or from different results of similar analyses (as in a meta-analysis). The test also assumes that the tables are independent (subjects or entities are in one and only one table).

Example 6.5

Mantel-Haenszel Analysis

A classic data set illustrating the use of the Mantel-Haenszel test is data collected at the University of California at Berkeley concerning gender patterns in graduate admissions (Bickel & O'Connell, 1975). The crosstabulated data for acceptance (no or yes) versus gender is given in Table 6.11 for five separate departments along with row percentages, showing the percentage of each gender that was admitted within each program. From this table, it can be seen that while Department 1 seems to have higher admission rates than the other departments, the comparative acceptance rates for males and females are about the same within departments, with there being a slight tendency for females to be admitted at a higher rate.

Table 6.11   Berkeley Graduate Admissions Data

Gender * Accepted * Department Crosstabulation

Department					Accepted No	Accepted Yes	Total
1	Gender	Female		Count	8	17	25
				% Within Gender	32.0%	68.0%	100.0%
		Male		Count	207	353	560
				% Within Gender	37.0%	63.0%	100.0%
	Total			Count	215	370	585
				% Within Gender	36.8%	63.2%	100.0%
2	Gender	Female		Count	391	202	593
				% Within Gender	65.9%	34.1%	100.0%
		Male		Count	205	120	325
				% Within Gender	63.1%	36.9%	100.0%
	Total			Count	596	322	918
				% Within Gender	64.9%	35.1%	100.0%
3	Gender	Female		Count	244	131	375
				% Within Gender	65.1%	34.9%	100.0%

(Continued)

Table 6.11 (Continued)

Department				Accepted		
				No	Yes	Total
		Male	Count	279	138	417
			% Within Gender	66.9%	33.1%	100.0%
	Total		Count	523	269	792
			% Within Gender	66.0%	34.0%	100.0%
4	Gender	Female	Count	299	94	393
			% Within Gender	76.1%	23.9%	100.0%
		Male	Count	138	53	191
			% Within Gender	72.3%	27.7%	100.0%
	Total		Count	437	147	584
			% Within Gender	74.8%	25.2%	100.0%
5	Gender	Female	Count	317	24	341
			% Within Gender	93.0%	7.0%	100.0%
		Male	Count	351	22	373
			% Within Gender	94.1%	5.9%	100.0%
	Total		Count	668	46	714
			% Within Gender	93.6%	6.4%	100.0%
Total	Gender	Female	Count	1259	468	1727
			% Within Gender	72.9%	27.1%	100.0%
		Male	Count	1180	686	1866
			% Within Gender	63.2%	36.8%	100.0%
	Total		Count	2439	1154	3593
			% Within Gender	67.9%	32.1%	100.0%

The Mantel-Haenszel analysis can be used to test the following hypotheses:

H_0: Controlling for (or within departments), there is no relationship between gender and acceptance.

H_a: Controlling for (or within departments), there is a relationship between gender and acceptance.

To produce the information in Table 6.11 and an appropriate Mantel-Haenszel analysis, follow these steps:

SPSS Step-By-Step. EXAMPLE 6.5: Mantel-Haenszel Analysis of Berkeley Graduate Admissions Data

1. Open the data file BIAS.SAV. Notice that the data set consists of three categorical variables (*Department, Gender,* and *Accepted*) and a *Count* variable.

2. Because data are in counts, you need to tell SPSS this before doing an analysis. Select **Data/Weight Cases** and select the radio button "Weight cases by" and put the *Count* variable in the Frequency variable box. Click OK.

3. Select **Analyze/Descriptive Statistics/Crosstabs**. . . .

4. Select *Gender* as the Row(s) variable and *Accepted* as the Column(s) variable. Select *Department* as the "Layer 1 of 1" variable.

5. Click the Statistics button and check the "Cochran's and Mantel-Haenszel Statistics" checkbox (leave common odds ratio as 1) and Continue.

6. Click the Cells button and select Row in the Percentages section and Continue.

7. Click OK and the output includes the information in Tables 6.11 and 6.12.

The preliminary results for the Mantel-Haenszel test are shown in Table 6.12, where it can be seen that $p = 0.756$, indicating that controlling for departments, there is no reason to conclude that there is a difference between male versus female admission rates. As mentioned previously, the consistent pattern is that the admission rates for males and females are about the same for each department, with perhaps

Table 6.12   Mantel-Haenszel Results for Berkeley Graduate Admissions Data

Tests of Conditional Independence

	Chi-Squared	df	Asymp. Sig. (2-Sided)
Cochran's	.125	1	.724
Mantel-Haenszel	.096	1	.756

a slight tendency for females to have a higher rate of admission. Cochran's test is similar to the Mantel-Haenszel test but is not commonly reported. In this example, Cochran's test gives results consistent with the Mantel-Haenszel test.

Reporting Results of a Mantel-Haenszel Analysis

Narrative for the Methods Section

"Controlling for department, the relationship between gender and acceptance is examined using a Mantel-Haenszel analysis."

Narrative for the Results Section

"Adjusting or controlling for department, no significant difference was found between male and female acceptance rates, $\chi^2(1, N = 3,593) = 0.10$, $p = 0.76$."

Tips and Caveats for Mantel-Haenszel Analysis

Simpson's Paradox

Historically, the real interest in the Berkeley admissions data set (and the reason for Bickel and O'Connell's 1975 article in *Science*) is the apparent inconsistency

Table 6.13   Berkeley Graduate Admissions Data Combined Across Departments

Gender * Accepted Crosstabulation

			Accepted		Total
			No	Yes	
Gender	Female	Count	1259	468	1727
		% Within Gender	72.9%	27.1%	100.0%
	Male	Count	1180	686	1866
		% Within Gender	63.2%	36.8%	100.0%
	Total	Count	2439	1154	3593
		% Within Gender	67.9%	32.1%	100.0%

between the conclusions based on evidence of a possible bias against females using the combined data (see Table 6.13) and the conclusions obtained previously based on the departmental data in Table 6.11 (i.e., within departments, the acceptance rates for men and women were not significantly different). In Table 6.13, we show an overall comparison between gender and admission combined over the five departments. Interestingly, in Table 6.13, the overall admission rates for males is 37% (686/1,866), while for females, it is only 27% (468/1,727). In addition, for this 2×2 table, the chi-square test for independence (computer output not shown here) gives $p < 0.001$, indicating a relationship between gender and admission. On the surface, these data seem to indicate a sex bias against women.

To explain the reasons for these seeming contradictions, note that admissions rates into Department 1 were substantially higher than were those for the other four majors. Further examination of the data in Table 6.11 indicates that males applied in greater numbers to Department 1, while females applied in greater numbers to departments into which admission was more difficult. The important point is that relationships between variables within subgroups can be entirely reversed when the data are combined across subgroups. (As indicated by *Simpson's paradox*.) Clearly, analysis of these data by department, as shown in Table 6.11, provides a better picture of the relationship between gender and admission than does use of the combined data in Table 6.13.

Tests of Interrater Reliability

Interrater reliability is a measure used to examine the agreement between two raters or observers on the assignment of categories of a categorical variable. It is an important measure in determining how well an implementation of some coding or measurement system works.

Appropriate Applications of Interrater Reliability

- *Classifying types of fractures*. Type of fracture of the tibia, classed as an A, B, or C type fracture (where classifications are not ordinal).
- *Tumor severity evaluation*. Different people read and rate the severity (from 0 to 4) of a tumor based on a magnetic resonance imaging (MRI) scan.
- *Ice-skating judging*. Several judges score competitors at an ice-skating competition on an integer scale of 1 to 5.

A statistical measure of interrater reliability is Cohen's kappa (κ), which ranges from -1.0 to 1.0, where large positive numbers mean better reliability, values near zero suggest that agreement is attributable to chance, and values less than zero signify that agreement is even less than that which could be attributed to chance.

Effect Size

Landis and Koch (1977) suggest the following effect size interpretation of kappa (κ):

- $\kappa < 0$ indicates no agreement
- $\kappa > 0$ and < 0.2 indicates slight agreement
- $\kappa > 0.20$ and < 0.40 indicates fair agreement
- $\kappa > 0.40$ and < 0.60 indicates moderate agreement
- $\kappa > 0.60$ and < 0.80 indicates substantial agreement
- $\kappa > 0.80$ indicates almost perfect agreement

Example 6.6

Interrater Reliability Analysis

Using an example from Fleiss (2000, p. 213), suppose you have 100 subjects whose diagnoses are rated by two raters on a scale that rates each subject's disorder as being psychological, neurological, or organic. The data are given in Table 6.14.

Table 6.14 Data for Interrater Reliability Analysis

		Rater A		
		Psychological	Neurological	Organic
Rater B	Psychological	75	1	4
	Neurological	5	4	1
	Organic	0	0	10

Source: Data from Fleiss (2000).

To analyze this data follow these steps:

1. Open the file KAPPA.SAV. Notice that the data are in count form with categorical variables *Rater_A, Rater_B*, and *Count*. Figure 6.4 shows this data file.

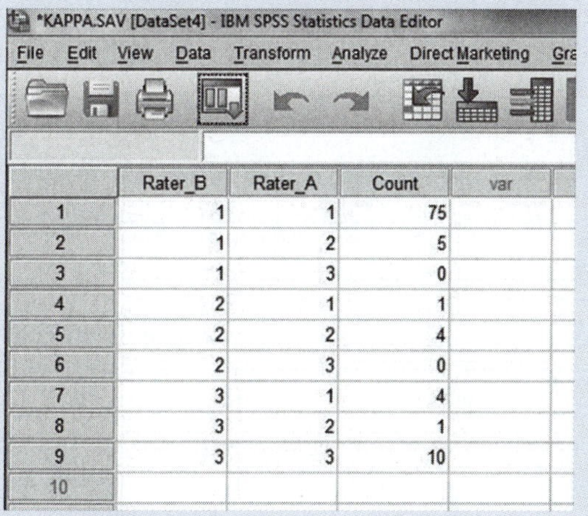

	Rater_B	Rater_A	Count	var
1	1	1	75	
2	1	2	5	
3	1	3	0	
4	2	1	1	
5	2	2	4	
6	2	3	0	
7	3	1	4	
8	3	2	1	
9	3	3	10	
10				

Figure 6.4 Interrater Reliability Data in SPSS

2. Before performing the analysis on this summarized data, you must tell SPSS that the *Count* variable is a "weighted" variable. Select **Data/Weight Cases** . . . and select the "weight cases by" option with *Count* as the Frequency variable. Click OK..

3. To perform the analysis, select **Analyze/Descriptive Statistics/Crosstabs**. . . .

4. Select *Rater_A* as Row, *Rater_B* as Col.

5. Click on the Statistics button, select Kappa and Continue.

6. Click OK to display the results for the Kappa test in Table 6.15.

Table 6.15   Results for Interrater Reliability Analysis

Symmetric Measures

		Value	Asymp. Std. Error[a]	Approx. T[b]	Approx. Sig.
Measure of Agreement	Kappa	.676	.088	8.879	.000
N of Valid Cases		100			

a. Not assuming the null hypothesis.

b. Using the asymptotic standard error assuming the null hypothesis.

The results of the interrater analysis are given in Table 6.15, where Kappa = 0.676 with $p < 0.001$ (Approx Sig.). Based on the effect size classification, this value indicates substantial agreement. Although not displayed in the output, you can find a 95% confidence interval using the generic formula for 95% confidence intervals:

$$\text{Estimate} \pm 1.96\ SE$$

Using this formula and the results in Table 6.15, an approximate 95% confidence interval on kappa is [0.504, 0.848].

Note that in this diagnosis example the categories are not ordered. In cases where categories are ordered (as in examples 2 and 3 of the bulleted list above), a weighted Kappa analysis is preferred. The weighted Kappa allows "close" ratings to not simply be counted as "misses." However, SPSS does not calculate weighted Kappa. (See SAS or WINKS SDA software for weighted Kappa Analysis.)

Reporting the Results of an Interrater Reliability Analysis

The following illustrates how you might report this interrater analysis in a publication format.

Narrative for the Methods Section

"An interrater reliability analysis using the Kappa statistic was performed to determine consistency among raters."

Narrative for the Results Section

"The interrater reliability for the raters was found to have substantial agreement where kappa = 0.68 ($p < .0001$), 95% CI [0.504, 0.848]."

Goodness-of-Fit Test

A goodness-of-fit test is used to ascertain whether the distribution of observed counts in the various categories of a categorical variable matches the expected distribution of counts under a hypothetical model for the data.

Appropriate Applications of the Goodness-of-Fit Test

The following are examples of situations in which a chi-square goodness-of-fit test would be appropriate.

- *Does a genetic theory apply?* Genetic theory indicates that the result of crossing two flowering plants to create a number of progeny should result in flowers that are 50% red, 25% yellow, and 25% white. When the cross-bred flowers bloom, the observed number of each color is compared with the numbers expected under the theory to see whether the genetic theory seems to apply in this case.

- *Is there a directional preference in nest positioning?* A zoologist wants to know whether there is a directional preference in the positioning of nests for a particular species of birds. A sample of 300 nests is observed, and each nest is categorized as facing north, northeast, and so on. The counts for each of the eight directions are compared with the counts expected if there is no directional preference.

- *Is there a change in educational attainment?* The U.S. Bureau of Labor Statistics provides the percentages of U.S. full-time workers in 1996 who fell into the following five categories: less than high school, high school degree—no college, some college, bachelor's degree, and advanced degree. A sample of 1,000 full-time workers is selected this year to determine whether the distribution of educational attainment has changed since 1996.

Design Considerations for a Goodness-of-Fit Test

1. The test assumes that a random sample of observations is taken from the population of interest.

2. The appropriate use of the chi-square to approximate the distribution of the goodness-of-fit test statistic depends on both the sample size and the number of cells. A widely used rule of thumb suggested by Cochran (1954) is that the approximation is adequate if no expected cell frequencies are less than 1 and no more than 20% are less than 5.

Hypotheses for a Goodness-of-Fit Test

The hypotheses being tested in this setting are as follows:

H_0: The population (from which the sample is selected) follows the hypothesized distribution.

H_a: The population does not follow the hypothesized distribution.

To test these hypotheses, a chi-squared test statistic is used that compares the observed frequencies with what is expected if the hypothesized model under the null is correct. Large values of the test statistic suggest that the alternative is true, while small values are supportive of the null. A low *p*-value suggests rejection of the null hypothesis and leads to the conclusion that the data do not follow the hypothesized, or theoretical, distribution.

Tips and Caveats for a Goodness-of-Fit Test

No One-Sided Tests

There are no one-sided/two-sided decisions to be made regarding these tests. The tests are inherently nondirectional ("sort of two-sided") in the sense that the chi-square test is simply testing whether the observed frequencies and expected frequencies agree without regard to whether particular observed frequencies are above or below the corresponding expected frequencies. If the null hypothesis is rejected, then a good interpretation of the results will involve a discussion of differences that were found.

Example 6.7

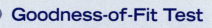

Goodness-of-Fit Test

As an illustration of the goodness-of-fit test, we consider a classic experiment in genetics. Gregor Mendel, a Czechoslovakian monk in the 19th century, identified some basic principles that control heredity. For example, Mendel's theory suggests that the phenotypic frequencies resulting from a dihybrid cross of two independent genes, where each gene shows simple dominant/recessive inheritance, will be expected to be in a 9:3:3:1 ratio. In Mendel's classic experiment using the garden pea, he predicted that the frequencies of smooth yellow peas, smooth green peas, wrinkled yellow peas, and wrinkled green peas would be in a 9:3:3:1 ratio. The hypotheses being tested in this setting are the following:

H_0: The population frequencies of smooth yellow, smooth green, wrinkled yellow, and wrinkled green peas will be in a 9:3:3:1 ratio.

H_a: The population frequencies will not follow this pattern.

Mendel's experiment yielded 556 offspring, so the expected frequencies would be

(9/16) x 556 = 312.75 smooth yellow

(3/16) x 556 = 104.25 smooth green

(3/16) x 556 = 104.25 wrinkled yellow

(1/16) x 556 = 34.75 wrinkled green

The frequencies that Mendel actually observed were 315, 108, 101, and 32 respectively (i.e., quite close to those expected). To perform an analysis testing his hypothesis, follow these steps:

SPSS Step-By-Step. EXAMPLE 6.7: Goodness-of-Fit Test Using Mendel's Data

This data set can be set up in two ways. If you know the counts in each category, you can set up a data set consisting specifically of these counts. If you have a standard casewise data set, then you can also run a goodness-of-fit test using that file directly.

The file MENDELCNT.SAV contains the actual counts Mendel obtained as shown in Figure 6.5. (You can either create the data set using the instructions in this example, or open the already created data set named MENDELCNT.SAV.)

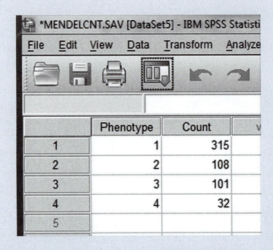

Figure 6.5   Mendel Data for Goodness-of-Fit Analysis

In order to create a data set consisting of the counts and perform the goodness-of-fit test in SPSS, follow these steps:

1. Select **File/New/Data** . . . (or open MENDELCNT.SAV and skip to item 3).

2. This new data set will have two numeric variables: *Phenotype* and *Count*. In the first column (i.e., for the *Phenotype* variable), enter the numbers 1 for smooth yellow, 2 for smooth green, 3 for wrinkled yellow, and 4 for wrinkled green, and in the second column, enter the corresponding counts (i.e., 315, 108, 101, and 32). Click on the Variable View and enter the variable names *Phenotype* and *Count*. In the Values column, specify Value Labels associated with the *Phenotype* codes (i.e., 1 = Smooth Yellow, etc.). Also, make sure the *Phenotype* variable is set as a Nominal measure. (See Appendix A: "A Brief Tutorial for Using IBM SPSS for Windows" if you do not know how to do this.)

3. Select **Data/Weight Cases** . . . and select the "weight case by" option with *Count* as the Frequency variable. Click OK..

4. Select **Analyze/Nonparametric Tests/Legacy Dialogs/Chi Square** . . . and select *Phenotype* as the Test variable.

5. In Expected Values, click on the Values radio button. Enter the theorized proportions in the order you entered the data. Thus, enter a 9 and click Add, enter 3 and click Add, and enter another 3 and click Add, and finally enter 1 and click Add. This specifies the theoretical 9:3:3:1 ratio.

6. Click OK to display the output shown in Table 6.16.

Table 6.16 Goodness-of-Fit Analysis for Mendel's Data

Phenotype

	Observed N	Expected N	Residual
Smooth Yellow	315	312.8	2.3
Smooth Green	108	104.3	3.8
Wrinkled Yellow	101	104.3	−3.3
Wrinkled Green	32	34.8	−2.8
Total	556		

Test Statistics

	Phenotype
Chi-Square	.470[a]
df	3
Asymp. Sig.	.925

a. 0 cells (0.0%) have expected frequencies less than 5. The minimum expected cell frequency is 34.8.

In Table 6.16, we show the results for this analysis where you can see the observed and expected frequencies. The chi-square statistic is 0.470 with 3 degrees of freedom and $p = .925$. That is, the observed phenotypic ratios followed the expected pattern quite well, and you would not reject the null hypothesis. There is no evidence to suggest that the theory is not correct. In general, if the *p*-value for this test is significant, it means that there is evidence that the observed data *do not* fit the theorized ratios.

Reporting the Results of a Chi-Square Goodness-of-Fit Analysis

The following examples illustrate how you might report this goodness-of-fit test in a publication format.

Narrative for the Methods Section

"A chi-square goodness-of-fit test was performed to test the null hypothesis that the population frequencies of smooth yellow, smooth green, wrinkled yellow, and wrinkled green peas will be in a 9:3:3:1 ratio."

Narrative for the Results Section

"The results were not statistically significant, and there is no reason to reject the claim that Mendel's theory applies to this dihybrid cross, $\chi^2 (3, N = 556) = 0.470, p = 0.925$."

Program Comments

- In Example 6.7 notice that we entered 9, 3, 3, and 1 as the expected frequencies. You can enter any set of numbers as long as they are multiples of the expected proportions—in this case, 9/16, 3/16, 3/16, and 1/16. So, for example, you could enter 18, 6, 6, and 2 and still obtain the same results. A natural set of expected frequencies to use is 312.75, 104.25, 104.25, and 34.75, which are the expected frequencies out of 556. However, SPSS does not allow an entry as long as 312.75. SPSS will accept 312.8 and so forth, and use of these rounded expected frequencies results in very minor differences from the results in Table 6.16.

- If you have a data set (such as the example described earlier involving the directional preference in the positioning of nests for a certain species of bird), you would select "All categories equal" in the "Expected Values" section.

- The chi-square procedure in SPSS does not recognize string (text) variables. This is the reason we assigned *Phenotype* to be a numeric variable and assigned the associated value labels rather than simply specifying *Phenotype* as a string variable and using the four phenotypes as observed values.

Other Measures of Association for Categorical Data

Several other statistical tests can be performed on categorical data. The test performed depends on the type of categorical variables and the intent of the analysis. The following list describes several of these briefly.

Correlation. If both the rows and columns of your table contain ordered numerical values, you can produce a Spearman's rho or other nonparametric correlations. See Chapter 8: Nonparametric Analysis Procedures for a discussion of nonparametric procedures.

Nominal measures. A number of other specialty measures can be calculated for crosstabulation tables in which both variables are nominal. These include the following:

- *Contingency coefficient.* This is a measure designed for larger tables. Some statisticians recommend that the table be at least 5 by 5. The values of the contingency coefficient range from 0 to 1, with 1 indicating high association. For smaller tables, this statistic is not recommended.

- *Phi.* The phi coefficient is a measure of association that is adjusted according to sample size. Specifically, it is the square root of the calculated chi-square statistic divided by n, the sample size. Phi ranges from -1 to 1 for 2×2 tables and, for larger tables, from 0 to the square root of the minimum of $r - 1$ or $c - 1$, where r and c denote the number of rows and columns, respectively. Phi is most often used in a 2×2 table where the variable forms true dichotomies. In the case of 2×2 tables, the phi coefficient is equal to Pearson's correlation coefficient.

- *Cramer's V.* This is a measure of association based on chi-square, where the upper limit is always 1. In a 2×2 table, Cramer's V is equal to the absolute value of the phi coefficient.

- *Lambda.* Also called the Goodman-Kruskal index, lambda is a measure of association where a high value of lambda (up to 1) indicates that the independent variable does a good job of predicting the dependent variable and where a low value of lambda (down to 0) indicates that it is of no help in predicting the dependent variable.

- *Uncertainty coefficient.* Sometimes called the entropy coefficient, this is a measure of association that indicates the proportional reduction in error (or uncertainty) when predicting the dependent variable. SPSS calculates symmetric and asymmetric versions of the uncertainty coefficient.

Ordinal Measures. Ordinal measures of association are appropriate when the two variables in the contingency table both have an inherent order.

- *Gamma.* This statistic ranges between -1 and 1 and is interpreted similarly to a Pearson's correlation. For two-way tables, zero-order gammas are displayed. For three-way to n-way tables, conditional gammas are displayed.

- *Somer's d*. This measure of association ranges between −1 and 1. It is an asymmetric extension of gamma. Asymmetric values are generated according to which variable is considered to be the dependent variable.

- *Kendall's tau-b*. This is a measure of correlation for ordinal or ranked measures where ties are taken into account. It is most appropriate when the number of columns and rows are equal. Values range from −1 to 1.

- *Kendall's tau-c*. This is similar to tau-b, except this measure ignores ties.

- *Eta*. This is a measure of association that is appropriate when the dependent variable is a quantitative measure (such as age or income) and the independent variable is categorical (nominal or ordinal). Eta ranges from 0 to 1, with low values indicating less association and high values indicating a high degree of association. SPSS calculates two eta values, one that treats the row variable as the quantitative variable and one that treats the column variable as the quantitative variable.

SUMMARY

This chapter explains how to analyze categorical data using a variety of techniques for measuring association and goodness-of-fit. The following chapter examines a comparison of three or more means.

REFERENCES

Bickel, P. J., & O'Connell, J. W. (1975). Is there a sex bias in graduate admissions? *Science, 187*, 398–404.

Cochran, W. G. (1954). Some methods for strengthening the common chi-square test. *Biometrics, 10*, 417–451.

Cooper, H., Hedges, L. V., & Valentine, J. C., eds. (2009). *The handbook of research synthesis and meta-analysis*. New York, NY: Russell Sage Foundation.

Fleiss, J. L. (2000). *Statistical methods for rates & proportions* (2nd ed.). New York, NY: John Wiley. (Data used by permission.)

Landis, J. R., & Koch, G. G. (1977). The measurement of observer agreement for categorical data. *Biometrics, 33*(1), 159–174.

Royston, P., Altman, D. G., & Sauerbrei, W. (2006). Dichotomizing continuous predictors in multiple regression: A bad idea. *Statistics in Medicine, 25.1*, 127–141.

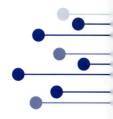

Analysis of Variance and Covariance

Sometimes, that "keep it simple" principle just doesn't meet your needs. Occasionally, you've got to make the leap from simple models to the more complex. This chapter takes the leap from the *t*-test to a series of tests designed to compare three or more means at a time or to compare means that are adjusted by some covariate. And even though it's a bit more involved than the *t*-test chapter, we'll try to keep it as simple and straightforward as possible. Specifically, this chapter discusses the following analyses:

- *One-way analysis of variance (ANOVA)*: an extension of the two-sample *t*-test used to determine whether there are differences among more than two group means
- *One-way analysis of variance with a test for trend*: used to test for a polynomial trend in the group means
- *Two-way analysis of variance*: used to evaluate the combined effect of two experimental factors
- *Repeated-measures analysis of variance*: an extension of the paired *t*-test for comparing means of the same or related subjects or objects over time or in differing circumstances
- *Analysis of covariance*: a one-way ANOVA in which the group means are adjusted by a covariate

These sections include discussion of multiple comparisons and graphs where appropriate. Although this chapter covers the most commonly used analysis of variance models, there are in fact a smorgasbord of analyses that can be classified under this umbrella. However, if you find that your experimental design goes beyond what is covered here, or if you do not understand how these models work, we suggest that you check out the references at the end of the chapter. Even better advice is to consult a statistician.

One-Way ANOVA

The one-way ANOVA (also called a one-factor ANOVA or completely randomized design) is a staple of almost every research discipline. It is widely used and, as you will see, relatively easy to perform and interpret. This model is a direct extension of the two-sample (independent group) *t*-test covered in Chapter 4: Comparing One or Two Means Using the *t*-Test. It is used to determine whether there are differences among the group means.

Appropriate Applications for a One-Way ANOVA

Examples of research that might use this design include the following:

- *Length of hospital stay.* Anorexic patients in a psychiatric ward are randomly grouped into a control treatment group (standard treatment) and two experimental treatment groups to determine whether either of the two experimental treatments reduces the average length of stay.
- *Which is the best brand?* The shear strengths of bolts manufactured by four different companies are compared to establish whether there are differences in the average shear strength.
- *What is the best package color?* A marketing study attempts to find out whether average sales are different for three choices of packaging color.

Design Considerations for a One-Way ANOVA

The design of a one-way ANOVA is similar to that for a two-sample (independent group) *t*-test, except that there are more than two groups. The key factors in designing such an analysis include the following:

The One-Way ANOVA Assumptions

1. *Independent samples.* The groups contain observed subjects (or objects) that are split into groups but are not paired or matched in any way. The groups are typically obtained in one of two ways:

   a. *Random split.* Subjects (or items) all come from the same population and are randomly split into groups. Each group is exposed to identical conditions, except for a "treatment" that may be a medical treatment, a marketing design factor, exposure to a stimulus, and so on.

   b. *Random selection.* Subjects are randomly selected from separate populations (i.e., by race, stores by region, machine by manufacturer, etc.).

2. *Normality.* A standard assumption for the one-way ANOVA to be valid is that the measurement variable is normally distributed within each group. That is, when graphed as a histogram, the shape approximates a bell curve (see Chapter 2: Describing and Examining Data).

3. *Equal variances.* Another assumption is that the within-group variances are the same for each of the groups.

    a. *How stringent are these assumptions?* As in the case of the *t*-test discussed in Chapter 4, studies have shown the one-way ANOVA to be robust against some departures from assumptions. Generally, slight departures from normality are of less concern than data that are highly nonnormal (i.e., a bimodal or highly skewed distribution). If you have equal or near-equal sample sizes in each group, the equal variance assumption becomes less important. However, the assumption of independence of the subjects is critical (Glass, Peckham, & Sanders, 1972).

    b. *An ANOVA tests the hypothesis of equal means.* Your outcome variable must be a quantitative variable such as height, weight, amount spent, or grade. (If you can make an assumption of normality for your data, it must at first at least be quantitative.)

    c. *Control group.* The groups to be compared may or may not include a control group. That is, one "control" group may receive a standard treatment or no treatment, while the others receive experimental treatments. If the experimental treatments are better than the control, then this may add more credibility to their use than if they are simply compared to other experimental groups.

    d. *Predefined comparisons.* The experimenter may have a special interest in certain comparisons among group means. These can be tested using contrasts. This topic is discussed later in this chapter.

    e. *Are group sample sizes equal?* The sample sizes in each group need not be equal, but if they are not equal, then care must often be taken when performing the post hoc analysis, as will be demonstrated in Example 7.1. In general, it is usually best to design your experiment so there is an equal (or almost equal) number of subjects in each group.

    f. *Are the groups ordered?* If groups have an inherent ordering such as age groups (0–15, 16–30, 31–50, 51 and above), torque pressure (mild, medium, strong), or dose (four increasingly strong levels), then your analysis could include an analysis of trend. The analysis in Example 7.2 includes a trend analysis.

Hypotheses for a One-Way ANOVA

The hypotheses for the comparison of the means in a one-way ANOVA are as follows:

$H_0: \mu_1 = \mu_2 = \ldots = \mu_k$ (the population means of all groups are the same).

H_a: $\mu_i \neq \mu_j$ for some $i \neq j$ (the population means of at least two groups are different).

Tips and Caveats for a One-Way ANOVA

- *Sample size considerations.* Inadequate sample sizes can result in a test without adequate power and can produce a nonsignificant finding, even if there are meaningful differences in the group population means. Also, small sample sizes cause the normality assumption to be more important and more difficult to assess.

- *Why not simply do several t-tests?* Since a one-way ANOVA usually involves examining pairwise comparisons, you may wonder why you would not simply perform the *t*-tests in the first place and make the analysis simpler. These comparisons are done within the context of an ANOVA to control the level of significance. For example, if you took four independent samples from the same population (i.e., the null hypothesis is true) and made all possible comparisons using *t*-tests, then there would be six total comparisons, each performed at the 0.05 level of significance. However, using this procedure, it can be shown that there is a $1 - (0.95)^6 = 0.26$ probability that at least one of the six comparisons will result in finding of a significant difference. That is, there is a 0.26 probability of rejecting the null hypothesis (which in this case is true). That is, the overall significance level is no longer 0.05 but has increased dramatically. By using the controlled environment of the one-way ANOVA, you preserve the error rate for the experiment. No knowledgeable statistician would use multiple *t*-tests in lieu of an appropriate ANOVA. See Chapter 1: Introduction for more discussion of these issues.

Example 7.1

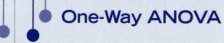

One-Way ANOVA

Describing the Problem

A university is experimenting with teaching a statistics course using three different methods, including the classical 3-day-a-week lecture, 1-day-a-week lecture plus CD lessons (including recorded lectures), and 1-day-a-week lecture plus online (Internet) tutorials. Students are randomly placed into one of the three methods, and all three methods are taught by the same instructor. Identical 100-point final exams are given to each section of the course. We will use the one-way ANOVA to compare the average learning (as measured by the final exam) for these three types of classes. Although it is highly desirable to have the same sample size in each group, it often doesn't work out that way in practice. In this example, 98 students signed up for the course, which means that the three groups will not have equal sample sizes if we use all of the students.

- Before performing the analysis, you should check out the assumptions listed earlier: For example, examine histograms or Q-Q plots to check normality.
- The students in each section are independent and randomly assigned.
- The assumption of equal variances will be tested as a part of the analysis.

To perform the analysis for this data, follow these steps:

SPSS Step-By-Step. EXAMPLE 7.1: One-Way ANOVA

1. Open the data set COURSES.SAV and select **Analyze/Compare Means/One-Way ANOVA**. . . .

2. Select *Section* as the Factor and *Grade* as the Dependent Variable. (Note that *Section*, the Factor variable, must be of nominal or ordinal measure.)

3. Click Options to select Descriptive and Homogeniety of Variance test and click Continue.

4. Click Post Hoc and select the Tukey multiple comparison test (for this example). Click Continue and OK to display results.

In the output for this analysis, first observe the descriptive statistics shown in Table 7.1.

Notice that the standard deviations are 10.16, 12.70, and 12.61 which don't cause much concern regarding the assumption of equal variances (remember that the variance is the square of the standard deviation). For further confirmation, a statistical test such as Levene's test for homogeneity of variances may be used. In this case, Levene's test, also shown in Table 7.1, yields a nonsignificant $p = 0.23$ for the comparison of these three variances, so the assumption of equal variance is not rejected.

Table 7.1   Descriptive Statistics for a One-Way ANOVA

Descriptives

GRADE								
					95% Confidence Interval for Mean			
	N	Mean	Std.Deviation	Std.Error	Lower Bound	Upper Bound	Minimum	Maximam
Standard	33	83.5455	10.16148	1.76889	79.9424	87.1486	58.00	1000.00
Internet	32	74.4688	12.70251	2.24551	69.8890	79.0485	45.00	94.00
CD Lessons	33	78.7879	12.60644	2.19450	74.3178	83.2579	49.00	100.00
Total	98	78.9796	12.32379	1.24489	76.5088	81.4504	45.00	100.00

Test of Homogeneity of Variances

GRADE			
Levene Statistic	df1	df1	Sig
1.492	2	95	.230

It is also helps to look at a graphical comparison of the groups. One way to do this is with side-by-side boxplots. The following steps produce this plot:

1. Using the COURSES.SAV data set select **Graphs/Chart Builder**. . . .

2. Select Boxplot from the chart types and drag the Simple Boxplot (left icon) into the Chart Preview box.

3. Drag *Grade* to the Y-axis and *Section* to the X-axis. (Note that the *Section* variable is Nominal. It must be either nominal or ordinal to be used here.)

4. Click OK and the plot shown in Figure 7.1 will be displayed.

The boxplot graph that includes medians and ranges shown in Figure 7.1 provides a visual comparison of the groups. In it, there is no evidence of any sizeable outliers or any obvious difference in variability among the three groups. The graph also shows (visually) that the final exam scores for the standard course were somewhat higher in general than for the two newer teaching methods but that there was considerable overlap among the distributions. Until further analysis, we cannot draw conclusions about significance of the differences in the mean final exam scores for the three methods.

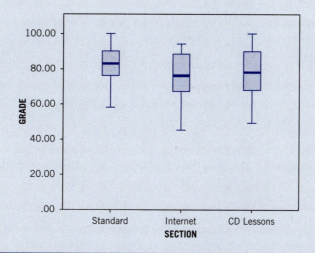

Figure 7.1 Boxplots for Course Data

Since there are no apparent violations of the assumptions, we next examine the ANOVA table in Table 7.2. This table provides an omnibus test of equality of means (labeled the "between-group" test). In this case, the ANOVA table reports an F-statistic of 4.754 with 2 and 95 degrees of freedom and $p = 0.011$. Because this p-value is less than 0.05, we reject the null hypothesis that all means are equal and conclude that there are some differences among the means. If the p-value had been nonsignificant, we would not conclude that there are differences in the means. No further multiple comparisons would be performed.

> Failing to reject the null hypothesis does not indicate a finding that there are no differences among the means. It simply indicates that we have been unable to detect differences. See the section in Chapter 1 titled "Understanding Hypothesis Testing, Power, and Sample Size."

Table 7.2 ANOVA Table for COURSE.SAV Data

ANOVA

GRADE					
	Sum of Squares	df	Mean Square	F	Sig.
Between Groups	1340.293	2	670.147	4.754	.011
Within Groups	13391.666	95	140.965		
Total	14731.959	97			

Since the ANOVA table indicates an overall significant difference among means, we now further investigate these differences using multiple comparisons. In this case, with three groups, there are three possible comparisons: standard versus Internet, standard versus CD, and Internet versus CD.

Most common of all post hoc tests is a comparison of all possible pairs of means. These are called multiple comparison tests. There is an alphabet soup of these tests available (most named after the statistician who came up with the technique). These include tests by the names of Tukey, Bonferroni, Duncan, Scheffé, R-E-G-W-F, and others. These tests each have their own characteristics (e.g., Bonferroni's test is quite conservative), and there are many opinions about which test to use and when. In this example, we limit our discussion to the use of Tukey's procedure to exemplify the technique. In practice, you may want to consider others. You may want to familiarize yourself with which techniques are commonly used in your disipline.

The multiple comparison results, based on the Tukey procedure, are reported in Tables 7.3 and 7.4. Using this procedure, two means are considered to be significantly different if the absolute difference in their corresponding sample means is greater than a specific threshold value. When sample sizes are equal, the formula for this threshold value involves this common sample size. When the sample sizes are not equal, the harmonic mean (32.66) of the corresponding sample sizes is typically used. Note that the harmonic mean is reported in Table 7.4.

In Table 7.3, all pairwise comparisons are listed along with their mean differences, standard errors, p-values, and 95% confidence intervals. For example, the first comparison is standard section versus Internet. The mean difference (Std Error) is 9.08 (2.95), the p-value testing the null hypothesis of no difference is $p = 0.008$, and the 95% confidence interval is [2.06, 16.09]. (This p-value reported in the table is already adjusted by the Tukey procedure according to how many comparisons are made in this table.) This indicates that there is a statistically significant difference between the mean for the standard versus Internet groups. In fact, this is the only statistically significant result in this table.

Another way to illustrate the Tukey multiple comparison in a table is shown in Table 7.4. In this table, the groups are listed in ascending order according to group means (Internet, CD, and standard). The columns labeled "Subset for alpha = 0.05" categorize the means into groups that are not significantly different from each other as subsets. (The 0.05 level used in this table has been adjusted by the Tukey procedure to account for how many comparisons are being made.) Thus, Internet and CD groups (which are both in column 1) form one subset, while CD and standard formed the other subset. Since the Internet and standard groups do not both appear in the same subset, they are significantly different from each other at the 0.05 significance level. Spend a moment to see how Table 7.3 and Table 7.4 are reporting the same results. Notice that SPSS warns that unequal sample sizes may compromise the results ("Type I error levels are not guaranteed"). In this case, with the sample sizes nearly equal, this is not an important concern.

To summarize, the overall ANOVA table results reported that at the $p = 0.011$ level of significance, there was at least one mean that was different from another. The post hoc Tukey test (performed at the 0.05 level of significance) examined all possible pairwise comparisons and determined that there

Table 7.3 Tukey Multiple Comparison Results

Multiple Comparisons

DependentVariable: GRADE

Tukey HSD

(I) SECTION	(J) SECTION	Mean Difference (I-J)	Std. Error	Sig.	95% Confidence Interval	
					Lower Bound	Upper Bound
Standard	Internet	9.07670*	2.94564	.008	2.0631	16.0903
	CD Lessons	4.75758	2.92290	.239	−2.2018	11.7170
Internet	Standard	−9.07670*	2.94564	.008	−16.0903	−2.0631
	CD Lessons	−4.31913	2.94564	.312	−11.3327	2.6944
CD Lessons	Standard	−4.75753	2.92290	.239	−11.7170	2.20138
	Internet	4.31913	2.94564	.312	−2.6944	11.3327

*.The mean difference is significant at the 0.05 level.

Table 7.4 Tukey Multiple Comparison Results as Reported by SPSS

Homogeneous Subsets

GRADE

Tukey HSD[a,b]

SECTION	N	Subset for alpha = 0.05	
		1	2
Internet	32	74.4688	
CD Lessons	33	78.7879	78.7879
Standard	33		83.5455
Sig.		.310	.243

Means for groups in homogeneous subsets are displayed.

a. Uses Harmonic Mean Sample Size = 32.660

b. The group sizes are unequal. The harmonic mean of the group sizes is used. Type I error levels are not guaranteed.

was a statistically significant difference in the mean scores of the standard versus the Internet groups. Specifically, the standard teaching method seems to have better average final exam performance than use of the Internet. The standard method also has a higher mean score than the CD method, although the difference is not statistically significant.

Reporting Results of a One-Way ANOVA

The following illustrates how you might report these one-way ANOVA results in a publication format.

Narrative for the Methods Section

"A one-way ANOVA was performed to test the hypothesis that the average final grades for the three course methods were equal. Multiple comparisons were performed using the Tukey procedure."

Narrative for the Results Section

"The average grades were found to be different across methods, $F(2, 95) = 4.75$, $p = 0.011$. Tukey multiple comparisons performed at a 0.05 significance level found that the average grade for the standard section is significantly higher than that for the Internet section."

Or, to be more complete,

"The average grades were found to be different across methods, $F(2, 95) = 4.75$, $p = 0.011$. The Tukey multiple comparisons performed at the 0.05 significance level found that the mean final exam grade for the standard course section ($M = 83.5$, $SD = 10.16$, $N = 33$) was significantly higher than that for the Internet section ($M = 74.5$, $SD = 12.7$, $N = 32$) but not significantly higher than the CD section ($M = 78.8$, $SD = 12.6$, $N = 33$). Mean exam grades for the CD and Internet sections were not found to be significantly different from each other."

Other Comparison Tests for a One-Way ANOVA

There are times when the standard "all-possible multiple comparisons" tests for a one-way ANOVA are not really what you want. Three alternatives to the all-possible comparisons are briefly discussed here:

- Dunnett's test
- Specified contrasts
- Trend analysis

Dunnett's Test. Dunnett's test is appropriate when the purpose of your analysis is to compare one group (usually the standard or control) against all other groups. For instance, in the previous example, we were interested in comparing all courses with each other. However, the real interest may be only the comparison between the standard course and the new methods. Thus, the standard method would be the control group to which the other two methods are compared. The preliminary analysis of variance would be performed exactly as above, and Dunnett's test is a post hoc test designed specifically for comparing treatment groups to a control group.

Example 7.1 (continued) With Dunnett's Comparison

1. Continuing with Example 7.1, select Analyze/Compare Means/One-Way ANOVA . . . and redo the analysis making these changes: In the Post Hoc section, select Dunnett, and indicate First for the Category Control (which is the standard group) as shown in Figure 7.2. This specifies the Standard group as the Control group. Uncheck the Tukey option.

2. Click Continue and OK to produce the Dunnett's results shown in Figure 7.2.

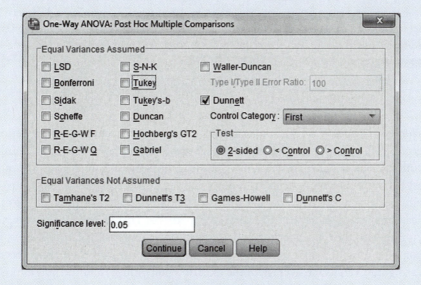

Figure 7.2 Indicate Dunnett's Test in Dialog Box

It should be noted that for Dunnett's test, you can use two-sided or one-sided tests. In this example, we will use a two-sided test if there is a question concerning whether to expect the new sections to do better or worse. The Dunnett's test results are shown in Table 7.5.

Table 7.5   Dunnett's Test Results

Multiple Comparisons

DependentVahable: GRADE
Dunnett t(2-sided)[a]

(I) SECTION	(J) SECTION	Mean Difference (I-J)	Std. Error	Sig.	95% Confidence Interval	
					Lower Bound	Upper Bound
Internet	Standard	−9.07670*	2.94564	.005	−15.6923	−2.4611
CD Lessons	Standard	−4.75758	2.92290	.187	−11.3221	1.8069

*. The mean difference is significant at the 0.05 level.

a. Dunnett t-tests treat one group as a control, and compare all other groups against it.

The results reported in Table 7.5 are specifically for the comparison of the Internet and CD Lessons sections against the Standard section. The "Sig." column shows there is a significant difference between the Internet section and the Standard section ($p = 0.005$) but no difference between the CD Lessons section and the Standard ($p = 0.187$). These findings are consistent with those obtained using Tukey multiple comparisons previously.

Contrasts for a one-way ANOVA. In some cases, you may simply want to examine certain specific group comparisons. Customized comparisons (planned contrasts) can be built around specific comparisons rather than simply investigating all-pairwise comparisons that are typical of the post hoc multiple comparison procedures. For example, suppose in the "course data" experiment, our alternative hypothesis is that the standard teaching method results in a higher mean final exam grade than the other two methods. That is, we want to compare the standard group with the two experimental groups in one comparison. To do that, we would need to combine, in some sense, the experimental groups. Thus, our comparison becomes the standard group versus the average of the experimental groups, and the null hypothesis of interest is H_0: $\mu_S = (\mu_I + \mu_C)/2$; that is, H_0: $\mu_S - (\mu_I + \mu_C)/2 = 0$, where μ_S, μ_I, and μ_C denote the population means for the standard, Internet, and CD sections, respectively.

A contrast is a weighted sum of means. The tricky part in designing a contrast is to assign weights (called contrast codes) to each group. These weights specify how the comparison will be made. In general, you assign a positive weight to one group or groups and negative weights to the remaining groups so that the weights add to zero. Based on the second form of the null hypothesis in the preceding paragraph, it makes sense to assign a weight (i.e., contrast code) of 1 to the standard group and a –0.5 to each of the other teaching methods. Multiplying a set of contrast codes by a constant gives another set of contrast codes that are equivalent. For example, you could also use 2 for the standard group and a –1 for each of the other teaching methods. To perform this contrast using example 7.1, perform the analysis as above, adding these steps:

Example 7.1 (Continued) With Contrasts

1. Redo the analysis in Example 7.1 (select Analyze/Compare Means/One-Way ANOVA . . .) with these changes: In the One-Way ANOVA dialog box, select the Contrast button.

2. In the One-Way ANOVA Contrasts dialog box, enter the contrast coefficients 1, –0.5, and –0.5 using the following technique: Enter 1 in the Coefficient box. Click Add. Enter –0.5 and click Add and enter –0.5 and click Add. This specifies the complete contrast as shown in Figure 7.3. (The order of the contrast coefficients indicate that the first group mean [Standard] will be contrasted with the average of the Internet and CD sections combined.) Click Continue.

3. Click OK to complete the analysis. The results based on the contrast codes 1, –.5, .–5 are shown in Table 7.6.

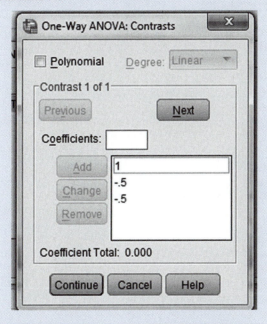

Figure 7.3   Contrasts for Course Data

Table 7.6   Contrasts for Course Data

Contrast Tests

		Contrast	Value of Contrast	Std. Error	t	df	Sig. (2-tailed)
GRADE	Assume equal variances	1	6.9171	2.53789	2.726	95	.008
	Does not assume equal variances	1	6.9171	2.36506	2.925	77.731	.005

Two versions of the contrast test are given, one that assumes equal variances and one that does not. Since we have already examined the variances and found them similar, the equal variances test is sufficient. In this case, $p = 0.008$, so we conclude that the mean grade of the standard course is significantly different (higher) than the average of the mean grades of the other two methods combined. If there is any question about the equality of variances, you should use the unequal variance option, which in this case gives a smaller p-value ($p = 0.005$) and leads to the same conclusion.

Example 7.2

One-Way ANOVA With Trend Analysis

Describing the Problem

A wholesale nursery is experimenting with a plant supplement that is designed to increase the number of flowers produced on a plant. To determine whether the supplement works and what strength to use, the nursery randomly selects 12 plants for five different commercially available strengths (1 to 5) of the supplement. After 2 weeks, the number of opened flowers per plant is counted. Table 7.7 gives the number of flowers counted for the 60 plants. It should be noted that there is no pairing of the data in this table. For example, the first entry under Strength 1 is not related in any way to the first entry under Strength 2.

We present this table here to make a point that will be clearer in the next section. For this example, notice that the way the data are presented in Table 7.7 is not the format in which it should be entered into the computer program. Rule 2 in "Guidelines for Creating Data Sets" given in Chapter 1 states that (usually) each line (row) of your data should contain the observations from a single subject. Each row in Table 7.7 contains observations from five separate plants that are not related to each other in any way. In general, the 60 observations in that table represent 60 randomly selected plants. The computer data file structure for a one-way ANOVA should take the form shown in Figure 7.4, which contains one subject (plant) per row and contains a "grouping" variable called *Strength* to indicate the concentration of the supplement that was used for that plant. For this data set, there are 60 rows, one for each plant.

Table 7.7 One-Way ANOVA Data for Example 7.2

Strength				
1	2	3	4	5
25	45	51	45	56
36	36	38	54	43
41	40	38	45	49
39	32	48	44	40
28	37	45	47	53
44	28	50	52	57
36	32	46	59	56
33	38	45	59	38
40	44	42	54	45
26	40	48	59	57
42	45	49	51	42
41	39	36	54	55

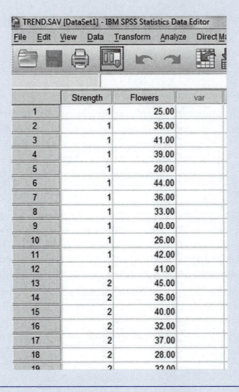

Figure 7.4 Data Entered for a One-Way ANOVA

What makes this analysis different from a typical one-way ANOVA is that the groups have an order (i.e., the strength 1 to 5). For this case, you may want to perform a trend analysis rather than use nonordered pairwise comparisons. A trend analysis tests the hypothesis that the means of the ordered groups change in a linear or higher order (e.g., quadratic or cubic) fashion. Figure 7.5 shows a plot of the mean number of flowers for each supplement strength.

It appears that the number of flowers increases as the strength of the supplement increases (up to a point). To perform this ANOVA with a trend analysis, follow these steps:

SPSS Step-By-Step. EXAMPLE 7.2: One-Way ANOVA With Trend

1. Open the data set TREND.SAV and select **Analyze/Compare Means/One-Way ANOVA**. . . . (Notice how the data are set up with one flower per row and with *Strength* as a grouping [factor] variable in Figure 7.4.)

2. Select *Strength* for Factor and *Flowers* for Dependent variable.

3. Click the Options checkbox to select the means plot and the Descriptive checkbox to select descriptive statistics and click Continue.

4. To specify the trend analysis, click on Contrasts and click the Polynomial checkbox. From the drop down box, select Cubic as the Degree as shown in Figure 7.6. Click Continue and OK, and the output in Table 7.8 and the means plot in Figure 7.5 appears.

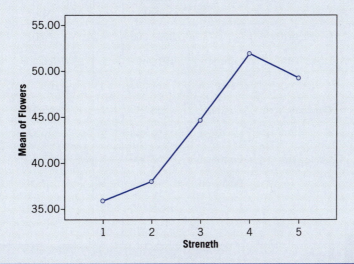

Figure 7.5   Mean Number of Flowers by Supplement Strength

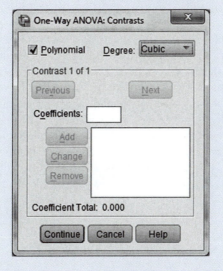

Figure 7.6   Specify Trend Analysis

Table 7.8 Test for Trend

ANOVA

Flowers

			Sum of Squares	df	Mean Square	F	Sig.
Between Groups	(Combined)		2304.100	4	576.025	15.851	.000
	Linear Term	Contrast	1976.408	1	1976.408	54.385	.000
		Deviation	327.692	3	109.231	3.006	.038
	Quadratic Term	Contrast	68.149	1	68.149	1.875	.176
		Deviation	259.543	2	129.771	3.571	.035
	Cubic Term	Contrast	252.300	1	252.300	6.943	.011
		Deviation	7.243	1	7.243	.199	.657
Within Groups			1998.750	55	36.341		
Total			4302.850	59			

The resulting output, shown in the ANOVA table in Table 7.8, includes tests for a linear, quadratic, and cubic trends. A quadratic trend is one that has a consistent curving pattern either upward or downward, while a cubic trend is characterized by a shift in curvature from upward to downward or vice versa.

Here is how to interpret the information in this table. The "Between Groups (Combined)" test is the same as the standard ANOVA test, and it shows that there is a difference among means across levels of strength ($p = < 0.001$). "Deviation" ($p = 0.038$) tests for the existence of a more complex trend. In this case, the results indicate that there is a more complex trend than linear. Therefore, we go to the quadratic trend and find that there is not a significant quadratic (single curve) trend ($p = 0.176$), but there is still a more complex trend ($p = 0.035$). That more complex trend is the cubic term ($p = 0.011$) and nothing more complex ($p = .657$). The results of this analysis suggest that there is a somewhat linear increase in mean flower production as the level of the supplement increases. The cubic term suggests (from examination of the plot) that there is a faster increase as the strength is increased from 2 to 3 and a downturn in flower production when the strength reaches 5, probably indicating strengths beyond this level are detrimental.

Two-Way Analysis of Variance

A two-way ANOVA is an analysis that allows you to evaluate the combined effect of two experimental variables (factors). Each factor is a "grouping" variable such as type of treatment, gender, brand, and so on. The two-way ANOVA tests to see if the factors are important (significant) either separately (called main effects) or in combination (via an interaction). Table 7.9 shows a typical setup for a two-way ANOVA. The two factors are *Color* and *Height* of sales displays, and each cell of the table contains the observed sales for displays containing that particular combination of characteristics (factors).

It is important to point out that this design, like the one-way ANOVA above, is based on the assumption that the observations in the cells are independent within and between cells. There are no repeated objects or subjects in any factor combination. Sometimes a two-way ANOVA is referred to as a $p \times q$ factorial design, where there are p levels of one factor and q levels of the other.

Appropriate Applications for a Two-Way ANOVA

- *Discrimination*? How do age and gender affect the salaries of 10-year employees at a national department store?
- *Product display strategies*. A manufacturer who displays products for sale wants to understand how the height of a display and the color of the display (or the combined effects of both height and color) affect sales.
- *Effectiveness of cholesterol-lowering drug*. Investigators want to know the roles of dosage and gender on the effectiveness of a cholesterol-lowering drug.

Design Considerations for a Two-Way ANOVA

When conducting a two-way ANOVA, there are several design considerations you should keep in mind. Most of these are extensions of those mentioned previously for the one-way ANOVA. These include the following:

Two-Way ANOVA Assumptions

1. *Independent samples*. Subjects should be randomly assigned to treatment combinations, that is, to the $p \times q$ possible combinations of factors (cells). Observations are independent in that there are no repeated objects or subjects in any factor combination.

2. *Normality*. Data within each cell of the design are assumed to be normally distributed.

3. *Equal variances*. The population variances within each combination of factors should be equal.

- *How stringent are the assumptions?* As in the previous discussion for the one-way ANOVA, studies have shown that ANOVA models are robust against moderate departures from the assumptions of normality and equal variances. In particular, the ANOVA is quite robust to the equal variance assumption if the cell sizes are equal or nearly equal (Glass et al., 1972). As with the *t*-test and one-way ANOVA, the assumption of independence of the subjects is critically important.

- *Comparing means.* Your outcome variable must be a quantitative variable such as height, weight, amount spent, or grade. (If you can make an assumption of normality, then your data are by definition quantitative.)

- *Are sample sizes equal for each cell?* The sample sizes in each group do not have to be equal, but if they are not, then care must often be taken in performing the analysis.

- *Are factor categories random or fixed?* In this guidebook, we discuss only a fixed factor analysis. That is, the factor levels are selected by the experimenter, such as a selection of specific doses of an experimental drug. In some cases, factor categories are randomly selected from a larger list of possible categories (a random selection of cities, for example). Random effects models and mixed models (i.e., with fixed and random effects) are not discussed here. For a discussion of random effects or mixed models, we recommend Winer (1971); Kutner, Neter, Nachtsheim, and Li (2004); and Keppel and Wickens (2004).

Hypotheses for a Two-Way ANOVA

The statistical model for the two-way ANOVA includes the main effects (i.e., the additive effects of each factor) along with an interaction effect. Interaction measures the extent to which the combined effects of the factors are *not* additive. To illustrate the effect of interaction, suppose your outcome variable is annual income (in thousands) and your two factors are gender and job category, as shown in Figure 7.7, where the four means (hourly-male, hourly-female, salaried-male, salaried-female) are plotted for two hypothetical scenarios.

The right-hand graph illustrates a situation in which the combined effects of the two factors are additive and there is no interaction effect. In this case, the salaried employees (both male and female) make about $55,000 to $60,000 per year more than the corresponding hourly employees of the same sex. Also, for each job category, the males make $5,000 to $10,000 more per year than the female employees on average. The result of this additive behavior is that the lines are almost parallel.

The left-hand graph shows an interaction effect. Specifically, for hourly employees, males and females have approximately the same average salaries. However, for salaried employees, males

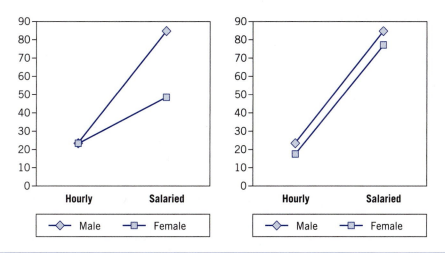

Figure 7.7 Interaction Plots

make about $35,000 more per year on average. This behavior is known as an interaction, and in the presence of such an interaction, you cannot make a blanket statement comparing the effect of gender on salary that applies to both job types. Instead, if you want to discuss the effect of gender on salary, you will need to consider each job category separately. Similarly, the effect that employee type (hourly vs. salaried) has on salary is only really understood when it is considered separately for males and females.

If you do not have a significant interaction (such as the right-hand graph), you can meaningfully test the main effects of job type and gender. However, if you have a significant interaction, such blanket statements may be meaningless since these two factors are interrelated (i.e., they "interact").

The testing procedure in a two-way ANOVA is as follows:

1. First Test for Interaction

The interaction hypotheses are as follows:

H_0: There is no interaction effect.

H_a: There is an interaction effect.

2. Test for Main Effects

If there is not a significant interaction, then test the following hypotheses regarding main effects:

The "main effects" hypotheses are

    a. For Factor A:

        H_0: Population means are equal across levels of Factor A.

        H_a: Population means are not equal across levels of Factor A.

    b. For Factor B:

        H_0: Population means are equal across levels of Factor B.

        H_a: Population means are not equal across levels of Factor B.

These three tests (interaction and two main effects tests) are performed in an analysis of variance table as F-tests. A low p-value (usually less than 0.05) for a test indicates evidence to reject the null hypothesis in favor of the alternative. It may be useful to refer to a standard textbook on the subject (e.g., Kutner et al., 2004; Winer, 2012) for more discussion of the actual statistical model.

Tips and Caveats for a Two-Way ANOVA

Unequal Sample Sizes Within Cells

A number of calculation and interpretation problems arise when you have an unequal number of observations in the cells of a two-way ANOVA. In SPSS, for example, if cell sizes are unequal, then it is important that the calculations be performed using the Type III ANOVA sum of squares (the default in SPSS). Small departures from equal cell sizes are not a serious concern, but you should examine why such unequal sizes exist. For example, if your sampling procedure has caused some values in some cells to be systematically eliminated, then you may be introducing bias into the model (see Elliott & Woodward, 1986).

Significant Interactions

If an interaction exists, the effects of the factors should not be interpreted in isolation from each other, and tests for main effects will often not be meaningful. It will usually be more appropriate, for example, to compare effects of the first factor within levels of the second factor and vice versa. That is, compare cell means rather than marginal means. A variety of methods could be used, including some that make use of the mean square error from the ANOVA table and others that involve considering each cell as a sample and performing a series of t-tests with a Bonferroni type p-value adjustment. For more details, see Kutner et al. (2004) and Keppel and Wickens (2004).

Example 7.3

Two-Way ANOVA

Describing the Problem

A manufacturer of a consumer retail product wants to examine the effectiveness of display strategies on sales. Six different displays are designed, which include three different highlight colors (red, blue, and black) and two different heights: short (45 inches) and tall (60 inches). To compare sales for each combination of height and color, one of the six display combinations is randomly placed at each of five discount department stores, a total of 30 different locations. After 2 months, the sales from each combination are compared. The data for this analysis are given in Table 7.9, and we assume the data in each cell are normally distributed.

Table 7.9   Two-Way ANOVA Data

Height/Color	Blue	Red	Black
Short	24	31	35
	25	28	32
	30	33	31
	28	35	38
	25	32	35
Tall	31	36	41
	32	32	36
	33	33	34
	36	41	32
	32	34	39

Descriptive statistics for the data are shown in Table 7.10. This table is created as a part of the following example. To perform an analysis on this data, follow these steps:

Table 7.10   Descriptive Statistics for Two-Way ANOVA

Descriptive Statistics

DependentVariable: Sales

Display Height	Display Color	Mean	Std. Deviation	N
Short	Blue	26.40	2.510	5
	Red	31.80	2.588	5
	Black	34.20	2.775	5
	Total	30.80	4.161	15
Tall	Blue	32.80	1.924	5
	Red	35.20	3.564	5
	Black	36.40	3.647	5
	Total	34.80	3.299	15
Total	Blue	29.60	3.978	10
	Red	33.50	3.440	10
	Black	35.30	3.268	10
	Total	32.80	4.213	30

SPSS Step-By-Step. EXAMPLE 7.3: Two-Way ANOVA

1. Open the data set named DISPLAY.SAV and select **Analyze/General Linear Models/ Univariate**. . . .

2. Select *Sales* as the Dependent variable and *Height* and *Color* as Fixed Factors.

3. Click on Plots and select *Height* for the Horizontal Axis and *Color* for Separate Lines and click Add. Next select *Color* for the Horizontal Axis and *Height* for Separate Lines and click Add. The completed dialog is shown in Figure 7.8. Click Continue.

4. Click Post Hoc test and select Color for Post Hoc tests. Select the Tukey (or your favorite test under the equal variances assumed list). We won't need a post hoc comparison for Height since there are only two heights. Click Continue.

5. Click Options and select means for *Height, Color,* and *Height*Color*. Select Descriptive Statistics, Estimates of effect size, and whatever other statistics you desire. Click Continue. Click OK to create output which includes Tables 7.10 and 7.11.

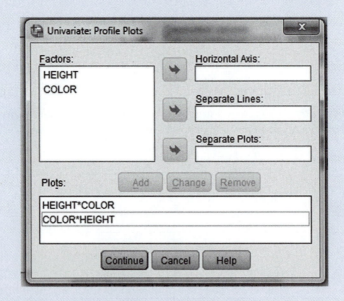

Figure 7.8   Select Plots for Two-Way ANOVA

The ANOVA results are shown in Table 7.11. To interpret the ANOVA table, you should first look at the interaction term (*Height * Color*). The nonsignificant $p = 0.268$ indicates that the interaction term is not statistically significant. A graph (sometimes called an interaction plot) to visually examine the possibility of an interaction effect is included in the output and is shown in Figure 7.9.

Table 7.11 Table for Two-Way ANOVA

Tests of Between-Subjects Effects

Dependent Variable: Sales

Source	Type III Sum of Squares	df	Mean Square	F	Sig.
Corrected Model	313.200[a]	5	62.640	7.457	.000
Intercept	32275.200	1	32275.200	3842.286	.000
HEIGHT	120.000	1	120.000	14.286	.001
COLOR	169.800	2	84.900	10.107	.001
HEIGHT * COLOR	23.400	2	11.700	1.393	.268
Error	201.600	24	8.400		
Total	32790.000	30			
Corrected Total	514.800	29			

a. R Squared = .608 (Adjusted R Squared = .527)

The lines showing the means for *Sales* by *Height* and color are fairly close to parallel (as measured by the interaction p-value [$p = 0.268$]), so the assumption of no interaction (i.e., that the effects are additive) seems plausible. Thus, it is appropriate to test for main effects, that is, to compare *Sales* by *Color* and *Sales* by *Height*. This graph helps explain the main effects tests. To give you another look at the interaction, a second plot that has height as the horizontal axis and separate lines for short and tall is included in your output. Note that the associated curves are fairly parallel. Before examining the statistical results, note that from Table 7.10 and the two interaction plots it can be seen that tall displays tend to have higher *Sales* (at all *Colors*) and that at each height, black displays yield the highest average sales followed by red and blue, in that order. The significance of these differences will be examined below.

The main effect for height is significant ($F = 14.286$ with 1 and 24 degrees of freedom, $p = 0.001$). This indicates that there is a statistically significant difference in *Sales* by *Height*. Thus, taller displays produced significantly greater *Sales*. It should be noted that post hoc tests are not needed since there are only two levels of *Height*.

The main effect for *Color* is also significant ($F = 10.107$ with 2 and 24 degrees of freedom, $p = 0.001$). This indicates that there is a statistically significant difference in *Sales* by *Color*. However, post hoc tests are needed to determine which differences are significant, although it is a safe conjecture that black displays (top line in Figure 7.9) are significantly higher than blue displays (bottom line).

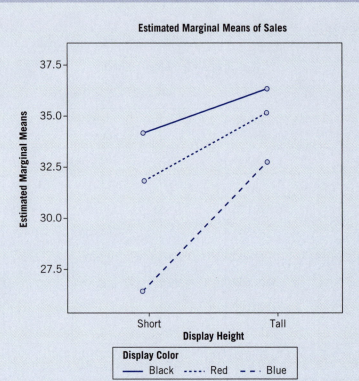

Estimated Marginal Means of Sales

Figure 7.9 Graph of Two-Way Interactions

6. To test for significant findings for this main effect for color, select Analyze/General Linear Models/Univariate and select PostHoc. Choose Height and Color as the factors and select the Tukey option. Click Continue and OK.

Table 7.12 shows the results of Tukey's test to identify specific differences. In the table, it can be seen that sales for red and black displays were not significantly different from each other, but both were significantly higher than sales for the blue display. Specifically, the p-value for the Blue versus Red comparison is 0.016 and the p-value for the Blue versus Black comparison is 0.001.

In summary, the conclusion from this analysis is that taller displays are better and that red and black displays are better than blue displays.

Reporting the Results of a Two-Way ANOVA

The following illustrates how you might report these two-way ANOVA results in a publication format.

Table 7.12   Tukey Comparisons for Sales by Display Color in a Two-Way ANOVA

Display Height * Display Color

Multiple Comparisons
Dependent Variable: Sales
Tukey HSD

(I)Display Color	(J) Display Color	Mean Difference (I-J)	Std. Error	Sig.	95% Confidence Interval	
					Lower Bound	Upper Bound
Blue	Red	–3.90*	1.296	.016	–7.14	–.66
	Black	–5.70*	1.296	.001	–8.94	–2.46
Red	Blue	3.90*	1.296	.016	.66	7.14
	Black	–1.80	1.296	.362	–5.04	1.44
Black	Blue	5.70*	1.296	.001	2.46	8.94
	Red	1.80	1.296	.362	–1.44	5.04

Based on observed means.
The error term is Mean Square (Error) = 8.400.
*The mean difference is significant at the 0.05 level.

Narrative for the Methods Section

"A two-way ANOVA was performed to determine if there is a difference in average sales for displays with different heights or highlight colors. In the presence of a significant difference, multiple comparisons were performed using the Tukey procedure at the $\alpha = 0.05$ significance level."

Narrative for the Results Section

"The test for interaction was not significant, $F(2, 24) = 1.393$, $p = 0.268$. Since there was no significant interaction, we tested main effects. The main effect for height was significant, $F(1, 24) = 14.286$, $p = 0.001$, where it is seen that taller displays have higher average sales. The main effect for color was also significant, $F(2, 24) = 10.107$, $p = 0.001$. Multiple comparisons using Tukey's test indicate that black and red displays have higher average sales than blue displays. Statistics are displayed in Table 7.13."

Table 7.13   Example Table Showing Descriptive Statistics for a Two-Way ANOVA

Height/Color	Blue		Red		Black		Marginal	
	Mean	SD	Mean	SD	Mean	SD	Mean	SD
Short	26.4	2.51	31.8	2.59	34.2	2.78	30.8	4.17
Tall	32.8	1.92	35.2	3.56	36.4	3.65	34.8	3.30
Marginal	29.6	3.98	33.5	3.44	35.3	3.27	32.8	4.21

Note: N for each cell is 5.

If an interaction exists, the effects of the factors should not be interpreted in isolation from each other, and tests for main effects will often not be meaningful. It will usually be more appropriate, for example, to compare effects of the first factor within levels of the second factor and vice versa. That is, compare cell means rather than marginal means.

Note that Table 7.13, which contains summary statistics, was created using a word processor and is not a part of the SPSS output. Sometimes it is necessary to summarize your results in a custom table that you make yourself rather than relying solely on the program's output.

Repeated-Measures Analysis of Variance

A repeated-measures ANOVA (and its close cousin, the randomized complete block design, or sometimes called the randomized block design) is an extension of the paired t-test in the sense that observations are paired, dependent, or linked together. The one-way and two-way ANOVA models discussed previously are sometimes referred to as "independent group" ANOVAs since there is no such pairing. In a repeated-measures ANOVA, observations are taken from the same or related subjects or objects over time or in differing circumstances. (In the randomized complete block design, we consider several "blocks" of subjects or objects that are similar in some respect. Then within a block, investigators randomly assign each treatment so that a different treatment is applied to each subject or object within the block.)

Appropriate Applications for a Repeated-Measures ANOVA

- *Which drug is best?* Four drugs to control high blood pressure are given to a group of individuals. Each subject receives the drugs in a random order with a washout period between doses.

- *What type of music increases sales?* A study is designed to examine the effects of playing background music in grocery stores. Ten stores participate in the study, and three music genres are tested (country, hip-hop, and oldies). Each store cycles through the three genres in a randomly assigned order, using each genre for a 1-month period. The researcher wants to know if the music selection influences sales.

- *Effectiveness of gasoline additive.* Five different gasoline additives are compared regarding their ability to improve gas mileage. Four cars are chosen for testing, and each additive is used once (in random order) for each car.

Design Considerations for a Repeated-Measures ANOVA

Repeated Measurements May Increase the Ability to Detect Differences

An advantage of a repeated-measures design is that each subject acts as his or her own control, and this can increase the ability to detect differences. That is, suppose a measurement is to be made on the cholesterol level at four time points (1 month, 3 months, 6 months, 1 year) after receiving a particular statin drug. Suppose we want 10 cholesterol readings at each of the four times. One method for doing this would be to use one-way ANOVA and select 40 patients on the medication and randomly select 10 to have their cholesterol readings taken at the end of 1 month, select 10 other patients to have cholesterol readings at the end of 3 months, and so on. This is clearly a poor design since any time differences in cholesterol readings may be obscured by the patient-to-patient variability in cholesterol levels. It makes more sense to take, say, 10 patients and measure each patient at the four times (repeated-measures design). Using this method, we more directly measure the effect of the medication over time.

Two Steps in the Analysis

As in the one-way ANOVA, the analysis has two steps. First, an *F*-test is used to test for a significant difference among the means across the repeated measure. If a difference is detected, then post hoc tests are used to determine where the differences lie.

Normality and Equal Variance Assumptions

The repeated-measures ANOVA assumes that the outcome measure is a normal variable and that the variances across repeated measures are equal. As with other versions of the ANOVA, the test is robust against moderate departures from the assumptions of normality and equality of variances. An additional assumption is that of sphericity, which assumes that the pairwise differences between treatment levels all have equal population variances. Mauchly's test for sphericity is commonly used to test this assumption (see Keppel & Wickens, 2004).

Randomization

This model also assumes that the participants are randomly selected from the population of interest.

Hypotheses for a Repeated-Measures ANOVA

The primary hypotheses for a repeated-measures ANOVA are written as follows:

H_0: There is no difference among means of the repeated measures.

H_a: At least one pair of means are different.

Tips and Caveats for a Repeated-Measures ANOVA

- *Don't confuse one-way ANOVA types.* Be careful not to confuse an independent group (i.e., one-way and two-way) ANOVA with a repeated-measures ANOVA. Use of an independent group ANOVA procedure to analyze data that should be analyzed as a repeated measure is incorrect—don't do it.

- *Sample size.* As with other analyses, small sample sizes can lead to nonsignificant results even when a difference exists (see Moher, Dulberg, & Wells, 1994).

Example 7.4

Repeated-Measures ANOVA

Describing the Problem

A researcher is interested in comparing four different drugs that are believed to temporarily reduce the amount of snoring. Eight patients are given the drugs in a random order for 1 week. The number of minutes snoring was compared to the results of each individual's previous sleep test (baseline), and a snoring index was calculated where 100 means no reduction from baseline, less than 100 is a decrease, and more than 100 is an increase.

Between each episode of drug therapy there is a 1 week period of washout with no drug. Figure 7.10 shows the SPSS data file SNORING.SAV. It should be noted that, for example, the first entries (those in row 1) under each drug are linked together since they all are measurements on the same person. This should be contrasted with the one-way ANOVA data in Table 7.7 in which the entries under each treatment (strength) are unrelated to (independent of) each other. In this "snoring data" repeated-measures example, each subject has four observations—thus four "drug" entries per row in the data file; whereas in the data file for one-way ANOVA shown in Figure 7.2, each subject (plant) has only a single observation (number of flowers) and there is only one observation per row (plus a grouping value). A plot of the mean values for each drug is shown in Figure 7.11. This plot will be produced as a part of the following example.

SNORING.SAV [DataSet2] - IBM SPSS Statistics Data Editor

File   Edit   View   Data   Transform   Analyze   Direct Marketing   Graphs   Utilities   Add

	Subject	DRUG1	DRUG2	DRUG3	DRUG4	var
1	1	89	78	79	98	
2	2	88	74	75	89	
3	3	80	75	76	94	
4	4	79	71	77	95	
5	5	91	68	83	91	
6	6	85	81	77	86	
7	7	87	73	73	104	
8	8	86	76	76	93	

Figure 7.10   Data for Repeated-Measures ANOVA

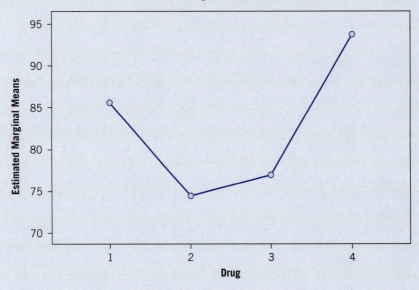

Figure 7.11   Plot of Means for Snoring Data

SPSS Step-By-Step. EXAMPLE 7.4: Repeated-Measures ANOVA

To perform the previous example in SPSS, follow these instructions:

1. Open the data set SNORING.SAV and select **Analyze/General Linear Model/ Repeated Measures**. . . .

2. For the Within-Subject Factor name, enter *DRUG* and 4 for number of levels. Click Add. In the Measure Name box enter SNORING. Click Add and click Define. See Figure 7.12.

3. For the Within-Subjects Variables, select (in order) *Drug1* (drag to location or click on right arrow), *Drug2* (click or drag), *Drug3* (click or drag), and *Drug4* (click or drag). See Figure 7.13.

4. Click on Options and place the *DRUG* factor in the Display Means for box. Select the Descriptive Statistics checkbox and any other measures you want to observe. Check the Compare main effects checkbox and select Bonferroni Confidence interval adjustment. (This produces the pairwise comparisons.) See Figure 7.14. Click Continue.

5. To produce the means plot, click on the Plots button and place the *DRUG* factor in the Horizontal Axis list and click Add and Continue.

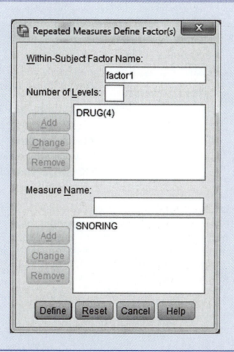

Figure 7.12   Defining Drug Levels

Figure 7.13   Defining the Within-Subject Variables

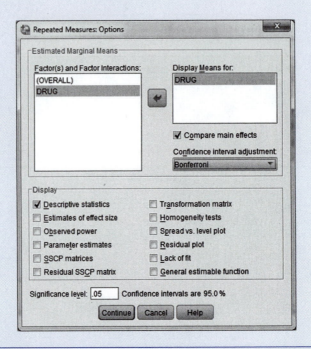

Figure 7.14 Define Repeated-Measures Options

6. Click OK to produce all of the output used in the example along with additional output we will not discuss here.

Before examining the results of the repeated-measures ANOVA to determine if there are any differences among the drugs in the effect on snoring, you should check the assumptions. A test for sphericity (a test that the variance-covariance matrix is spherical in form—similar to a test of equality of variances) is performed using the Mauchly's Test of Sphericity is shown in Table 7.14. For these data, Mauchly's test yields $p = 0.786$ (in the table's Sig. column) which indicates that we can safely assume sphericity.

The ANOVA results given in Table 7.15 are presented in four versions. If sphericity is a plausible assumption, the standard F-test on the top row (Sphericity Assumed) of Table 7.15 can be used to test for a drug effect, and this gives $F = 30.289$ with 3 and 21 degrees of freedom and $p = 0.000$. Because of the low p-value for the F-test on the drug effect, we reject the null hypothesis that the drugs are equivalent and conclude that there is a difference in means for the drugs. The other three tests in Table 7.15 are adjustments for the standard F-test and are used if the assumption of sphericity is not acceptable. Note that these alternative versions of the test give results consistent with the standard F-test in this case.

Table 7.14   Mauchly's Test of Sphericity

Mauchly's Test of Sphericity[a]

Measure: SNORING

Within Subjects Effect	Mauchly's W	Approx. Chi-Square	df	Sig.	Epsilon[b]		
					Greenhouse-Geisser	Huynh-Feldt	Lower-bound
DRUG	.851	2.454	5	.786	.812	1.000	.333

Tests the null hypothesis that the error covariance matrix of the orthonorrnalized transformed dependent variables is proportional to an identity matrix.

   a. Design: Intercept

     Within Subjects Design: DRUG

   b. May be used to adjust the degrees of freedom for the averaged tests of significance. Corrected tests are displayed in the Tests of Within-Subjects Effects table.

Table 7.15   ANOVA Results for Repeated-Measures Analysis

Tests of Within-Subjects Effects

Measure: SNORING

Source		Type III Sum of Squares	df	Mean Square	F	Sig.
DRUG	Sphericity Assumed	1843.094	3	614.365	30.239	.000
	Greenhouse-Geisser	1843.094	2.437	756 269	30.239	.000
	Huynh-Feldt	1843.094	3.000	614.365	30.239	.000
	Lower-bound	1843.094	1.000	1843.094	30.239	.001
Error(DRUG)	Sphericity Assumed	426.656	21	20.317		
	Greenhouse-Geisser	426.656	17.060	25.010		
	Huynh-Feldt	426.656	21.000	20.317		
	Lower-bound	426.656	7.000	60.951		

Part two of this ANOVA analysis is to determine where these differences lie. As in other ANOVA models, the differences can be examined using pairwise comparisons. Table 7.16 shows SPSS output of pairwise comparisons using the Bonferroni method.

Table 7.16 Bonferroni Comparisons for Repeated-Measures ANOVA

Pairwise Comparisions

Measure: SNORING

(I) DRUG	(J) DRUG	Mean Difference (I-J)	Std. Error	Sig.[b]	95% Confidence Interval for Difference[b]	
					Lower Bound	Upper Bound
1	2	11.125*	2.142	.008	3.338	18.912
	3	8.625*	1.451	.003	3.350	13.900
	4	−8.125	2 4B2	.082	−17.148	.898
2	1	−11.125*	2.142	.008	−18.912	−3.338
	3	−2.500	2.027	1.000	−9.868	4.868
	4	−19.250*	2.678	.001	−28.985	−9.515
3	1	−8.625*	1.451	.003	−13.900	−3.350
	2	2.500	2.027	1.000	−4.868	9.868
	4	−16.750*	2.520	.002	−25.911	−7.589
4	1	8.125	2 482	.082	−.898	17.148
	2	19.250*	2.678	.001	9.515	28.985
	3	16.750*	2.520	.002	7.589	25.911

Based on estimated marginal means

*. The mean difference is significant at the .05 level.

b. Adjustment for multiple comparisons: Bonferroni.

This table compares each pair of means for each drug. For example, the comparison of *Drug1* to *Drug2* gives a mean difference of 11.125 and a *p*-value of 0.008. The overall conclusion of the pairwise comparisons is that there is no significant difference between *Drug2* and *Drug3* (*p* = 1.0), and Drugs 2 and 3 are both significantly different from Drugs 1 and 4. Also, we see that Drug 1 and Drug 4 are not significantly different from each other (p=0.082). Since *Drug2* and *Drug3* have the lowest means, our conclusion is that both *Drug2* and *Drug3* are better at decreasing snoring than *Drug1* and *Drug4*, but we don't have sufficient evidence to choose between *Drug2* and *Drug3*.

Reporting Results of a Repeated-Measures ANOVA

The following illustrates how you might report this repeated-measures ANOVA in a publication format.

Narrative for the Methods Section

"A repeated-measures analysis of variance was performed to compare the ability of each of the four drugs to reduce snoring (decrease the snoring index). The assumption of sphericity was checked using Mauchly's test, and the Bonferroni method was used to perform pairwise comparisons following a significant overall test result."

Narrative for the Results Section

"Mauchly's test found that an assumption of sphericity is plausible ($p = 0.79$). The overall test for differences in means in the repeated-measures ANOVA was significant, $F(3, 21) = 30.2$, $p < 0.001$. Pairwise comparisons indicate at the overall 0.05 level that Drug2 ($M = 74.5$, $SD = 4.04$) and Drug3 ($M = 77.0$, $SD = 3.0$) were better at reducing snoring than Drug1 ($M = 85.6$, $SD = 4.21$) or Drug4 ($M = 93.8$, $SD = 5.55$). However, no significant difference was found between Drug2 and Drug3 or Drug1 and Drug2."

You might choose to include the comparison results in a graphical display such as the one illustrated in Figure 7.15 to summarize the pairwise comparisons. This graph is not created in SPSS, so you must create it on your own. The interpretation of the graph is that any two drugs that are underlined with the same line are not significantly different. Thus, the display quickly and succinctly illustrates that Drug2 and Drug3 are not significantly different from each other and that Drug1 and Drug4 are also not significantly different from each other. However, the means for Drug2 and Drug3 are both significantly lower than the means for Drug1 and Drug4.

DRUG 2	DRUG 3	DRUG 1	DRUG 4
74.5	77.0	85.6	93.8

Figure 7.15   A Graphical Comparison of Mean Differences, the Results of the Bonferroni Comparison

Analysis of Covariance

The final topic for this chapter is really a combination of analysis of variance and regression. We consider a one-way analysis of covariance (ANCOVA), which is essentially a one-way ANOVA with a twist. That twist is that the means across groups are not compared directly. Instead, the means are adjusted by some other quantitative variable called a covariate. Notice that the covariate variable is not a value controlled by the researcher but is instead a value that is intrinsic to the subject (or entity) observed. When an appropriate covariate is used, an ANCOVA is an improvement over the corresponding ANOVA model since it explains additional variability and thus results in a more precise analysis.

Appropriate Applications for Analysis of Covariance

- *Which promotion is most effective?* A car dealership wants to know if placing trucks, SUVs, or sports cars in his outside display area affects the number of customers who enter the showroom. However, he is also aware that outside temperature may affect the number of customers. His study compares customer traffic for the three different display options with daily high temperature as a covariate.

- *Which drug is best?* A researcher is comparing three drugs for decreasing triglyceride levels and suspects that the effectiveness of the drugs is related to the subject's age. Therefore, she uses age as a covariate in the comparison.

- *Which teaching method is better?* A school system is trying to decide among three proposed methods for teaching math. The teaching methods are allocated to randomly selected sections, and performance is evaluated using the final exam. To standardize the comparisons, a pretest (covariate) is given to each student at the beginning of the year.

Design Considerations for an Analysis of Covariance

Because an analysis of covariance is a combination of one-way ANOVA and regression, considerations from both perspectives should be made when performing this type of analysis:

1. *Normality.* A standard assumption for the ANOVA model to be valid is that the measurement variable is normally distributed within each group. See Chapter 2: Describing and Examining Data for discussion concerning how to assess these characteristics for a variable.

2. *The groups must be independent.* Each subject (or entity) in each group should be different. Subjects should be randomly assigned to each group.

3. *The covariate must be quantitative and should be linearly related to the outcome measure in each group or treatment level.* If the covariate is not correlated with the outcome measure, it will be of little use in the analysis. This assumption implies that for each treatment level, there is a regression line relating the covariate with the response variable.

4. *Homogeneity of regressions.* A key assumption in ANCOVA is that the slopes of the regression lines discussed in Item 3 above are equal. That is, this assumption specifies that these regression lines are parallel.

5. *Other considerations.* As in all analysis of variance models, it is assumed that the variances across groups are equal and error terms are uncorrelated. It is also assumed that the treatments do not affect the covariates.

The covariate (also called a concomitant variable) should be something that is observed prior to the study, or it should be a variable that is not influenced by the study. Typical covariates include age, pretest scores, IQ, and so on. As with the analysis of variance and t-test, the procedure is robust against moderate departures from normality and variance assumptions, particularly if the sample size per group is moderately large. The independent group assumption should not be violated.

Hypotheses for an Analysis of Covariance

An analysis of covariance model consists of two components: (1) the component specifying the group effect as in an ANOVA model and (2) a component indicating the linear relationship between the dependent variable and the covariate. Typically, analysis of covariance testing proceeds in two steps:

1. *Homogeneity of regressions.* The null hypothesis is tested that the regression lines relating the dependent variable and the covariate have the same slopes in all groups.

2. *Group effects.* If the null hypothesis in Item 1 is not rejected, then we test the group effect by testing the null hypothesis that the group regression lines are not only parallel but also are actually equal to each other. If they are determined to be separate lines, then this is an indication of a group effect after adjusting for the covariate.

The hypotheses related to the homogeneity of regressions assumption are given as follows:

H_0: The regression lines for each group are parallel.

H_a: At least two of the regression lines for groups are not parallel.

If the F-test for testing these hypotheses is not rejected, then we move on to test for a group effect. These hypotheses can be stated very informally as follows:

H_0: All group means (adjusted by the covariate) are equal.

H_a: At least two means (adjusted by the covariate) are not equal.

An F-test is used to test for differences in adjusted group means. As with a one-way ANOVA, if differences are found and there are more than two groups, you may want to use a multiple comparison procedure to identify the differences. For more discussion of ANCOVA models, see Keppel and Wickens (2004).

Example 7.5

Analysis of Covariance

Describing the Problem

A school system is choosing among three proposed methods of teaching math in the fifth grade. Nine classes are randomized to the three methods and are taught for 3 months. Pretest and posttest scores are compared. Using the pretest score as a covariate, an analysis is performed to determine if there are any differences and, if so, which method or methods are best. Before performing an Analysis of Covariance on the data, first examine the data graphically. To perform this analysis, follow these steps.

SPSS Step-By-Step. EXAMPLE 7.5:
Analysis of Covariance

1. Open the data set MATH.SAV and select **Graphs/Chart Builder**. Select the **Scatter/Dot** chart type and drag the **Simple Scatter** (leftmost) icon into the Chart Preview box.

2. Drag *Posttest* to the Y-axis and *Pretest* to the X-axis. To choose the grouping variable, click on the Groups/Point ID tab and check Grouping/stacking variable. A Set Color box appears in the Chart Preview box. Drag *Method* into this box. Click OK to display the preliminary graph. (Note that your Set Color variable, *Method* in this case, must be of nominal or ordinal type.)

3. Double-click on the graph to enter the Chart Editor. In the Chart Editor, select **Elements/Fit Line at Subgroups**. In the Properties dialog box, uncheck the Attach label to line option and click Apply. In the Chart Editor, choose **Options/X-Axis Reference Line**. Back in the Properties dialog box, and in the Scale Axis position text box, enter 33.06. Click Apply. (We'll discuss the purpose of this line later in the example.) Close the Properties dialog box and exit the Chart Editor. The comparison graph will be displayed in the output, as shown in Figure 7.16.

It is always a good idea to study a plot of your data before performing your analysis. In this case, you are interested in determining if the lines are parallel and, if so, whether some are different from others (i.e., that some teaching methods produce higher scores adjusted for a pretest). In the graph, you can see three lines, each representing one of the methods. The top line represents Method 3, and the other two lines represent Methods 1 and 2. Visually, we see that these lines are not perfectly parallel but that the slopes are quite similar. In addition, we see that two of the lines (for Methods 1 and 2) are quite similar, while the line for Method 3 seems to be distinct and stays above the other two lines. This suggests that Method 3 is preferable to the other two methods and that Methods 1 and 2 are very similar to each other. Analysis of covariance is a formalized method for checking these observations. The following steps are used to perform the analysis of covariance:

A. An *F*-test is used to determine if the regression lines are parallel. This is similar to an interaction test in a two-way analysis. The model required to create this output is

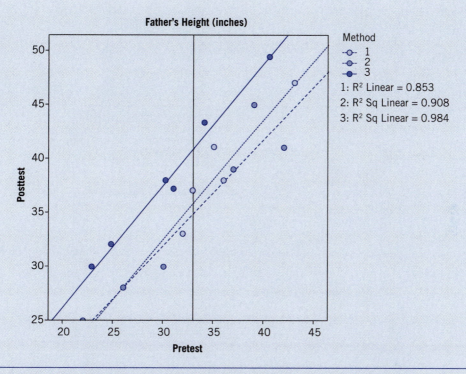

Figure 7.16 Analysis of Covariance Comparison Plot With Reference Line for Pretest

one that contains the fixed factor (*Method*), the covariate (*Pretest*), and an interaction term (*Method*Pretest*).

B. If the assumption of parallel regression lines is not rejected, then another *F*-test is used to compare the adjusted means to determine if any are different. (If the slopes are different, the ANCOVA assumptions are not met making the analysis more difficult. We suggest you consult a statistician.)

C. If there are significant differences among the adjusted means, then a pairwise comparison is performed to determine which methods are different.

1. To perform the analysis of covariance on the MATH.SAV data, select **Analyze/General Linear Model/Univariate** . . . and then select *Posttest* as the dependent variable (this is your outcome variable), *Method* as a Fixed Factor, and *Pretest* as a covariate.

2. To calculate the model containing the interaction term, click on the Model button and select the Custom radio button. Click on *Method* and the right arrow and *Pretest* and the right

arrow. Make sure the Build Terms option in the middle of the dialog box is set at Interaction. While holding down the CTRL key, select both *Method* and *Pretest* and then click on the right arrow. In the Model box, you should have three terms—*Method, Pretest,* and *Method*Pretest* as shown in Figure 7.17. Click Continue.

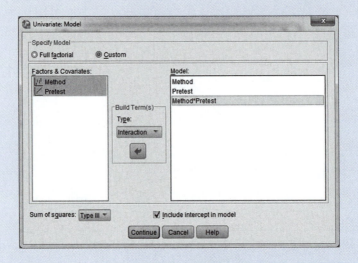

Figure 7.17 Dialog Box Specifying Terms for the ANCOVA Model

ANCOVA Step A

3. Click OK to display the preliminary *F*-test to test for parallelism (What we call Step A.) In this case, this test yields a *p*-value of 0.683 which means that you can proceed to create a table of comparisons for means.

4. Table 7.17 shows SPSS output related to this step. The table provides output for the ANCOVA model containing the terms *Method, Pretest,* and *Method*Pretest.* The test for the significance of the interaction term (i.e., *Method*Pretest*) is the only test to consider at this stage to test the assumption of parallel slopes (lines). Since $p = 0.683$ for this *F*-test, we conclude that the assumption of parallel slopes for the lines is reasonable, and we can proceed to Step B, the test for differences in the adjusted means.

ANCOVA Step B

5. Go back to the analysis setup (**Analyze/General Linear Model/Univariate**) and click on the Model button. Click on the *Method*Pretest* term and the left arrow to remove this term from the model. Click Continue and OK. The results are shown in Table 7.18.

Table 7.17 ANCOVA Analysis Containing Test for Equal Slopes

Tests of Between-Subjects Effects

Dependent Variable: Posttest

Source	Type III Sum of Squares	df	Mean Square	F	Sig.
Corrected Model	698.179[a]	5	139.636	33.633	.000
Intercept	1.326	1	1.326	.319	.582
Method	.820	2	.410	.099	.907
Pretest	476.450	1	476.450	114.759	.000
Method * Pretest	3.262	2	1.631	.393	.683
Error	49.821	12	4.152		
Total	25836.000	18			
Corrected Total	748.000	17			

a. R Squared = .933 (Adjusted R Squared = .906)

The *F*-test designed to test for differences among adjusted means (assuming parallelism) is given in Table 7.18, which is similar to Table 7.17 but does not have an interaction term. In this case, we are interested in the term labeled *Method* since that is the term that compares the three teaching methods. we see that F=13.976 and $p < 0.001$ for this test, so we reject the null hypothesis that the adjusted means are equal and conclude that there is at least one pair of adjusted means that are different.

ANCOVA Step C

5. To create the pairwise comparisons, go back to the analysis setup (**Analyze/General Linear Model/Univariate**) one more time. Click the Options button. Place Method in the Display Means for box. Select the Compare Main Effects checkbox and select the Bonferroni (or your choice) of multiple comparison procedure in the Confidence Interval Selection box. Check the Descriptive Statistics checkbox and any others that you want displayed. Click Continue and OK to produce the results in Table 7.19.

Since we found a difference among adjusted means, pairwise comparisons (Table 7.19) can be used to identify which adjusted means are different. In this case, the Bonferroni procedure is utilized to make the comparisons as shown in Table 7.19. In this case, it can be seen that at the overall 0.05 level of significance, Method 3 is significantly different from Method 1 and Method 2, (Bonferroni adjusted

Table 7.18 Analysis of Covariance Test for Group Effects (on Method)

Tests of Between-Subjects Effects

Dependent Variable: Posttest

Source	Type III Sum of Squares	df	Mean Square	F	Sig.
Corrected Model	694.917[a]	3	231.639	61.092	.000
Intercept	4.152	1	4.152	1.095	.313
Method	105.981	2	52.990	13.976	.000
Pretest	627.917	1	627.917	165.605	.000
Error	53.083	14	3.792		
Total	25836.000	18			
Corrected Total	748.000	17			

a. R Squared = .929 (Adjusted R Squared = .914)

p-values are $p = 0.005$ and $p = 0.001$ respectively), but Methods 1 and 2 are not significantly different (Bonferroni adjusted $p = 1.0$). It is clear from this analysis that Method 3 has a higher overall adjusted mean on the standardized math test than either Methods 1 or 2 which is consistent with our initial visual observations.

For illustrative purposes, Figure 7.15 includes a vertical reference line that represents the mean of *Pretest* (33.06). The adjusted means, which are used to compare the groups under the ANCOVA model, are the values on the vertical scale at which the reference line intersects the three regression lines. These adjusted posttest means are given in Table 7.20.

The covariate has an important effect on the comparison among methods for these data. Without the covariate model, the (unadjusted) means for the *Posttest* scores are 39.17, 34.67, and 38.17 for teaching Methods 1, 2, and 3, respectively. It should be noted that if a one-way analysis of variance were performed on the *Posttest* variable without using *Pretest* as a covariate, the (unadjusted) means would not be significantly different ($p = 0.50$). These results are in contrast to the results in Table 7.20 and in Figure 7.8, in which it can be seen that the adjusted means are 40.8 for Method 3 and 36.1 and 35.1 for Methods 1 and 2, respectively. That is, Method 3 yields a significantly higher adjusted mean score, even though its associated raw mean score was slightly lower than the mean for Method 1. Thus, the covariate model reveals a difference that would not have been evident without an adjustment based on the mathematical ability/preparation of these students in the class (as measured by the pretest).

Table 7.19 Analysis of Covariance Pairwise Comparisons

Pairwise Comparisons

Dependent Variable: Posttest

(I) Method	(J) Method	Mean Difference (I-J)	Std. Error	Sig.[b]	95% Confidence Interval for Difference[b]	
					Lower Bound	Upper Bound
1	2	1.022	1.156	1.000	−2.120	4.165
	3	−4.738*	1.209	.005	-8.025	−1.451
2	1	−1.022	1.156	1.000	-4.165	2.120
	3	−5.761*	1.138	.001	-8.853	−2.668
3	1	4.738*	1.209	.005	1.451	8.025
	2	5.761*	1.138	.001	2.668	8.853

Based on estimated marginal means

*. The mean difference is significant at the .05 level.

b. Adjustment for multiple comparisons: Bonferroni.

Reporting Results for an Analysis of Covariance

The following examples illustrate how you might report this analysis of covariance in a publication format.

Narrative for the Methods Section

"An analysis of covariance (ANCOVA) was used to compare final math scores by teaching method using a pretest as a covariate. Bonferroni pairwise comparisons were used to determine significant differences in the groups."

Narrative for the Results Section

"The ANCOVA test for parallel within-group regression lines was not significant ($F = 0.39$ with 2 and 12 df, $p = 0.68$). The resulting test for equality of adjusted means found a significant difference ($F = 13.98$ with 2 and 14 df, $p = < .001$). The Bonferroni pairwise comparisons found that at the overall 0.05 level, the adjusted mean posttest under Method 3 ($M_{adj} = 40.8$, $SE = 0.82$) is significantly different from Method 1 ($M_{adj} = 36.1$, $SE = 0.83$) and Method 2 ($M_{adj} = 35.1$, $SE = 0.80$), but Methods 1 and 2 are not different from each other. It is clear from this analysis that Method 3 produced a higher overall improvement in score on the standardized math test than either Method 1 or 2 when adjusted for pretest scores."

Table 7.20 Adjusted Means for Analysis of Covariance

Estimates

Dependent Variable: Posttest

| Method | Mean | Std. Error | 95% Confidence Interval | |
			Lower Bound	Upper Bound
1	36.095[a]	.830	34.314	37.875
2	35.072[a]	.796	33.366	36.779
3	40.833[a]	.822	39.071	42.595

[a]Covariates appearing in the model are evaluated at the following values: Pretest = 33.06.

SUMMARY

This chapter explains the most common types of analysis of variance. For more information on topics, including power and sample size for these types of analyses, see Keppel and Wickens (2004). The next chapter introduces nonparametric analyses.

REFERENCE

Elliott, A. C., & Woodward, W. A. (1986). Analysis of an unbalanced two-way ANOVA on the microcomputer. *Communications in Statistics*, B15(1), 215–225.

Glass, G. V., Peckham, P. D., & Sanders, J. R. (1972). Consequences of failure to meet assumptions underlying the fixed effects analysis of variance and covariance. *Review of Educational Research*, 42, 239–323.

Keppel, G., & Wickens, T. D. (2004). *Design and analysis: A researcher's handbook* (4th ed.). Upper Saddle River, NJ: Pearson Prentice Hall.

Kutner, M. H., Neter, K., Nachtshei, C. J., & Li, W. (2004). *Applied linear statistical models*. Homewood, IL: McGraw-Hill Education.

Moher, D., Dulberg, C. S., & Wells, G. A. (1994). Statistical power, sample size, and their reporting in randomized controlled trials. *Journal of the American Medical Association*, 272, 122–124.

Winer, B. J. (1971). *Statistical principles in experimental design, Second Edition*. New York, NY: McGraw-Hill. Literary Licensing, LLC.

CHAPTER

8

Nonparametric Analysis Procedures

When "Plan A" doesn't work out, it's always good to have a "Plan B." The good news is that when the normality assumption for a standard parametric procedure such as the *t*-test, correlation, ANOVA, or others is not met, you have other options. A nonparametric procedure can often be used in place of a parametric procedure.

The basic technique used by nonparametric procedures to get around the normality assumption is that they do not use the raw data. Instead, in a nonparametric procedure, the ordered or ranked values are commonly used in the analysis. That is, the smallest value receives a rank of 1, the next smallest a rank of 2, and so on. There will be some instances in which the data are ranked with respect to the entire data set and others in which the ranking will be done within groups. For more discussion on the use of ranks (e.g., how they are used in the case of ties, etc.), you should check a text with a good discussion of nonparametric analysis. Several good ones are Hollander, Wolfe, and Chicken (2013); Gibbons (2011); and Sprent and Smeeton (2007). Nonparametric procedures are also useful if you don't have exact data values but you know how the data are ordered. This chapter presents descriptions of several commonly used and reported nonparametric statistical procedures. They include the following:

- *Spearman's rank correlation (measure association between two variables)*: a nonparametric alternative to Pearson's correlation
- *Mann-Whitney U (compare two independent groups)*: a nonparametric alternative to a two-sample *t*-test
- *Kruskal-Wallis (compare two or more independent groups)*: a nonparametric alternative to a one-way analysis of variance
- *Sign test or Wilcoxon test (compare two repeated measures)*: a nonparametric alternative to the paired *t*-test
- *Friedman's test (compare two or more repeated measures)*: a nonparametric alternative to a repeated-measures analysis of variance

The chi-square tests (e.g., for association and for goodness of fit) can also be considered to be nonparametric tests. These are covered in Chapter 6: Analysis of Categorical Data.

In this chapter, you will learn when, why, and how to perform a nonparametric test and how to present your results. The descriptions of the statistical tests in this chapter are sometimes abbreviated compared to other chapters because these procedures often mimic many of the design considerations of their parametric cousins.

Spearman's Rho

Spearman's rho (sometimes called Spearman's rank correlation) is a substitute for Pearson's correlation coefficient discussed in Chapter 5: Correlation and Regression when the normality assumptions for that measure cannot be assumed. Spearman's rho measures the strength of an increasing or decreasing relationship between two variables. Instead of using the raw observed data, Spearman's rho is based on the ranked data. Like Pearson's correlation, Spearman's rho takes on values from –1 to 1 and is interpreted in much the same way as Pearson's correlation. In fact, Spearman's rho is computationally equal to Pearson's correlation calculated on the ranks instead of the original data.

SIDEBAR

Pearson's correlation is a measure of the linear correlation between two variables, and Spearman's correlation is a measure of the increasing or decreasing (monotonic) strength of association between two variables. This relationship need not be linear.

Appropriate Applications for Spearman's Rho

- *Is your car a status symbol*? Examine the association between people from five categories of socioeconomic level and model year of car driven. Note that socioeconomic level is an ordinal variable that may not satisfy the requirements of a quantitative variable. For discussion of variable types, see Chapter 2: Describing and Examining Data.

- *Tennis rankings*. Measure the correlation between tennis rankings of American tennis players and amount of income earned playing tennis (again, the tennis ranking variable is ordinal).

- *Is crime rate related to education*? A criminologist collects data on the crime rates and median educational level for a sample of U.S. cities to examine the relationship. There is concern that the variables may not be normal and that outliers may have too strong an effect on Pearson's correlation.

Design Considerations for Spearman's Rho

Situations in which Spearman's rho would be chosen over Pearson's correlation are as follows:

- *Data benefits from ranking.* When data values contain a few unusual values or outliers, we showed in Chapter 5: Correlation and Regression that the Pearson correlation can be unduly influenced by these values. Using Spearman's rho (which is based on ranks) in these situations can give a clearer measure of the actual strength of the association by minimizing the influence of the extreme values.

- *Data observed as ordinal variables.* When data are observed in ordered values such as tiny, small, medium, large, very large, or < 10, 11–20, 21–30, 31–40, > 40, and so on, then Pearson's correlation is not appropriate, whereas Spearman's rho can still be correctly used.

- *Sample size and/or normality issues.* A measure of association between two variables is needed in a situation in which sample size is small and the normality of at least one of the variables is questionable.

Hypotheses for Spearman's Rho

The hypotheses being tested are the following:

H_0: There is no monotonic relationship between the two variables.

H_a: There is a monotonic relationship between the two variables.

Tips and Caveats for Spearman's Rho

- *Check the feasibility of results with a graph.* As illustrated in Chapter 5, you should always visually examine the relationship associated with your measure of the correlation using a scatterplot.

- *Correlation does not imply cause and effect.* The finding of a significant correlation (either Pearson's or Spearman's) does not justify the conclusion of a cause-and-effect relationship.

- *Could data be transformed?* If you are using Spearman's rho instead of a Pearson's correlation because your data distribution is nonnormal, another strategy might be to transform to data that are more nearly normal using a transformation such as the square root, logarithm, and so on.

Example 8.1

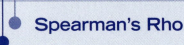

Spearman's Rho

Describing the Problem

An educator wants to know how attendance (recorded as the percentage of classes attended) is related to the final letter grade received by freshmen students in an American history class at a community college. Because the grades are given as A, B, C, D, and F (recorded as 1, 2, 3, 4, and 5), Spearman's rho is used to measure the association. A scatterplot of the data is shown in Figure 8.1 and is created in the following example.

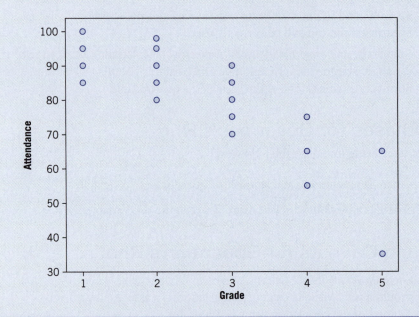

Figure 8.1   Scatterplot of Grade Versus Attendance Data

SPSS Step-By-Step. EXAMPLE 8.1: Spearman's Rho

To perform the analysis and generate the plot in SPSS follow these steps:

1. Open the data set ATTENDANCE.SAV and select **Analyze/Correlate/Bivariate**.

2. Select *Grade* and *Attendance* as the variables to analyze.

3. Check the Spearman's checkbox and click OK to display the preliminary output shown for Spearman's rho in Table 8.1.

4. To create the scatterplot shown in Figure 8.1, select **Graph/Chart Builder**. Select the **Scatter/Dot** type chart and drag the Simple Scatter icon into the Chart Preview box.

5. Select *Attendance* for the Y-axis and *Grade* for the X-axis and click OK.

Table 8.1 Output for Spearman's Rho

Correlations

			Grade	Attendance
Spearman's rho	Grade	Correlation Coefficient	1.000	−.852**
		Sig. (2-tailed)	.	.000
		N	22	22
	Attendance	Correlation Coefficient	−.852**	1.000
		Sig. (2-tailed)	.000	.
		N	22	22

**. Correlation is significant at the 0.01 level (2-tailed).

In the SPSS output shown in Table 8.1, the Spearman's rho is −0.852 with $p < 0.001$. Spearman's rho is appropriate in this case because the letter grades (although coded with numbers) might not be considered to be of equal distance apart (depending on the grading criteria).

Reporting Results for Spearman's Rho

The following example illustrates how you might report this test result in a publication format.

Narrative for the Methods Section

"Spearman's correlation was used to examine the association between final letter grades and course attendance because *Grade* was considered an ordinal variable."

Narrative for the Results Section

"Spearman's rho for grade and course attendance was rho = −0.85, $p < 0.001$. This indicates that students with worse attendance tended to have lower final grades in the course and vice versa."

Mann-Whitney-Wilcoxon (Two Independent Groups Test)

The Mann-Whitney-Wilcoxon test (referred to in SPSS as the Mann-Whitney U) is similar to the two-sample t-test without the normality or equal variance assumption. However, the data must meet the requirement that the two samples are independent. Like other nonparametric procedures we will discuss, the Mann-Whitney procedure uses ranks instead of the raw data values. Specifically, the data values are assigned ranks relative to both samples combined, and Mann-Whitney's test is designed to test whether observations in one population tend to have higher values (and therefore higher ranks) than those from the other population.

Typical settings appropriate for use of the Mann-Whitney test are those in which

- the sample sizes are small and normality is questionable;
- the data contain outliers or extreme values that, because of their magnitude, distort the mean values and affect the outcome of the comparison; and
- the data are ordinal.

Hypotheses for a Mann-Whitney Test

The hypotheses being tested by the Mann-Whitney test are the following:

H_0: The two populations have the same distribution.

H_a: The two populations do not have the same distribution.

Note that the Mann-Whitney procedure tests equality of the distributions rather than means, as was the case in the two-sample t-test. Medians are usually reported for this type of data, but the Mann-Whitney test is not simply a test comparing medians unless the only difference in the two distributions is a shift in location.

Example 8.2

● Mann-Whitney Test

Describing the Problem

A researcher wants to know if one fertilizer (Brand 1) causes plants to grow faster than another brand of fertilizer (Brand 2). Starting with seeds, he grows plants in identical conditions and randomly assigns fertilizer Brand 1 to seven plants and fertilizer Brand 2 to six plants. Note: This is the same data set used in Example 4.2.

SPSS Step-By-Step. EXAMPLE 8.2: Mann-Whitney Test

To create the output for the Mann-Whitney test, follow these steps:

1. Open the data set FERTILIZER.SAV and select **Analyze/Nonparametric Test/ Independent Samples**. . . . You are presented with three options (on the Objective tab of the Nonparametric test dialog box):

   • Automatically compare distributions across groups
   • Compare medians across groups
   • Customize analysis

Select the first option "Automatically compare. . . ."

2. Click on the Fields tab. Select *Height* as the Test Field and *Type* as the Group variable. Click the Run button to perform the Mann-Whitney analysis. The output is shown in Table 8.2.

Table 8.2   Mann-Whitney Analysis (Version 1)

Hypothesis Test Summary

	Null Hypothesis	Test	Sig.	Decision
1	The distribution of HEIGHT is the same across categories of TYPE.	Independent-Samples Mann-Whitney U Test	.234[1]	Retain the null hypothesis.

Asymptotic significances are displayed. The significance level is .05.

1. Exact significance is displayed for this test.

3. To produce the Legacy Version of the Mann-Whitney output (which in this case contains additional information), select **Analyze/Nonparametric Test/Legacy Dialogs/2 Independent Samples**.

4. Select *Height* as the Test Variable and *Type* as the Group variable. (SPSS requires *Type* to be a numeric variable in this analysis.) To specify the range of values for the grouping variable, click Define Groups. Enter 1 for Group 1 and 2 for Group 2 (corresponding to the codes used for the two groups) and Continue. Check the Mann-Whitney checkbox and click OK. The output from this analysis is in Table 8.3.

Table 8.3 Mann-Whitney Analysis (Legacy Version 2)

Rank

	TYPE	N	Mean Rank	Sum of Ranks
HEIGHT	1	7	5.79	40.50
	2	6	8.42	50.50
	Total	13		

Test Statistics[a]

	HEIGHT
Mann-Whitney U	12.500
Wilcoxon W	40.500
Z	−1.219
Asymp. Slg. (2-talled)	.223
Exact Sig. [2*(1-tailed Sig.)]	.234[b]

a. Grouping Variable: TYPE

b. Not corrected for ties.

In the legacy output (Table 8.2), the "Ranks" table gives mean ranks for each group. Thus, the mean ranks are compared rather than the actual means of the data. The "Test Statistics" table shows a Mann-Whitney U statistic value of $U = 12.5$ and an exact p-value of $p = 0.234$ (as reported in both versions of the output). The asymptotic p-value is an approximation for large sample sizes. In this case, with sample sizes of 7 and 6, you should use the "exact" p-value. The Mann-Whitney test and the Wilcoxon rank sum test are different test statistics formed using the ranked data that yield equivalent p-values. It is most common to refer to this as the Mann-Whitney U test. It is interesting to note that these results (i.e., not finding a significant difference between fertilizers) are consistent with those found in Example 4.2 using the two-sample t-test.

Reporting Results for a Mann-Whitney Test

The following sample write-ups illustrate how you might report this Mann-Whitney test in publication format.

Narrative for the Methods Section

"A Mann-Whitney test was used to test the hypothesis that the distribution of heights of the plants for the two types of fertilizer was equal because height was not considered normally distributed."

Narrative for the Results Section

"The distribution of plant heights given fertilizer Brand 1 was not significantly different from that given fertilizer Brand 2, Mann-Whitney $U = 12.5$, $p = 0.23$."

Kruskal-Wallis Test

The Kruskal-Wallis test is the nonparametric counterpart to the one-way analysis of variance. With the Kruskal-Wallis test, there are no normality assumptions. Otherwise, the design considerations and data collection issues are the same as those for the one-way ANOVA discussed in Chapter 7: Analysis of Variance and Covariance. For more information on the appropriate applications for this type of analysis, refer to the description of the one-way ANOVA in Chapter 7.

SIDEBAR
As with the Mann-Whitney test, care should be taken not to describe the Kruskal-Wallis test as a test for a difference in medians.

Hypotheses for a Kruskal-Wallis Test

The hypotheses being tested are as follows:

H_0: There are no differences in the distributions of the groups.

H_a: There are differences in the distributions of the groups.

Example 8.3

Kruskal-Wallis Test

Describing the Problem

An agricultural researcher wants to know which of four possible feeds is best in producing weight gain for sheep. Twenty-eight sheep are randomly divided into four "feed" groups. Because the groups are small, the normality of the data cannot be adequately tested. Therefore, a Kruskal-Wallis test is used to compare the four groups. The data for this analysis (in the SPSS data editor) are shown in Figure 8.2. Notice how these data have been entered in the same way as the *t*-test or analysis of variance data in that there is one observation per line and there is a grouping variable (*Feed* in this case) that specifies a group identity for each observation. To perform the analysis on these data, do the following steps. Two ways of doing the analysis are shown:

	FEED	WEIGHT	var	v
1	1	50.80		
2	1	57.00		
3	1	44.60		
4	1	51.70		
5	1	48.20		
6	1	51.30		
7	1	49.00		
8	2	68.70		
9	2	67.70		
10	2	66.30		
11	2	69.80		
12	2	66.90		
13	2	65.20		
14	2	62.00		
15	3	82.60		
16	3	74.10		
17	3	80.30		
18	3	80.50		
19	3	81.50		
20	3	78.60		
21	3	76.10		
22	4	76.90		
23	4	72.20		
24	4	73.70		
25	4	74.20		
26	4	70.60		
27	4	75.30		
28	4	69.80		

Figure 8.2   Data for Kruskal-Wallis Example

SPSS Step-By-Step. EXAMPLE 8.3: Kruskal-Wallis Test

1. Open the data set FEED.SAV and select **Analyze/Nonparametric tests/Independent samples**. You are presented with three options (on the Objective tab of the Nonparametric test dialog box):

   - Automatically compare distributions across groups
   - Compare medians across groups
   - Customize analysis

Select the first option "Automatically compare. . . ."

2. Click on the Fields Tab. Select *Weight* as the Test Variable and *Feed* as the Groups Variable. Click the Run button to perform the Kruskal-Wallis analysis. The output is shown in Table 8.4. In this table, the test is performed at the 0.05 significance level. Since the observed significance (the Sig column) is 0.000 (report as $p < .0001$), the null hypothesis is rejected (Decision column).

Table 8.4   Output for Kruskal-Wallis Analysis (Version 1)

Hypothesis Test Summary

	Null Hypothesis	Test	Sig.	Decision
1	The distribution of WEIGHT is the same across categories of FEED.	Independent-Samples Kruskal-Wallis Test	.000	Reject the null hypothesis.

Asymptotic significances are displayed. The significance level is .05.

3. To produce more detailed (legacy) output for this test, use these steps. Select **Analyze/Nonparametric Test/Legacy Dialogs/K Independent Samples**.

4. Select *Weight* as the Test Variable and *Feed* as the Grouping Variable. To specify the range of values for the grouping variable, click Define Range. Enter 1 as the minimum and 4 as the maximum (corresponding to the codes used for the four feeds) and click Continue.

5. Click OK to display the output for the Kruskal-Wallis test. The output for this analysis is shown in Table 8.5.

In Table 8.5, the "Ranks" table shows the mean ranks for each group, and the "Test Statistics" table reports the chi-square test statistic and associated *p*-value. It should be noted that the ranking for the Kruskal-Wallis

Table 8.5 Output for Kruskal-Wallis Analysis (Legacy Version 2)

Ranks

	FEED	N	Mean Rank
WEIGHT	1	7	4.00
	2	7	11.07
	3	7	24.43
	4	7	18.50
	Total	28	

Test Statistics[a,b]

	WEIGHT
Chi-Square	24.481
df	3
Asymp. Sig.	.000

a. Kruskal-Wallis Test

b. Grouping Variable: FEED

procedure is done on the basis of all 28 observations. Thus, the smallest value in the list, that is, 44.6 in Feed Group 1 (the third value from the top) in Figure 8.2, is assigned Rank 1; 48.2 (also in Group 1) is assigned Rank 2; and so on, and the largest value in the list, 82.6 (in Group 3), is assigned the largest rank of 28. It is interesting to note that the weights in Feed Group 1 have a mean rank of 4. Because 4 is the mean of the ranks 1, 2, . . . , 7, this implies that the seven smallest weights were in Feed Group 1, a fact that can be verified by examining the data in Figure 8.2. This information seems to suggest that weights in Feed Group 1 are smaller than those in other groups, and this leads us to believe that the null hypothesis is not true. In fact, from the table, we see that $p < 0.001$ (in Tables 8.4 and 8.5 it is reported as .000), verifying our observations. There is sufficient evidence to reject the null hypothesis that the groups are the same and conclude that there is a statistically significant difference in the weight gains by feed.

SPSS does not offer a multiple comparison test for the Kruskal-Wallis test. Because the results are significant, you can safely conclude that the weight gains for Feed 3 (MEDIAN = 80.3) are significantly higher than the weight gains for Feed 1 (MEDIAN = 50.8). A description of how to do Tukey-style multiple comparisons for a Kruskal-Wallis test can be found in Zar (2009). In general, after obtaining a significant Kruskal-Wallis test, you could use multiple Mann-Whitney tests to examine pairwise differences. There would be six such comparisons. A conservative approach (Bonferroni) would be to perform these comparisons at the $0.05/6 = 0.0083$ level (Miller, 1981). We will not go into this analysis here.

Another nonparametric analysis for these data would be to perform a median test. The steps are almost identical to those shown in this example except you would select the median comparison rather than Kruskal-Wallis. In the median test, the null hypothesis is that there is no difference in medians across groups. The medians test should not be used unless you have reason to believe that the only differences among the distributions is the median (and not the shape.)

Reporting Results for a Kruskal-Wallis Test

The following example illustrates how you might report this Kruskal-Wallis test in a publication format.

Narrative for the Methods Section

> "A Kruskal-Wallis test was used to test for differences among feeds because normality was questionable and sample sizes within each group are small."

Narrative for the Results Section

> "The Kruskal-Wallis test for comparison of feeds indicates that there is a statistically significant difference in the distribution of weight gain between the groups, X^2 (3) = 24.5 and $p < 0.001$."

Sign Test and Wilcoxon Signed-Rank Test for Matched Pairs

The sign test and the Wilcoxon Signed-Rank (WSR) test can be used to compare paired data as nonparametric alternatives to the paired t-test. These tests are used when you cannot justify a normality assumption for the differences. Otherwise, the design considerations for these tests are the same as for the paired t-test described in Chapter 4. Applications of paired-data analysis are given in Chapter 4 and are applicable here.

The sign test is very simple in that it counts the number of differences that are positive and those that are negative and makes a decision based on these counts. The sign test can be used when the differences are ordinal or quantitative. The Wilcoxon signed-rank test goes one step further in that it uses information about the magnitude of the differences.

Specifically, the absolute values of the differences are ranked from smallest to largest, and then the sum of the ranks associated with positive differences is compared with the sum of the ranks for the negative differences. It should be pointed out that the Wilcoxon signed-rank test assumes that the differenced data are quantitative and the distribution of the differences is symmetric. The sign test is less powerful than the Wilcoxon signed-rank test and many statisticians prefer the WSR test.

Hypotheses for a Sign Test

The hypotheses being tested by the sign test are as follows:

H_0: The probability of a positive difference is equal to the probability of a negative difference.

H_a: The probability of a positive difference is not equal to the probability of a negative difference.

Hypotheses for a Wilcoxon Signed-Rank Test

The hypotheses being tested by a Wilcoxon signed-rank test are as follows:

H_0: The median difference between pairs of observations is zero.

H_a: The median difference between pairs of observations is not zero.

Example 8.4

Wilcoxon Signed-Rank Test and Sign Test

Using the Wilcoxon signed-rank test on the same "Diet" data that was used in Example 4.4 (analyzed in Chapter 4 as a paired *t*-test) is illustrated in the following steps:

SPSS Step-By-Step. EXAMPLE 8.4: Wilcoxon Signed-Rank and Sign Test

1. Open the data set DIET.SAV and select **Analyze/Nonparametric Tests/Related Samples**. . . . You may be presented with three options (on the Objective tab of the Nonparametric test dialog box):

   - Automatically compare observed data to hypothesized
   - Customize analysis

Select the first option "Automatically compare. . . ."

2. Click on the Fields tab and drag *Before* and *After* in the Test Fields box. Click Run. The output created is shown in Table 8.6.

Table 8.6   Results of the Wilcoxon Signed-Rank Test (First Version)

Hypothesis Test Summary

	Null Hypothesis	Test	Sig.	Decision
1	The median of differences between before and after equals 0.	Related-Samples Wilcoxon Signed-Rank Test	.035	Reject the null hypothesis.

Asymptotic significances are displayed. The significance level is .05.

The output shown in Table 8.6 indicates *p* = 0.035. Since the test is performed at the 0.05 significance level, the decision is to "Reject the null hypothesis." Therefore, you conclude that there is evidence that the two groups are different.

3. To create the legacy tables for the Wilcoxon signed-rank test, select **Analyze/ Nonparametric Tests/Legacy Dialogs** . . . **/2 Related Samples**.

4. Drag the *Before* variable into the Pair1/Variable1 box and *After* into the Pair1/Variable2 box as shown in Figure 8.3.

5. Make sure the Wilcoxon and Sign checkboxes are selected and click OK. The output shown in Table 8.7 is displayed. Note that by default, SPSS calculates the difference as "after – before" regardless of the order you enter the variables in step 2 above.

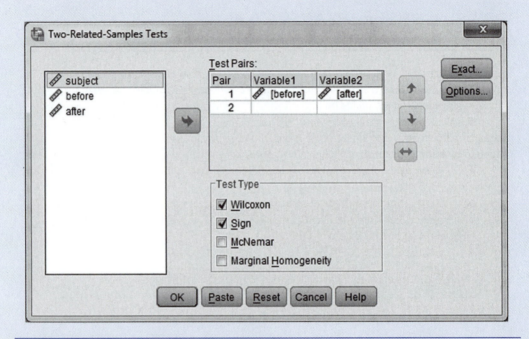

Figure 8.3   Dialog Box for Wilcoxon Signed-Rank Test

The Legacy Version of the output (Table 8.7) provides more detail in the "Ranks" table showing differences calculated as "after weight minus before weight." It also indicates that there were 10 negative differences, five positive differences, and no ties. The statistic calculated for the test is $Z = -2.108$ and $p = 0.035$. Similar output for the sign test (not shown) produces a p-value of 0.302. In this case, the Wilcoxon signed-rank test produced a significant result at the 0.05 level, and the less powerful sign test was not significant ($p = 0.302$). The Wilcoxon test is in general more powerful, and in this example, it detected a difference when the sign test did not. Given these somewhat contradictory results, you would use the Wilcoxon signed-rank test if you can reasonably make the assumption that the distribution of the differences is symmetric. You might choose the more conservative sign test if you are uncomfortable with this assumption. It should be noted that in Example 4.4 (where the data were analyzed using a paired t-test), the results were significant ($p = 0.02$).

Table 8.7 Results of the Wilcoxon Signed-Rank Test

Ranks

		N	Mean Rank	Sum of Ranks
after - before	Negative Ranks	10[a]	9.70	97.00
	Positive Ranks	5[b]	4.60	23.00
	Ties	0[c]		
	Total	15		

a. after < before

b. after > before

c. after = before

Test Statistics[a]

	after - before
Z	−2.108[b]
Asyrnp. Sig. (2-tailed)	.035

a. Wilcoxon Signed Ranks Test

b. Based on positive ranks.

Reporting the Results for a Wilcoxon Signed-Rank Test or Sign Test

The following illustrates how you might report the results of the Wilcoxon signed-rank test or sign test in a publication format.

Narrative for the Methods Section

"The Wilcoxon signed-rank test (or sign test) was used to ascertain whether the diet was effective since weight loss was not considered normally distributed."

Narrative for the Results Section

"The Wilcoxon test showed the diet to be effective, with 10 of 15 subjects losing weight ($p = 0.035$)."

or

"The sign test showed that the results were not significant, with 10 of 15 subjects losing weight ($p = 0.302$)."

Friedman's Test

Friedman's test is a nonparametric alternative to a repeated-measures analysis of variance used to compare observations repeated on the same subjects. Unlike the parametric repeated-measures ANOVA, this test makes no assumptions about the distribution of the data (e.g., normality). Friedman's test, like many nonparametric tests, uses the ranks of the data rather than their raw values to calculate the statistic.

The design considerations for this Friedman's test are similar to those for the repeated-measures ANOVA discussed in Chapter 7, except for the normality assumption. We recommend that you review that discussion to understand how and when Friedman's test should be used.

Hypotheses for Friedman's Test

The hypotheses being tested in Friedman's test are as follows:

H_0: The distributions are the same across repeated measures.

H_a: The distributions across repeated measures are different.

Example 8.5

Friedman's Test

We use Friedman's test to analyze the "Snoring" data in Example 7.4 (Chapter 7) where it was analyzed as a repeated-measures ANOVA. The data (shown in Figure 7.10, Chapter 7) compare the effects of four drugs on snoring for eight patients. To create the output for the Friedman's test example, follow these steps in SPSS:

SPSS Step-By-Step. EXAMPLE 8.5: Friedman's Test

1. Open the data set SNORING.SAV and select **Analyze/Nonparametric Tests/Related Samples**. . . . You may be presented with these options (on the Objective tab of the Nonparametric test dialog box):

   - Automatically compare observed data to hypothesized
   - Customize analysis

Select the first option "Automatically compare. . . ."

2. Click on the Fields tab and drag *Drug1, Drug2, Drug3*, and *Drug4* into the Test Fields box. Click Run. The output for Friedman's test is shown in Table 8.8.

Table 8.8 Output for Friedman's Test (Version 1)

Hypothesis Test Summary

	Null Hypothesis	Test	Sig.	Decision
1	The distributions of DRUG1, DRUG2, DRUG3 and DRUG4 are the same.	Related-Samples Friedman's Two-Way Analysis of Variance by Ranks	.000	Reject the null hypothesis.

Asymptotic significances are displayed. The significance level is .05.

The results shown in Table 8.8 indicate that $p < 0.001$ ($p = 0.000$). The test is performed at the 0.05 significance level and the decision is to "Reject the null hypothesis." Therefore, you have evidence to conclude that there is a difference in the distributions across the four drug variables.

3. To create the legacy output, select **Analyze/Nonparametric Tests/Legacy Dialogs/ K-Related Samples**.

4. Select *Drug1* to *Drug4* as the Test Variables. Make sure the Friedman checkbox is selected. Click OK to display the test results for the Friedman test as shown in Table 8.9.

Table 8.9 Output for Friedman's Test

Ranks

	Mean Rank
DRUG1	3.06
DRUG2	1.25
DRUG3	1.75
DRUG4	3.94

Test Statistics[a]

N	8
Chi-Square	22.48
df	1
Asymp.Sig.	.000

a. Friedman Test

5. Because the Friedman's test indicated that there was a difference across drugs, (Chi-Square = 22.48, $p < 0.001$) it is appropriate to perform multiple comparisons by comparing each drug against the others in a series of pairwise selections. This is similar to the multiple comparison tests illustrated in Chapter 7 for ANOVA. To perform these tests, select **Analyze/Nonparametric Tests/Legacy Dialogs/2-Related Samples**.

6. Specify the Test Pairs list by dragging *Drug1* and *Drug2* to the Pair 1 line, then *Drug1* and *Drug3* to Pair2, *Drug1* and *Drug4* to the third line, and so forth for all possible pairs (six in all). Make sure the Wilcoxon Test checkbox is selected as shown in Figure 8.4. Click OK to display the results of the pairwise comparisons. The pairwise comparisons are shown in Table 8.10.

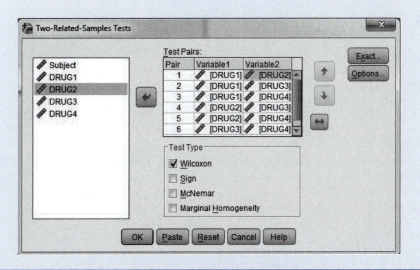

Figure 8.4 Selecting Pairwise Comparisons for Friedman's Analysis

Table 8.10 Multiple Comparisons for Friedman's Test

Test Statistics[a]

	DRUG2-DRUG1	DRUG3-DRUG1	DRUG4-DRUG1	DRUG3-DRUG2	DRUG4-DRUG2	DRUG4-DRUG3
Z	−2.524[b]	−2.527[b]	−2.371[c]	−1.378[c]	−2.521[c]	−2.524[c]
Asymp. Sig. (2-tailed)	.012	.012	.018	.168	.012	.012

a. Wilcoxon Signed-Rank Test

b. Based on positive ranks.

c. Based on negative ranks.

In the Friedman's legacy output (Table 8.9), the data are ranked within patients across drugs. For example, using the data in Figure 7.10 (Chapter 7), the snoring index for *Patient1* for *Drug1* through *Drug4* was 89, 78, 79, and 98, respectively. The resulting ranks are, then, *3, 1, 2,* and *4*, respectively. This ranking is done separately for each patient. If a certain drug tended to be assigned a preponderance of low ranks, then this would suggest it is better at reducing snoring. The output in Table 8.9 shows the ranks by drug along with a chi-square and associated *p*-value. In that table, we see that *Drug2* had a mean rank of 1.25, while *Drug4* had a mean rank of 3.94. These mean ranks are consistent with the findings for *Patient1* and suggest that there is a general tendency for *Drug2* to perform best and *Drug4* to perform worst.

Table 8.10 shows the results of the multiple comparisons test (six total comparisons). This analysis indicates a statistically significant difference between *Drug 1* and *Drug 2*, *Drug 1* and *Drug 3*, *Drug 2* and

. *Drug 4*, and *Drug 3* and *Drug 4* all at $p = 0.012$ and *Drug4* and *Drug1* at $p = 0.018$. The other pairwise comparison (*Drug2* and *Drug2*) is not statistically significant ($p = 0.168$). These results for these data are consistent with the findings for the repeated measures ANOVA in Example 7.4 (Chapter 7).

Reporting Results for Friedman's Test

The following illustrates how you might report this Friedman's test in a publication format.

Narrative for the Methods Section

"The difference among drugs was tested using Friedman's test because the assumption of normality could not be verified and the sample size for each group was small. In the presence of a significant overall test, follow-up pairwise comparisons were performed using the Wilcoxon signed-rank test, with the *p*-values adjusted using the Bonferroni correction to maintain an overall 0.05 comparison rate."

Narrative for the Results Section

"Friedman's test for comparison of drugs resulted in $X^2(3) = 22.5$ and $p < 0.001$. The drug producing the lowest snoring score was *Drug2*. Multiple comparisons indicate that *Drug2* and *Drug3* were more effective at reducing snoring than *Drug1* and *Drug4*, but there was no significant difference between *Drug2* and *Drug3*."

SUMMARY

Nonparametric tests are used when the assumptions for a standard parametric test cannot be reasonably assumed. They typically analyze the ranks of values instead of actual observed values and may therefore also be used when data are ordinal. The next chapter introduces logistic regression.

REFERENCES

Gibbons, G. D. (2011). *Nonparametric statistical inference, fifth edition*. Boca Raton, FL: Chapman & Hall/CRC.

Hollander, M., Wolfe, D. A., & Chicken, E. (2013). *Nonparametric statistical methods*. Vol. 751. Hoboken, NJ: John Wiley & Sons.

Miller, R. G. (1981). *Simultaneous statistical inference* (2nd ed.). New York, NY: Springer Verlag.

Sprent, P., & Smeeton, N. C. (2007). *Applied nonparametric statistical methods, Fourth Edition*. Boca Raton, FL: CRC Press.

Zar, J. H. (2009). *Biostatistics analysis* (5th ed.). Upper Saddle River, NJ: Prentice Hall.

Logistic Regression

Introduction to Logistic Regression

You've either got it or you don't. That's the point of logistic regression. Binary logistic regression is defined by a response variable that can take on only one of two values, typically 1 and 0 (often interpreted as yes or no, diseased or not diseased, alive or dead, etc.). Typical reasons a researcher would choose logistic regression for an analysis include the following:

- To predict the probability of an event occurring based on a list of one or more predictor variables
- To rank the relative importance of predictor variables in explaining the response variable
- To calculate an odds ratio that measures the importance of a predictor variable on the response

This chapter begins by describing simple logistic models and then discusses the more complicated process of selecting a model from a list of possible predictors and evaluating that model. Thus, the topics that are covered in this chapter include the following:

- *Simple logistic regression*: analyzing and interpreting a logistic regression model with one predictor variable
- *Multiple logistic regression*: developing of a logistic regression model based on more than one predictor variable, including the following:

  Model selection: selecting of the "best" variables to include in a model

  Model interpretation: interpreting of model coefficients and assessment of the model fit

  Prediction: using a logistic model for prediction

Although this chapter specifically covers binary logistic regression, there are also other types of logistic regression not discussed in this chapter, including multinomial logistic regression (where the dependent variable can have more than two outcomes) and ordinal logistic regression (where the dependent variable has two or more ordered categories). For the remainder of this chapter, the term *logistic regression* will refer to only binary logistic regression. To keep this discussion at the level of the rest of this book, we will discuss models that do not include interaction terms. However, although we've kept formulas to a minimum for most of the book, we felt it necessary to include a few more here than in previous chapters for explanatory purposes. If you need to delve deeper into this subject, we recommend that you refer to Cohen, Cohen, West, and Aiken (2002); Daniel and Cross (2013); Hosmer, Lemeshow, and Sturdivant (2013); Kleinbaum (2011); Kutner, Nachtsheim, and Neter (2004); and Tabachnick and Fidell (2012).

Appropriate Applications for Logistic Regression

- *What variables affect voting preference?* Investigators want to predict how a person will vote (two options) based on demographic characteristics of the individual.

- *Is this customer a good candidate for a loan?* A bank wants to predict whether a customer will default on a loan based on known demographic and financial information.

- *Will this patient develop coronary heart disease?* In a longitudinal study of 450 patients, the independent variables age, gender, smoking behavior, and blood pressure are used to predict whether patients will develop coronary heart disease during the study.

As you can see from these examples, the characteristic that distinguishes logistic regression from linear regression (discussed in Chapter 5: Correlation and Regression) is the *binary* response (dependent) variable. Otherwise, as in linear regression, the predictor (independent) variables can be quantitative or binary.

Simple Logistic Regression

Simple logistic regression is a logistic model based on a single *dependent (response) variable* that can be either dichotomous or quantitative. The logistic analysis determines if an independent variable (*predictor variable*) is a statistically significant predictor of the response. This section will examine the case in which the independent variable is quantitative. Understanding how to interpret the simple logistic model will help you understand the more complicated logistic regression equations later in this chapter. This simple logistic equation takes on the following form:

$$p = \frac{e^{\beta_0 + \beta_1 * Predictor}}{1 + e^{\beta_0 + \beta_1 * Predictor}} \, , \tag{9.1}$$

where p is the probability that the dependent variable is equal to 1, β_0 is the equation intercept (or constant), and β_1 is the coefficient for the predictor variable. Think of these coefficients in a similar way as those in a simple linear regression. As in simple linear regression, the parameters β_0 and β_1 are estimated from the data, and a statistical test is used to determine whether the coefficient β_1 can be considered to be nonzero.

Hypotheses for Simple Logistic Regression

The typical hypotheses tested in a simple logistic regression are the following:

H_0: $\beta_1 = 0$ (the predictor variable is not related to the probability of occurrence).
H_a: $\beta_1 \neq 0$ (the predictor variable is related to the probability of occurrence).

The role of β_1 is specified in Equation 9.1. If β_1 is zero, then the logistic equation shows that there is no logistic relationship between the predictor variable and the probability of occurrence. If β_1 is found to be nonzero, then the independent variable plays a role in predicting p.

Tips and Caveats for Simple Logistic Regression

Cause and Effect

As in linear regression, the detection of a significant predictor variable (i.e., β_1 is found to be nonzero) does not necessarily imply a cause-and-effect relationship between the predictor and the response.

Example 9.1

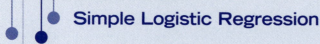

Simple Logistic Regression

Describing the Problem

A major automaker is experimenting with rebates on a new line of SUVs. At a local car show, 100 rebate coupons are handed out to attendees who are classified as strong prospects to purchase the SUV. Each coupon is randomly valued at anywhere between $250 and $5,150. During the following month, dealers keep track of which coupons were redeemed as part of the purchase of an SUV. The automaker is interested in knowing how the value of the rebate coupon is related to the probability that a customer will purchase the SUV.

Because the rebate values are large (up to $5,150), it will help us obtain a more understandable prediction equation if we create a new variable called *Rebate100*, which has the value *Rebate* ÷ 100. Otherwise, the coefficient for *Rebate* will be small and could lead to rounding errors for predictions. (This will be illustrated in the upcoming example.)

SPSS Step-By-Step. EXAMPLE 9.1:
Simple Logistic Regression

To produce the output for Example 9.1, follow these steps:

1. Open the data set REBATE.SAV and choose **Analyze/Regression/Binary Logistic**. . . .

2. Select *Purchase* as the dependent variable and *Rebate100* as the Covariate variable. (As shown in Figure 9.1.)

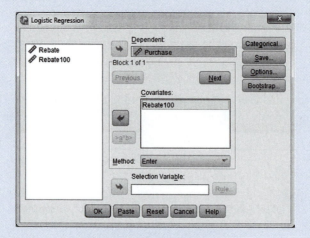

Figure 9.1   Dialog Box for Logistic Regression

3. To produce the confidence intervals, click on Options and check CI for Exp(B). Click Continue.

4. To produce the data used for the graph shown in Figure 9.2, click on the Save button and check the Probabilities checkbox. Click Continue.

5. Click OK to produce output that includes Table 9.1.

Table 9.1 Simple Logistic Regression Output

Variables in the Equation

		B	S.E.	Wald	df	Sig.	Exp(B)	95% C.I. for EXP(B) Lower	Upper
Step 1[a]	Rebate100	.214	.043	24.597	1	.000	1.239	1.138	1.349
	Constant	−5.900	1.254	22.137	1	.000	.003		

a. Variable(s) entered on step 1: Rebate100.

One way to make use of the information in Table 9.1 is to use the results to predict the probability that a customer will redeem a coupon. To calculate this value, use the prediction equation shown in Equation 9.1.

The second column in Table 9.1 (labeled "B") refers to the estimates of the β coefficients (β_0 and β_1 mentioned above in the logistic equation and hypotheses). We will use the notation b_0 and b_1 to denote estimates of β_0 and β_1, respectively. The *Rebate100* coefficient is $b_1 = 0.214$ with $p < 0.001$. This indicates that *Rebate100* is a statistically significant predictor of the probability of a purchase. Because β_1 is deemed nonzero, it is appropriate to use the information in the table to construct a predictive logistic equation. This simple logistic equation takes on the following form:

$$\hat{p} = \frac{e^{b_0 + b_1 * Rebate100}}{1 + e^{b_0 + b_1 * Rebate100}}$$

where $\hat{p}$ denotes the predictor of the probability of purchase, p. In this case, $b_0 = -5.9$ and $b_1 = 0.214$. For a \$3,000 coupon (i.e., 3000/100 = 30 is the value used in the equation), the predicted probability of purchase would be 0.627, as given by the following equation:

$$\hat{p} = \frac{e^{-5.9 + 0.214 * 30}}{1 + e^{-5.9 + 0.214 * 30}} = 0.627$$

A graphical technique for approximating the probabilities associated with this logistic regression without using Equation 9.1 is to produce the plot shown in Figure 9.2, a plot of the rebate values

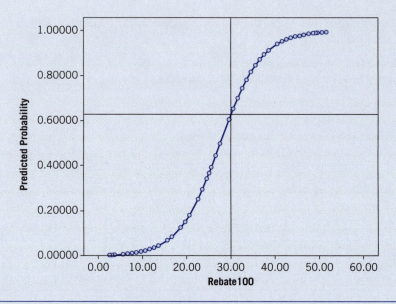

Figure 9.2 Graph of Logistic Regression for Car Rebate Data

and the predicted probabilities of purchase based on the model. Notice the vertical line we've drawn at *Rebate100* = 30. This line crosses the probability curve at about 0.63. This tells you that there is approximately a 63% chance that a customer with a $3,000 coupon will redeem this coupon, which is consistent with the results of the computation above (which yielded the probability 62.7%). (For more information on decision cutoff values, see the discussion at the end of the section "Multiple Logistic Regression.")

To produce the graph in Figure 9.2, follow these steps:

1. Select **Graphs/Chart Builder**. From the Gallery, choose Scatter/Dot and drag the Simple Scatter icon into the Chart Preview box.

2. Select *Predicted Probability* as the Y-axis and *Rebate100* as the X-axis. See Figure 9.3. Click OK to produce the preliminary graph.

3. Double-click on the graph to enter the SPSS Chart Editor.

4. From the Options menu, select an X reference line. Specify a value of 30 for the X-axis and click Close. Similarly from the Options menu, select a Y reference line with value 0.627. Click Apply and Close. (The Y reference line is drawn to assist your reader in visualizing the predicted probability.)

5. From the Elements menu, select Interpolation Line. Click Close.

6. Close the Chart Editor to display the graph shown in Figure 9.2.

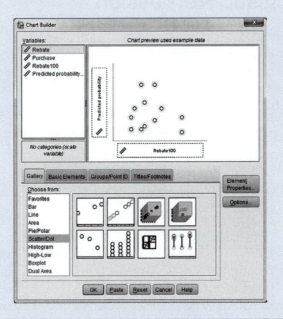

Figure 9.3 Dialog Box for Logistic Plot

Table 9.1 also contains information about the odds ratio (OR). The OR for *Rebate100* is given in the column headed Exp(B) and is equal to 1.239. A discussion of Odds Ratio is found in Chapter 6: Analysis of Categorical Data. (If we had used *Rebate* instead of *Rebate100*, the OR would have been 1.002, which would have been more difficult to interpret.) The corresponding 95% confidence interval for the OR is [1.138 to 1.349], which does not cover the value 1.0 and thus tells us that the OR is statistically significant (at the $\alpha = 0.05$ level). In this case, the OR is interpreted as the change in odds for each *unit change* in the predictor. That is, the odds of a customer purchasing an SUV are 1.239 times greater for each $100 increase in the rebate coupon.

These preliminary concepts for interpreting logistic regression provide an important foundation for the next section, which will discuss the development of a model that contains more than one predictor variable.

Reporting the Results of a Logistic Regression

The following illustrates how you might report the odds ratio for the logistic regression in a publication or report format.

Narrative for the Methods Section

"To examine the effect of coupon value on sales, we used a logistic regression."

Narrative for the Results Section

"The odds ratio of a customer purchasing an SUV is 1.239 ($p < 0.001$). This implies that every $100 unit increase in the size of the coupon yields a 23.9% estimated increase in the odds that a customer will use the coupon for a purchase."

Multiple Logistic Regression

A multiple logistic regression model has a *dependent (outcome or response) variable* that has two possible values (often coded with the values 0 and 1) and more than one *independent variable (predictor variables)*. A common setting is the situation in which there are several predictors to select from, and the task of the researcher is to select the best subset of possible predictors. Thus, the purpose of the logistic analysis includes the following:

- Determining which predictors are important and how they affect the response
- Creating a parsimonious and effective prediction equation

Tips and Caveats for Multiple Logistic Regression

Qualitative Predictor Variables

SIDEBAR

If you have a predictor variable that can take on only one of two values, it is common practice to code that variable using 0 and 1 values. If you use some other values, it will change the prediction equation and may make interpretation more challenging.

The predictor variables for a multiple logistic regression may be either binary or quantitative. If a potential categorical predictor variable has more than two categories such as race, brand of pickup truck, or socioeconomic status, the variable must be recoded into two or more binary indicator variables as in the multiple regression setting (also discussed in Chapter 5: Correlation and Regression). For example, suppose an observed variable is hair color, categorized as 1 = black, 2 = blonde, 3 = brown, and 4 = red. To recode this, you must create $c - 1$ (i.e., the number of categories minus 1) new binary variables. Let's call these variables *Black, Blonde,* and *Brown*. Thus, a person with black hair would have the following values: *Black* = 1, *Blonde* = 0, and *Brown* = 0. A person with brown hair would have the values *Black* = 0, *Blonde* = 0, and *Brown* = 1. A person with red hair would have the values *Black* = 0, *Blonde* = 0, and *Brown* = 0, and so forth. (Some people refer to this procedure as dummy coding and the indicator variables as dummy variables.) If you do not create indicator variables in this fashion, you can indicate that a variable is "Categorical" in the logistic analysis (in SPSS), and it will create automatic indicator variables (as shown in the upcoming example).

Variable Selection

The process used to select the best variables for the model is similar to the process used in multiple linear regression.

Predictor Variables with Large Values

If a continuous predictor variable contains values that are large in magnitude, it may cause the estimate of the corresponding β coefficient as well as the corresponding OR to be small. This small number can lead to round-off errors in predictions and make interpretation difficult. It is advisable to divide predictor variables with large numbers by a constant to create smaller values for a predictor variable. This was illustrated for the *Rebate* variable in Example 9.1 and for the *Price* variable in the upcoming example. Another strategy is to standardize predictor variables (i.e., subtract the mean and divide by the standard deviation). See Example 9.2 for more discussion of these topics.

Example 9.2

Multiple Logistic Regression

Describing the Problem

The sales director for a chain of appliance stores wants to find out what circumstances encourage customers to purchase extended warranties after a major appliance purchase. The response variable is an indicator of whether or not a warranty is purchased. The predictor variables they want to consider are the following:

- Customer gender
- Age of the customer
- Whether a gift is offered with the warranty
- Price of the appliance
- Race of customer

There are several strategies you can take to develop the "best" model for the data. It is recommended that you examine several models before determining which one is best for your analysis. Once you have identified a set of possible predictor variables (perhaps a subset of a larger number of variables), one approach to determine which should be included in a final (parsimonious) model is to use a hierarchical technique in which you select some predictor variables to be in the model based on your knowledge of the research problem. (For example, if your research question includes a comparison of gender differences, you would always include gender in your model. This is done using the Block option in SPSS as illustrated in the upcoming example.) Another approach is to allow the computer to select variables in the model using strictly statistical criteria. We recommend a blend of these approaches in most situations. In this example, we allow the computer to help specify important variables, but it is inadvisable to accept a computer-selected model without examining alternatives. For this example, we begin by examining the significance of each variable in a fully populated model.

> We recommend that if you have a large number of possible predictor variables, you first perform a preliminary analysis by examining each predictor variable separately in a series of simple logistic models. From these analyses, if a variable has no predictive relationship with the outcome variable (e.g., the p-value for the univariate model is greater than 0.20), you may choose to drop that variable from consideration, thus reducing the candidates you will use in the multivariate model selection. (We did not do this in the Example 9.2 because we started with a relatively small number of possible predictors.)

To perform this analysis using SPSS, follow these instructions:

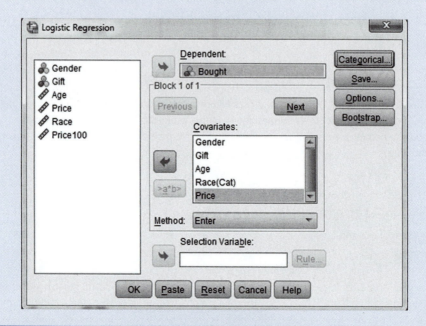

Figure 9.4   Dialog Box for Multiple Logistic Regression

SPSS Step-By-Step. EXAMPLE 9.2:
Multiple Logistic Regression

1. Open the data set WARRANTY.SAV and choose **Analyze/Regression/Binary Logistic**. . . .

2. Select *Bought* as the dependent variable and *Gender, Gift, Age, Price,* and *Race* as the covariates (i.e., the independent or predictor) variables (see Figure 9.4).

3. Click on the Categorical checkbox and specify *Race* as a categorical variable. Notice that the default reference category is set as "last" which means that other race categories will be compared to *Race* = 4. (Thus, SPSS creates a series of three indicator variables named *Race(1), Race(2),* and *Race(3)* from the four categories of *Race*.) Click Continue. Note that for this analysis, we are selecting the Method "Enter" which means that we will enter all of the variables in the model. Click OK to produce output that includes Table 9.2.

Notice that the *Race* variable, which was originally coded as 1 = White, 2 = African American, 3 = Hispanic, and 4 = Other, has been changed (by the SPSS logistic procedure) into three (4 − 1) indicator variables called *Race(1), Race(2),* and *Race(3)* since *Race* = 4 is the reference value. These three variables each enter the equation with their own coefficient and *p*-value, and there is an overall *p*-value given for *Race*.

The significance of each variable is measured using a Wald statistic. (Note that SPSS reports a Wald chi-square and not the Wald z that is more commonly used.) You can convert the Wald chi-square to a Wald z by taking the square root of the chi-square value and assigning the sign of the corresponding coefficient estimate, that is, b_i. Using $p = 0.10$ as a cutoff criterion for not including variables in the equation, it can be seen that *Gender* ($p = 0.142$) and *Race* ($p = 0.419$) do not seem to be important predictor variables. *Age* is marginal ($p = 0.104$), but we'll leave it in for the time being. The analysis is rerun without these "unimportant" variables, yielding the output in Table 9.3. Continue with the following steps to produce this output:

Table 9.2 Including All Predictor Variables in the Logistic Regression Equation

Variables in the Equation

		B	S.E.	Wald	df	Sig	Exp(B)
Step 1[a]	Gender	−3.772	2.568	2.158	1	.142	.023
	Gift	2.715	1.567	3.003	1	.083	15.112
	Age	.091	.056	2.683	1	.104	1.096
	Price	.001	.000	3.363	1	.067	1.001
	Race			2.827	3	.419	
	Race(1)	3.773	13.863	.074	1	.785	43.518
	Race(2)	1.163	13.739	.007	1	.933	3.199
	Race(3)	6.347	14.070	.203	1	.652	570.898
	Constant	−12.018	14.921	.649	1	.421	.000

a. Variable(s) entered on step 1: Gender, Gift, Age, Price, Race.

Table 9.3 Results of Reduced Model

Variables in the Equation

		B	S.E.	Wald	df	Sig.	Exp(B)
Step 1[a]	Gift	2.339	1.131	4.273	1	.039	10.368
	Age	.064	.032	4.132	1	.042	1.066
	Price	.000	.000	6.165	1	.013	1.000
	Constant	−6.096	2.142	8.096	1	.004	.002

a. Variable(s) entered on step 1: Gift, Age, Price.

4. To produce the "reduced" Table 9.3, again choose **Analyze/Regression/Binary Logistic** . . . , select *Bought* as the dependent variable and *Gift, Age, and Price* as the covariates (remove *Gender* and *Race*), and click OK.

This reduced model indicates that there is a significant predictive power for the variables *Gift* ($p = 0.039$), *Age* ($p = 0.042$), and *Price* ($p = 0.013$). Although the p-value for *Price* is small, notice that the OR = 1.000 and the coefficient for *Price* is zero to three decimal places. These seemingly contradictory bits of information (i.e., small p-value but OR = 1.000, etc.) are suggestive that the magnitudes of the values for *Price* are hiding the actual OR relationship. A solution is to create a new variable that is Price divided by 100. We've already done this and have named the variable *Price100*. Rerun the model following these steps:

5. Redo the Logistic analysis using the new Price100 variable by choosing **Analyze/ Regression/Binary Logistic** . . . , select *Bought* as the dependent variable and *Gift, Age,* and *Price100* as the covariates.

6. Click on the Options checkbox and select the Hosmer-Lemeshow goodness-of-fit. Click Continue and OK. This produces a lot of output that includes Tables 9.4 and 9.5.

In Table 9.4, observe that the odds ratio for Price100 is now 1.041 and the estimated coefficient is 0.040. All of the other values in the table remain the same. All we have done is to recode *Price* into a more usable number (similar to our creation of the *Rebate100* variable in Example 9.1). Another tactic often used is to standardize values such as *Price* by subtracting the mean and dividing by the standard deviation (see the section "Transforming, Recoding, and Categorizing Your Data" in Appendix A for information on how to do this). Using standardized scores eliminates the problem observed with the *Price* variable and also simplifies the comparison of odds ratios for different variables.

The results in Table 9.4 show that the odds that a customer who is offered a gift will purchase a warranty is 10 times greater than the corresponding odds for a customer having the same other characteristics but who is not offered a gift. We also observe that for each additional \$100 in *Price*, the

Table 9.4 Revised Model Using *Price100*

Variables in the Equation

		B	S.E.	Wald	df	Sig.	Exp(B)
Step 1[a]	Gift	2.339	1.131	4.273	1	.039	10.368
	Age	.064	.032	4.132	1	.042	1.066
	Price100	.040	.016	6.165	1	.013	1.041
	Constant	−6.096	2.142	8.096	1	.004	.002

a. Variable(s) entered on step 1: Gift, Age, Price100

odds that a customer will purchase a warranty increases by about 4%. This tells us that people tend to be more likely to purchase warranties for more expensive appliances. Finally, the OR for age, 1.066, tells us that older buyers are more likely to purchase a warranty.

One way to assess the model is to use the information in the Model Summary table shown in Table 9.5. In general, when comparing models, the lower the $-2*$(log likelihood) ($-2LL$) value, the better the fit. To determine whether the inclusion of an additional variable in a model gives a *significantly* better fit, you can use the difference in the $-2LL$ values for the two models to determine a chi-square test statistic. For example, for the model shown in Table 9.5, $-2LL = 22.278$. By removing the *Age* variable from the equation and rerunning the analysis, (not shown here) we get $-2LL = 27.44$. The difference (larger model $-2LL$ minus smaller model $-2LL$) has a chi-squared distribution with 1 degree of freedom, and if this value is larger than 3.84, the log-likelihood criterion suggests that the new variable should be included in the model. For this example,

$$\chi^2 = \text{Larger model } (-2LL) - \text{Smaller model } (-2LL)$$
$$= 27.44 - 22.278 = 5.162$$

and we conclude that the model including *Age* is a better model. Other criteria shown in Table 9.5 that can be used to assess the model are the Cox and Snell *R*-square and the Nagelkerke *R*-square, which are designed to provide information similar to the *R*-square in multiple regression.

Another model evaluation technique is the Hosmer-Lemeshow goodness-of-fit test. (Partial results are shown in Table 9.5.) This test divides the data into several groups based on $\hat{p}$ values, then computes a chi-square from observed and expected frequencies of subjects falling in the two categories of the binary response variable within these groups. Large chi-square values (and correspondingly small *p*-values) indicate a lack of fit for the model. In Table 9.5, we see that the Hosmer-Lemeshow chi-square test for the final warranty model yields a *p*-value of 0.987, thus suggesting a model that fits the data. Note that the Hosmer-Lemeshow chi-square test is not a test of importance of specific model

Table 9.5   Model Diagnostics

Hosmer and Lemeshow Test

Step	Chi-square	Df	Sig.
1	1.792	8	.987

Model Summary

Step	-2 Log likelihood	Cox & Snell R Square	Nagelkerke R Square
1	22.278[a]	.523	.753

a. Estimation terminated at iteration number 8 because parameter estimates changed by less than .001.

parameters (which may also appear in your computer printout). It is a separate post hoc test performed to evaluate the overall model's ability to fit the data.

Interpretation of the Multiple Logistic Regression Model

Once we are satisfied with the model, it can be used for prediction just as in the simple logistic example above. For this model, the prediction would be

$$\hat{p} = \frac{e^{-6.096+2.339*Gift+.064*Age+.04*Price100}}{1+e^{-6.096+2.339*Gift+.064*Age+.04*Price100}}$$

Using this prediction equation, we could predict the outcome for a customer having the following characteristics:

Age = 55

Price (of appliance) = $3,850

Gift = 1 (yes)

Placing these values in the equation yields the following:

$$\hat{p} = \frac{e^{-6.096+2.339*1+.064*55+.04*38.5}}{1+e^{-6.096+2.339*1+.064*55+.04*38.5}} = 0.786$$

Thus, there is 78.6% chance a customer with these characteristics will purchase a warranty if a gift is offered. If a gift is not offered (i.e., Gift = 0) while the other characteristics stay the same, the equation becomes

$$\hat{p} = \frac{e^{-6.096+2.339*0+.064*55+.04*38.5}}{1+e^{-6.096+2.339*0+.064*55+.04*38.5}} = 0.262$$

This information can be helpful in understanding the importance of the gift in selling a warranty for a particular age bracket or price. Using this information, it would be reasonable to predict that a person with the characteristics in the first example (i.e., Age = 55, Price = $3,850, and Gift = 1) would purchase a warranty because $\hat{p} = 0.786$, and the person in the second example (i.e., no gift offered) would not be predicted to purchase a warranty because $\hat{p} = 0.262$. The typical cutoff for the decision would be 0.5 (or 50%). Thus, using this cutoff, anyone whose $\hat{p}$ score was higher than 0.5 would be predicted to buy the warranty, and anyone with a lower score would be predicted to not buy the warranty. However, there may be times when you want to adjust this cutoff value. Kutner et al. (2004) suggest three ways to select a cutoff value:

- Use the standard 0.5 cutoff value.
- Determine a cutoff value that will give you the best predictive fit for your sample data. This is usually determined through trial and error.

- Select a cutoff value that will separate your sample data into a specific proportion of your two states based on a prior known proportion split in your population.

To choose a cutoff value other than the default 0.5, go back to the step-by step example and select Options (see Step 6) dialog box and enter the desired cutoff value in the box titled "Classification cutoff." For example, to use the second option for deciding on a cutoff value, examine the model classification table that is part of the SPSS logistic output, as shown in Table 9.6.

This table indicates that the final model correctly classifies 94% of the cases correctly. The model used the default 0.5 cutoff value to classify each subject's outcome. (Notice the footnote to the table: "The cut value is .500.") You can rerun the analysis with a series of cutoff values such as 0.4, 0.45, 0.55, and 0.65 to see if the cutoff value could be adjusted for a better fit. A "better" fit (selected by the researcher) may involve a desire to have the best predictive results appear in a particular cell. However, when you change the cutoff value to increase the percent correctly predicted in one cell, it will typically make the predictions in other cells worse. For example, you may be most interested in maximizing correct classifications in the "No/No" (Observed/Predicted) cell or minimizing incorrect classifications to the No/Yes cell. For this example, the default 0.5 cutoff value is deemed sufficient. (For more information about classification, see Cohen et al. [2002], p. 516.)

The following example shows how to force a specific variable (or variables) into the model and how to use an automated selection procedure to choose the remaining variables. Suppose, for example, that you always want to have the *Gift* variable in the Warranty data model.

SPSS Step-By-Step. EXAMPLE 9.2a: Multiple Logistic Regression: Specifying a Forced Variable and Using a Selection Procedure

1. Open the data set WARANTY.SAV and choose **Analyze/Regression/Binary Logistic**. . . .

Table 9.6   Model Classification

Classification Table[a]

			Predicated		
			Bought		Percentage Correct
Observed			No	Yes	
Step 1	Bought	No	12	2	85.7
		Yes	1	35	97.2
	Overall Percentage				94.0

a. The cut value is .500.

2. Select *Bought* as the dependent variable and *Gender, Age, Price100,* and *Race* as the covariates (i.e., the independent or predictor) variables. (Do not include *Gift in the list of covariates*.) Use the Categorical button to set *Race* as categorical as in the previous example.

3. Change the Method from Entry to Forward: Conditional. (You could also do this example using one of the other methods.) This tells SPSS to select variables from *Gender, Age, Price100,* and *Race.* Click the Options button and observe the Stepwise entry and removal criteria (set at 0.05 for Entry and 0.10 for Removal by default). Do not change these values, but be aware that you can change them if you want to adjust the significance criteria used for selection. Click Continue to return to the main logistic regression dialog box.

4. To force *Gift* to always be in the model, click the Next button (See Figure 9.4.) In this version of the dialog box, select *Gift* alone as a covariate and leave the Method as Entry. By doing this, you have indicated two sets of variables to enter into the model—one is forced (*Gift*) and the others are selected by an automated procedure.

5. Click OK to produce output that contains a "final" model, which is in the last table of the (considerable) amount of SPSS output. Note that this is the same model shown in Table 9.4. Study the SPSS output to see the steps SPSS used to select the variables that end up in the final model.

This example illustrated how to force a variable into the model and how to use an automatic selection procedure. You may not always get the same set of variables when you use different selection procedures, so we encourage you to examine and compare competing models using the −2*(log likelihood) or other methods to select a final model.

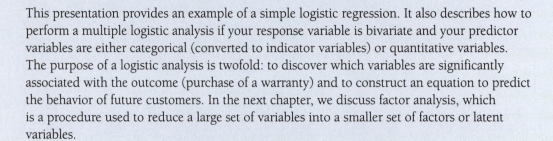

SUMMARY

This presentation provides an example of a simple logistic regression. It also describes how to perform a multiple logistic analysis if your response variable is bivariate and your predictor variables are either categorical (converted to indicator variables) or quantitative variables. The purpose of a logistic analysis is twofold: to discover which variables are significantly associated with the outcome (purchase of a warranty) and to construct an equation to predict the behavior of future customers. In the next chapter, we discuss factor analysis, which is a procedure used to reduce a large set of variables into a smaller set of factors or latent variables.

REFERENCES

Cohen, J., Cohen, P., West, S. G., & Aiken, L. S. (2002). *Applied multiple regression/correlation analysis for the behavioral sciences* (3rd ed.). Mahwah, NJ: Lawrence Erlbaum.

Daniel, W., & Cross C. L. (2013). *Biostatistics* (10th ed.). New York, NY: John Wiley.

Hosmer, D. W., Lemeshow, S., & Sturdivant, R. X. (2013). *Applied logistic regression* (3rd ed.). New York, NY: John Wiley.

Kleinbaum, D. G. (2011). *Logistic regression: A self-learning text* (3rd ed.). New York, NY: Springer-Verlag.

Kutner, M. H., Nachtsheim, C. J., Neter, J., & Li, W. (2004). *Applied linear statistical models*. Homewood, IL: McGraw-Hill, Irwin.

Tabachnick, B. G., & Fidell, L. S. (2012). *Using multivariate statistics* (6th ed.). Boston, MA: Allyn & Bacon.

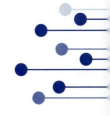

CHAPTER 10

FACTOR ANALYSIS
Introduction to Factor Analysis

Suppose you have collected data on a lot of variables for your subjects, and you want to summarize the information collected into a smaller set of features or factors. You might use this summarized information to create a more manageable collection of variables on which to do further analysis. You might also be interested in obtaining information on underlying latent variables (or factors) that cannot be directly measured. For example, Gardiner (2006) identifies several types of intelligence, two of which are Logical-Mathematical Intelligence (Number/Reasoning Smart) and Linguistic Intelligence (Word Smart). Each of these types of intelligence encompasses a variety of attributes. Someone who is Number/Reasoning Smart is good at performing calculations, using symbolic thought, logical reasoning, etc. Certainly there is not a single variable or measurement that can quantify a person's "Number/Reasoning Smartness." Quantifying the Number/Reasoning Smartness of an individual would require collecting data on a large number of variables/questions that measure various aspects of this type of intelligence. You might consider a study in which you collect many variables measuring a variety of aspects of "intelligence" in an attempt to either arrive at your own classification of intelligences or perhaps to see whether you can obtain measurements on the underlying intelligence factors identified by Gardiner. SPSS provides a variety of tools (under the general heading of "Dimension Reduction") that allow us to perform these types of analyses. The tool we will discuss in this chapter is *Factor Analysis*.

Factor Analysis can be divided into two approaches: Exploratory Factor Analysis and Confirmatory Factor Analysis.

- Exploratory factor analysis, as the name suggests, involves techniques for examining data sets for purposes of identifying factors or latent variables, examining which variables contribute most information, etc.
- Confirmatory factor analysis (which we will not discuss) involves a set of techniques for testing hypotheses to, again as the name suggests, try to confirm certain theories, etc.

In the remainder of this chapter, the term "Factor Analysis" will implicitly refer to "Exploratory Factor Analysis."

Related to Factor Analysis is the technique of Principal Component Analysis (PCA). These two methods are similar, but there are inherent differences in the settings.

- PCA is a technique for finding a few new variables, computed as linear combinations of the existing variables, which account for most of the variance (information) in the data.
- In Factor Analysis, the goal is to express the actual observed data as a *linear combination of a smaller number of underlying unobserved (latent) variables,* called *factors*. While PCA is based on explaining variance, factor analysis focuses on explaining the covariance/correlation structure among the observed variables.

In this chapter, we will discuss factor analysis using SPSS which offers several distinct methods for doing factor analysis. There is no universal agreement concerning which of these methods are best, but one of the most popular is the *principal axis factoring (principal factor method)*, which is related to PCA. Another popular method is maximum likelihood. In the examples in this chapter, we will use the principal factor method, but we note that for these two examples, the use of maximum likelihood yields very similar results.

The stages of a factor analysis solution are the following:

(a) Compute a covariance or correlation matrix for the variables to be used in the study.

(b) Extract the factors (which involves the decision concerning how many factors to extract).

(c) Rotate the factors for enhanced interpretation.

(d) Compute factor scores (if desired).

Appropriate Applications for a Factor Analysis

Possible applications of factor analysis were mentioned in the introduction and will be discussed further in the examples. Some applications are as follows:

- *Are there different types of intelligence?* Example 10.1 which follows addresses the issue of analyzing intelligence test results to determine whether there are a small number of components of intelligence.

- *Questionnaire analysis.* You might analyze the results of a questionnaire designed to study patient satisfaction with a treatment regimen in order to understand broad factors of satisfaction (such as, for example, convenience and comfort).

- *Olympic decathlon athletes*. In Example 10.2, we study data on results of the 10 events in the Olympic decathlon to determine if there seem to be underlying dimensions of athletic ability.

Design Considerations for Factor Analysis

Appropriate Sample Size

Several authors have studied the question of what sample size is needed for you to feel comfortable that your results generalize well. Some authors, e.g., Tabachnick and Fidell (2013), recommend 300 observations but would be comfortable with 150 in some situations. Other authors suggest that it is not the overall sample size that matters as much as the ratio of the number of observations to variables. Sample size recommendations for obtaining stable estimates range from at least 5 per variable and at least 100 overall, to 10–20 observations per observed variable.

Sufficient Correlation Structure Within the Data Set

Recall that factor analysis is a collection of techniques for examining the correlations among the variables in your data set in order to identify factors or underlying latent variables. Consequently, if correlations among all of your observed variables are small, then there is little hope that factor analysis will provide information on underlying latent factors. SPSS provides two tools for assessing the sufficiency of the correlation structure: Bartlett's test of sphericity and the Kaiser-Meyer-Olkin measure of sampling adequacy.

- *Bartlett's test of sphericity*: In Chapter 5: Correlation and Regression, it was noted that calculated (or sample) correlations are estimates of the true correlation between two variables. Bartlett's test of sphericity is a test of the null hypothesis that all true correlations between variables in the data set are zero, i.e., there is no actual correlation structure at all. In terms of the correlation matrix calculated in Stage (a) of the factor analysis procedure above, Bartlett's test of sphericity is a test of the null hypothesis that the off-diagonal elements of the theoretical correlation matrix are all 0's. SPSS provides an option to run Bartlett's test, and rejection of the null hypothesis is an indication that it is appropriate to continue on with a factor analysis.

- *Kaiser-Meyer-Olkin (KMO) measure of sampling adequacy*: KMO measures the extent to which correlation between pairs of variables can be explained by other variables. The maximum is 1 and a rule of thumb is to not do factor analysis if the KMO is less than 0.5.

Hypotheses for Factor Analysis

There are no hypothesis tests associated with (exploratory) factor analysis (except for Bartlett's test discussed earlier).

Tips and Caveats for Factor Analysis

Larger Samples Sizes Are Preferred

So, what's new? This is universal advice. However, since there are no specific hypotheses to be tested in exploratory factor analysis, EFA, you don't have the benefit of a decision rule to tell you whether you are justified in generalizing your results. Experience has shown, as discussed above, that reasonably large samples are usually required. Conclusions based on small samples may very well not be replicated in follow-up sampling.

Factor Analysis Is Tricky Business

There are many critics of factor analysis who point to the fact that solutions are not unique and there are several subjective steps in the process. As with all chapters in this book, but especially here, we emphasize the fact that this is not a textbook describing the techniques in detail, but we "cut to the chase" with the assumption that you know something about the topic itself. Reading this chapter and going through the examples will not make you an instant factor analysis expert.

Be Careful About Conclusions

The first two tips and caveats both point to the fact that factor analysis is quite subjective, and it is difficult to quantify the quality of factor analysis results. Johnson and Wichern (2007) say that assessment of the quality of results is often based on the "Wow" factor. That is, "If while scrutinizing the factor analysis, the investigator can shout 'Wow, I understand these factors,' the application is deemed successful."

Factor Analysis/Dimension Reduction

The stages (a) through (d) of a factor analysis listed previously are best described in the context of examples. The following two examples illustrate the use of factor analysis, using *principal axis factoring*, sometimes referred to as the *principal factor method*, on a synthetically constructed data set where we know the answers and on actual Olympic decathlon data.

Example 10.1

Factor Analysis of Intelligence Data

Describing the Problem

The data set INTEL.SAV contains a synthetically constructed set of intelligence data collected on 200 (hypothetical) subjects. Six variables were constructed to measure either Word Smartness or Numerical/Reasoning Smartness. These variables are all measured on a 10 point scale (0–10), and are considered to be scores on the following measurements or tests:

> *Computation*—Test on mathematical computations
>
> *Vocabulary*—A vocabulary test
>
> *Inference*—A test of the use of inductive and deductive inference
>
> *Reasoning*—A ctest of sequential reasoning
>
> *Writing*—A score on a writing sample
>
> *Grammar*—A test measuring proper grammar usage

We will use the techniques of factor analysis to determine whether the two components of intelligence, Word Smartness and Numerical Reasoning Smartness, can be extracted from the data.

SPSS Step-By-Step. EXAMPLE 10.1: Factor Analysis of Intelligence Data

In the following example, we show the steps involved in running factor analysis on SPSS.

1. Open the data set INTEL.SAV and select **Analyze/Dimension Reduction/Factor** as shown in Figure 10.1.

2. Select all six variables for analysis as shown in the Factor Analysis dialog box as shown in Figure 10.2

3. Click the Descriptives button, and you will see the dialog box in Figure 10.3. Select Univariate descriptives to see means, standard deviations, and number of observations on each of our variables. Also select Coefficients to request the correlation matrix, and select the KMO and Bartlett's test to request the tests discussed earlier that help us to determine whether a factor analysis is appropriate.

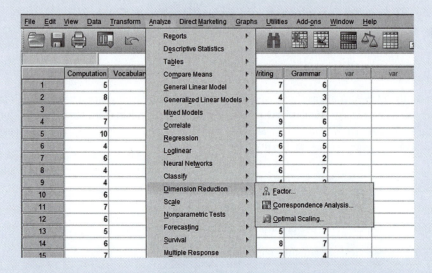

Figure 10.1 Analyze Menu Showing the Dimension Reduction Selection

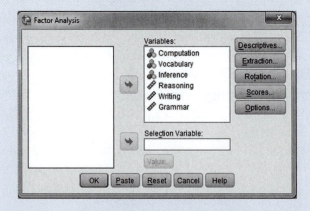

Figure 10.2 Factor Analysis Dialog Box

4. Select Continue at the bottom of the Descriptives menu and then OK, and you will see the output in Table 10.1 showing descriptive statistics, the correlation matrix shown in Table 10.2, and the results of the KMO and Bartlett's tests in Table 10.3.

In Table 10.1, it can be seen that all variables have similar means and standard deviations. The correlation matrix (see Chapter 5: Correlation and Regression) in Table 10.2, shows that there are high

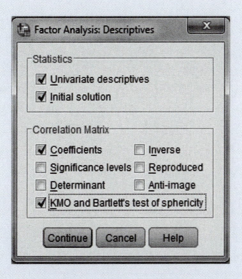

Figure 10.3 Options Under the Descriptives Tab

Table 10.1 Descriptive Statistics for the Synthetic Intelligence Data

Descriptive Statistics

	Mean	Std. Deviation	Analysis N
Computation	5.03	1.787	200
Vocabulary	5.25	1.691	200
Inference	4.34	1.676	200
Reasoning	4.63	1.940	200
Writing	5.00	1.995	200
Grammar	4.38	1.845	200

pairwise correlations among *Computation, Inference,* and *Reasoning* (to a lesser extent). These are the variables that seem to be measuring different aspects of Number/Reasoning Smartness. Similarly, the variables *Vocabulary, Writing,* and *Grammar* appear to be positively pairwise correlated and seem to be measuring aspects of Word Smartness. Based on these preliminary observations, we would expect an exploratory factor analysis procedure to detect two underlying factors. The KMO and Bartlett's test results shown in Table 10.3 indicate it is reasonable to run a factor analysis on the data.

5. In order to extract factors, we return to the Factor Analysis dialog box and this time select Extraction. As you can see in Figure 10.4, we have chosen to run Principal Axis Factoring based on the Correlation matrix. We have also instructed

Table 10.2 Correlation Matrix Among the Six Variables

Correlation Matrix

		Computation	Vocabulary	Inference	Reasoning	Writing	Grammar
Correlation	Computation	1.000	.132	.844	.531	.106	.105
	Vocabulary	.132	1.000	.040	.098	.752	.677
	Inference	.844	.040	1.000	.500	.057	.038
	Reasoning	.531	.098	.500	1.000	.148	.155
	Writing	.106	.752	.057	.148	1.000	.785
	Grammar	.105	.677	.038	.155	.785	1.000

Table 10.3 KMO and Bartlett's Test Results

KMO and Bartlett's Test

Kaiser-Meyer-Olkin Measure of Sampling Adequacy.		.687
Bartlett's Test of	Approx. Chi-Square	685.260
Sphericity	df	15
	Sig.	.000

Figure 10.4 Factor Analysis Extraction Dialog Box

SPSS to display the Unrotated factor solution and to display a Scree plot. We have also indicated that we want to extract those factors whose eigenvalues are greater than one, and we have set a limit of 25 on the number of iterations in the iterative solutions.

6. Select Continue at the bottom of the Extraction menu. Click on the Rotation button in the Factor Analysis dialog box and then select None on the Rotation menu as shown in Figure 10.5.

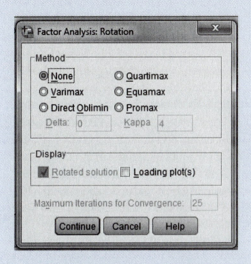

Figure 10.5 Factor Analysis Rotation Dialog Box

7. Select Continue, and then select OK. The output includes Tables 10.4 to 10.6 and Figure 10.6. These are discussed below.

You can perform factor analysis on the basis of the correlation matrix or the covariance matrix. The covariance matrix has the variances (squared standard deviations) of the variables along the main diagonal with covariances between variables as the off-diagonal elements. The correlation matrix is simply the covariance matrix calculated on standardized variables, all of which have mean zero and standard deviation 1. The correlation matrix is especially preferred when the variables are scored on different scales, etc. Even though our variables are all scaled similarly (0–10), we will use the correlation matrix.

> The covariance matrix has the variances (squared standard deviations) of the variables along the main diagonal with covariances between variables as the off-diagonal elements.

Table 10.4   Total Variance Explained by Initial Extraction

Total Variance Explained

Factor	Initial Eigenvalues			Extraction Sums of Squared Loadings		
	Total	% of Variance	Cumulative %	Total	% of Variance	Cumulative %
1	2.680	44.672	44.672	2.680	44.672	44.672
2	2.070	34.497	79.169	2.070	34.497	79.169
3	.582	9.693	88.862			
4	.320	5.340	94.202			
5	.203	3.384	97.586			
6	.145	2.414	100.000			

Extraction Method: Principal Component Analysis.

The Principal Axis factoring method uses PCA to obtain an initial estimate of the number of factors. PCA is based on explaining as much of the total variance as you can using as few components as is reasonable, where by total variance we mean the sum of the variances of the variables being used in the analysis. In our case, we have six variables, each of which has been standardized to have a variance of 1 (since we are using the correlation matrix). So, the total variance is 6. The first principal component, Y1, is the linear combination of the six variables (subject to the constraint that the sum of the squared coefficients in the linear combination is 1) that has the largest variance. This variance is called the eigenvalue associated with the first principal component. The second principal component, Y2, is the linear combination of the six variables (subject to the same constraint about the coefficients and for which Y1 and Y2 are uncorrelated) that has the next largest variance. The third, fourth, etc. principal components are obtained similarly with each new principal component being required to be uncorrelated with the ones previously obtained. (Aren't you glad SPSS will do this for you?) Table 10.4 summarizes this information.

It can be seen that the first principal component has a variance (eigenvalue) of 2.68, which is 44.672% of the total variance, 6. The second principal component has an eigenvalue of 2.07, which is 34.497% of the total variance. The first two principal components represent (or explain) 79.169% of the total variance. Recall that on the Factor Analysis option box we chose to extract components associated with eigenvalues greater than 1 (a common strategy). Notice that the third through sixth eigenvalues are all substantially less than 1. The strategy of selecting components with eigenvalues greater than 1 results in the extraction of two factors in this problem, which as we mentioned explain 79% of the total variance.

The Scree plot in Figure 10.6 plots the eigenvalues for the first through sixth principal components. It is obvious that there is a distinct break between the first two eigenvalues and the others. Consequently, a decision to keep two components again seems reasonable. (Remember—that's what we expected.)

The Communalities shown in Table 10.5 in the Extraction column are the proportion of the variance in each of the original six variables retained by keeping only two factors. The first column contains initial

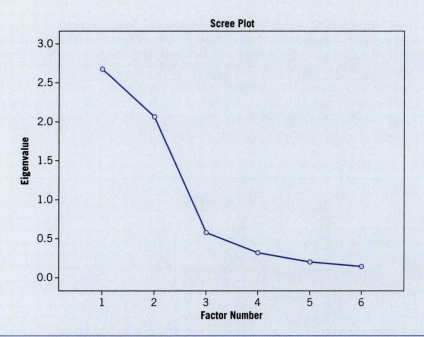

Figure 10.6 Scree Plot for Intelligence Data

estimates based on the principal axis factoring method. If we had selected the principal components extraction method (the first item in the extraction list), the initial communalities would have been set to 1.0 for each variable. Clearly all six of the variables are fairly well represented by the two factors, with variable *Reasoning* having the smallest communality, 0.324.

Table 10.5 Communalities for Intelligence Data Based on the 2-Factor Solution

Communalities

	Initial	Extraction
Computation	.737	.882
Vocabulary	.596	.646
Inference	.723	.813
Reasoning	.307	.324
Writing	.709	.869
Grammar	.637	.712

Extraction Method: Principal Axis Factoring.

Next, we examine the two factors that are obtained and determine whether additional information can be obtained by a rotation. The factor loadings are shown in Table 10.6. In the table, it can be seen that the first factor loads positively on all of the variables. This factor might be considered to be an *overall intelligence* measurement (based on only the two types of intelligence our variables measured). The second factor tends to differentiate between variables *Computation, Inference,* and *Reasoning* (the variables measuring Number/Reasoning Smartness) and *Vocabulary, Writing,* and *Grammar* (the variables that measured Word Smartness). It seems that rotating the axes might yield more interpretable results (since we actually *know* there are two factors—Word Smartness and Numerical/Reasoning Smartness).

Table 10.6   Unrotated Factor Matrix for Intelligence Data

Factor Matrix[a]

	Factor	
	1	2
Computation	.577	.741
Vocabulary	.699	−.397
Inference	.494	.754
Reasoning	.408	.397
Writing	.807	− 467
Grammar	.732	−.420

Extraction Method: Principal Axis Factoring.

a. 2 factors extracted. 12 iterations required.

8. To perform a rotation, return to the Factor Analysis: Rotation dialog box shown in Figure 10.5, and this time instead of selecting None, select Varimax, which is probably the most common rotation. Select Continue and then OK. In the resulting output, you will see Table 10.7, which is the same as Table 10.4 with the addition of three new columns giving information about the variance explained by the rotated factors. It can be seen that the first two rotated factors explain 37.2% and 33.6% of the variance, respectively.

The output also includes the factor matrix shown previously in Table 10.6 followed by the rotated factor matrix shown in Table 10.8 that shows loadings on the rotated factors.

The resulting rotated factor matrix is quite easily interpreted with Factor 1 seeming to measure Word Smartness and Factor 2 measuring Numerical/Reasoning Smartness seen by the fact that Factor 1 has heavy loadings on variables *Vocabulary, Writing, and Grammar*, while Factor 2 has large loadings on variables *Computation, Inference, and Reasoning*. Wow! I understand these factors (and in fact that's the way we generated the data).

Table 10.7 Total Variance by Rotated Factors for Intelligence Data

Total Variance Explained

Factor	Initial Eigenvalues			Extraction Sums of Squared Loadings			Rotation Sums of Squared Loadings		
	Total	% of Variance	Cumulative %	Total	% of Variance	Cumulative %	Total	% of Variance	Cumulative %
1	2.680	44.672	44.672	2.418	40.306	40.306	2.231	37.186	37.186
2	2.070	34.497	79.169	1.828	30.463	70.770	2.015	33.584	70.770
3	.582	9.693	88.862						
4	.320	5.340	94.202						
5	.203	3.384	97.586						
6	.145	2.414	100.000						

Extraction Method: Principal Axis Factoring.

Table 10.8 Rotated Factor Matrix for Intelligence Data Using Varimax Rotation

Rotated Factor Matrix

	Factor	
	1	2
Computation	.060	.937
Vocabulary	.801	.066
Inference	−.017	.901
Reasoning	.114	.558
Writing	.930	.068
Grammar	.842	.065

Extraction Method: Principal Axis Factoring.

Rotation Method: Varimax with Kaiser Normalization.

a. Rotation converged in 3 iterations.

SPSS provides a variety of other rotation options. Varimax is an example of an "orthogonal rotation." That is, the rotated factors are uncorrelated with each other. The Varimax, Quartimax, and Equamax options on the rotation menu shown in Figure 10.5 are all examples of orthogonal rotations. The Direct Oblimin and Promax options produce oblique rotations which are not subject to the constraint that the new rotated factors are orthogonal (uncorrelated). Again, this example is only for illustrative purposes, and you should look at books such as Stevens (2002), Johnson and Wichern (2007), and Johnson (1998) for more discussion of these concepts and the issues involved.

9. To calculate factor scores (Stage [d] in the Factor Analysis outline), select Scores from the Factor Analysis main dialog box shown in Figure 10.2. The Factor Score dialog box is shown in Figure 10.7 where it can be seen that we have chosen to save the factors as variables using the Regression method. Select Continue and then OK, and the factor scores will be saved on the data screen in two new columns (variables) called *FAC_1* and *FAC_2*. For each subject, *FAC1_1* is a measure of the Word Smartness (the higher the value the higher the Word Smartness) while *FAC2_1* measures the Numerical/Reasoning Smartness in a similar manner. These may or may not be needed in your analysis.

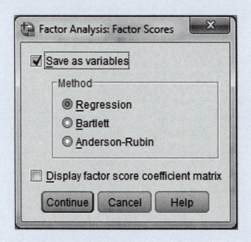

Figure 10.7   Select to Save Factor Scores as Variables

Reporting the Results of a Factor Analysis

Narrative for the Methods Section

"The intelligence data collected on the 200 (hypothetical) subjects were analyzed using factor analysis based on extraction using principal axis factoring with a varimax rotation."

Narrative for the Results Section

"We obtained two factors using the criterion that factors associated with eigenvalues greater than 1 are retained. We interpreted the rotated factors as Word Smartness and Numerical/Reasoning Smartness respectively. The Word Smartness factor accounted for 37.2% of the total variance, and the Numerical/Reasoning Smartness accounted for 33.6% yielding 70.8% of the variances being accounted for by these two rotated factors."

Example 10.2

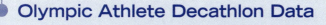

Olympic Athlete Decathlon Data

Describing the Problem

Data were collected on the 193 participants who completed all 10 decathlon events in the 1988 through 2012 Olympics. The 10 events in the decathlon are the 100 meter run, long jump, shot put, high jump, 400 meter run, 100 meter hurdles, discus, pole vault, javelin, and 1,500 meter run. These events are designed to measure a wide variety of athletic ability, and in fact, the Olympic decathlon winner is often referred to as the World's Greatest Athlete. In this example, we use factor analysis to explore whether there are a few (fewer than 10) underlying components or factors of athletic ability being measured by the decathlon events. It should be noted that the "times" in the running events are given negative signs so that "larger" values are better than "smaller" ones as is the case in the distance measurements. Also, the 1,500 meters results are given in (negative) seconds rather than the usual reporting of minutes and seconds. Additional variables in the data set include *year* (the year of the Olympic Games) and *ptotal* (the total number of points for that athlete based on the decathlon scoring system).

We use the procedure outlined in the previous example to run the factor analysis for the Olympic Athlete Data.

SPSS Step-By-Step. EXAMPLE 10.2: Olympic Athlete Decathlon Data

1. Open the data set OLYMPIC.SAV and select **Analyze/Dimension Reduction/Factor**.

2. On the resulting Factor Analysis dialog box (similar to that shown in Figure 10.2), select variables *100 Meters[run100]* through *1500 meter run[run1500s]*.

3. Select the Descriptives tab, and make the same selections as are indicated in Figure 10.3. (Univariate, Initial solution, Coefficents, and KMO.)

4. Select Continue and then OK to obtain the descriptive statistics (shown in Table 10.9), correlation matrix (Table 10.10), along with the KMO and Bartlett's test results in Table 10.11.

The KMO and Bartlett's test results suggest that a factor analysis is reasonable. In Table 10.10, it is interesting to note that there are some positive correlations (as would be expected) between times in the 100 meter and 400 meter run (0.621) and between the shot put and discus results (0.748). It is also interesting that the results in the 1,500 meter run has weak correlations with all other events, with the strongest correlation being with the 400 meter run (0.368).

5. To extract factors, select Extraction on the Factor Analysis menu and choose Principal Axis Factoring and the other options as shown in Figure 10.4. (Principal axis factoring, Correlation matrix, Unrotated factor solution, Scree, and Based on Eigenvales greater than 1.)

Table 10.9 Descriptive Statistics for Decathlon Data

Descriptive Statistics

	Mean	Std. Deviation	Analysis N
100 meters	−11.0240	.28081	193
long jump	7.2231	.35049	193
shot put	14.3291	1.23613	193
high jump	1.9858	.08587	193
400 meter run	−49.3312	1.28343	193
110 meter hurdles	−14.6980	.55508	193
discus	43.5870	4.20158	193
pole vault	4.7358	.34220	193
javelin	59.0330	6.37839	193
1500 meter run	−278.7472	13.17835	193

6. Select Continue at the bottom of the Extraction menu. Click on the Rotation button and select None as shown in Figure 10.5.

7. Select Continue then OK. The output includes Tables 10.12 to 10.14 and Figure 10.8. These are discussed below.

It can be seen that the first principal component has a variance (eigenvalue) of 4.15 which is 41.45% of the total variance (10). The second principal component has an eigenvalue of 1.53 which is 15.29% of the total variance, and the third principal component has eigenvalue 1.21 and accounts for 12.14% of the variation. The first three principal components represent (or explain) 68.88% of the total variance. Again, we have chosen to use the common strategy of extracting factors associated with eigenvalues greater than 1 which results in an initial selection of three factors. The Scree plot in Figure 10.8 gives a graphical view of the eigenvalues, and it can be seen that there is a fairly distinct break between the third eigenvalue and the remaining ones, which are all quite similar to each other.

The Communalities associated with the 3-factor solution based on principal axis factoring are shown in Table 10.13. It can be seen that all 10 variables are reasonably well represented by the three factors, with *javelin* having the smallest communality, 0.342.

Table 10.14 contains the factor matrix for the unrotated 3-factor solution. There it can be seen that the first factor has positive coefficients for each variable, with all of them being above 0.4 except for

Table 10.10 Correlation Matrix for Decathlon Data

Correlation Matrix

		100 meters	long jump	shot put	high jump	400 meter run	110 meter hurdles	discus	pole vault	javelin	1500 meter run
Correlation	100 meters	1.000	.625	.469	.221	.621	.692	.365	.326	.152	-.009
	long jump	.625	1.000	.372	.461	.542	.546	.324	.439	.313	.239
	shot put	.469	.372	1.000	.368	.198	.469	.748	.380	.407	-.112
	high jump	.221	.461	.363	1.000	.213	.320	.339	.340	.303	.217
	400 meter run	.621	.542	.198	.213	1.000	.518	.145	.317	.123	.368
	110 meter hurdles	.692	.546	.469	.320	.518	1.000	.370	.435	.283	.050
	discus	.365	.324	.748	.339	.145	.370	1.000	.267	.354	-.102
	pole vault	.326	.439	.380	.340	.317	.435	.267	1.000	.359	.157
	javelin	.152	.313	.407	.303	.123	.283	.354	.359	1.000	.167
	1500 meter run	-.009	.239	-.112	.217	.368	.050	-.102	.157	.167	1.000

Table 10.11 KMO and Bartlett's Test Results for Decathlon Data

KMO and Bartlett's Test

Kaiser-Meyer-Olkin Measure of Sampling Adequacy.		.795
Bartlett's Test of Sphericity	Approx. Chi-Square	813.506
	df	45
	Sig.	.000

Table 10.12 Total Variance Explained by Initial Extraction for Decathlon Data

Total Variance Explained

Factor	Initial Eigenvalues			Extraction Sums of Squared Loadings		
	Total	% of Variance	Cumulative %	Total	% of Variance	Cumulative %
1	4.145	41.448	41.448	3.777	37.770	37.770
2	1.528	15.285	56.732	1.150	11.496	49.266
3	1.214	12.144	68.876	.776	7.757	57.023
4	.720	7.203	76.080			
5	.671	6.705	82.785			
6	.541	5.408	88.192			
7	.405	4.054	92.246			
8	.329	3.294	95.541			
9	.240	2.494	98.034			
10	.197	1.966	100.000			

Extraction Method: Principal Axis Factoring.

the 1,500 meter run. Thus, this seems to be an overall measure of athletic ability, focusing on the first nine events. The other two factors are difficult to interpret. Based on these observations, it seems that rotation would be advisable.

8. Select the Rotation option from the Factor Analysis menu, and select Varimax rotation. Select Continue and then OK. In the resulting output, you will see Table 10.15 which is the same as Table 10.12 with the addition of three new columns giving information

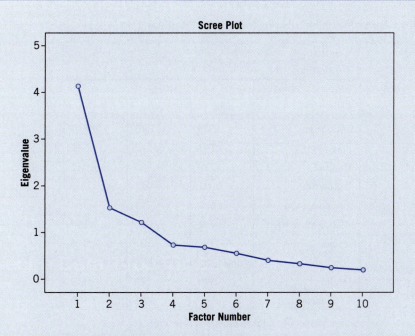

Figure 10.8 Scree Plot for Decathlon Data

Table 10.13 Communalities for 3-Factor Solution for Decathlon Data

Communalities

	Initial	Extraction
100 meters	.686	.963
long jump	.567	.614
shot put	.654	.824
high jump	.324	.359
400 meter run	.552	.617
110 meter hurdles	.562	.584
discus	.572	.616
pole vault	.320	.346
javelin	.285	.342
1500 meter run	.316	.438

Extraction Method: Principal Axis Factoring.

Table 10.14   Factor Matrix for 3-Factor Solution for Decathlon Data

Factor Matrix[a]

	Factor		
	1	2	3
100 meters	.805	.213	−.519
long jump	.743	.233	.088
shot put	.720	−.553	−.011
high jump	.501	−.043	.326
400 meter run	.607	.495	−.060
110 meter hurdles	.742	.093	−.155
discus	.599	−.507	.016
pole vault	.552	.021	.203
javelin	.444	−.173	.338
1500 meter run	.167	.448	.457

Extraction Method: Principal Axis Factoring,

a. 3 factors extracted. 20 iterations required.

Table 10.15   Total Variance by Rotated Factors for Decathlon Data

Total Variance Explained

Factor	Initial Eigenvalues			Extraction Sums of Squared Loadings			Rotation Sums of Squared Loadings		
	Total	% of Variance	Cumulative %	Total	% of Variance	Cumulative %	Total	% of Variance	Cumulative %
1	4.145	41.448	41.448	3.777	37.770	37.770	2.432	24.322	24.322
2	1.528	15.285	56.732	1.150	11.496	49.266	2.251	22.508	46.830
3	1.214	12.144	68.876	.776	7.757	57.023	1.019	10.193	57.023
4	.720	7.203	76.080						
5	.671	6.705	82.785						
6	.541	5.408	88.192						
7	.405	4.054	92.246						
8	.329	3.294	95.541						
9	.249	2.494	98.034						
10	.197	1.966	100.000						

Extraction Method: Principal Axis Factoring.

about the variance explained by the rotated factors. It can be seen that the first three rotated factors explain 24.3%, 22.5%, and 10.2% of the variance, respectively.

The output also includes the factor matrix shown previously (in Table 10.14) followed by the rotated factor matrix shown in Table 10.16 that shows loadings on the rotated factors.

Table 10.16 Rotated Factor Matrix Using Varimax Rotation on Decathlon Data

Rotated Factor Matrix[a]

	Factor		
	1	2	3
100 meters	.951	.209	−.122
long jump	.598	.367	.350
shot put	.281	.839	−.202
high jump	.174	.474	.323
400 meter run	.693	.051	.366
110 meter hurdles	.662	.375	.076
discus	.200	.738	−.177
pole vault	.304	.422	.276
javelin	.068	.527	.244
1500 meter run	.083	−.027	.656

Extraction Method: Principal Axis Factoring.
Rotation Method: Varimax with Kaiser Normalization.

a. Rotation converged in 5 iterations.

The first rotated factor seems to be heavily loaded on 100 meters, long jump, 400 meter run, and 110 meter hurdles. These events all focus on the legs, speed, and spring. Because of the fact that there are 10 variables, the factors are a bit difficult to visualize.

9. Select Options on the Factor Analysis main menu (see Figure 10.2). The Options dialog box is shown in Figure 10.9. The default option concerning handling of missing cases is to exclude cases listwise, which we have done in each of these two examples by simply not changing the default. Select Suppress small coefficients and change the value in the box to 0.4 which will help us visualize the factors in the rotated solution. Click Continue and then OK.

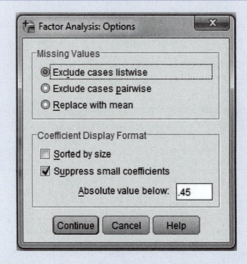

Figure 10.9 Options Dialog Box

The resulting rotated factor matrix, which suppresses coefficients less than 0.4, is given in Table 10.17. We think you will agree that the interpretation "pops out" more clearly in this case. Again we see

Table 10.17 Rotated Factor Matrix in Table 10.16 With Suppressed Coefficients

Rotated Factor Matrix[a]

	Factor		
	1	**2**	3
100 meters	.951		
long jump	.598		
shot put		.839	
high jump		.474	
400 meter run	.693		
110 meter hurdles	.662		
discus		.738	
pole vault			
javelin		527	
1500 meter run			.656

Extraction Method: Principal Axis Factoring.
Rotation Method: Varimax with Kaiser Normalization.

a. Rotation converged in 5 iterations.

the same interpretation given previously for Factor 1. Factor 2 seems to consist primarily of events that use arm strength, e.g., shot put, discuss pole vault, and javelin. Surprisingly, high jump also is included in this category. The only event with coefficient greater than 0.4 in Factor 3 is the 1,500 meter run. Recall that it is also the event that was basically uncorrelated with the other nine events on a pairwise basis as seen in the correlation matrix in Table 10.10. These interpretations are similar to, but not entirely the same as, those obtained by Johnson and Wichern (2007) based on a 4-factor analysis of data obtained on Olympic decathletes who participated in Olympics after World War II and prior to 1988.

Narrative for Factor Analysis

"The decathlon data set contains the results for the 193 participants who completed all 10 decathlon events in the 1988 through 2012 Olympics. The 10 events in the decathlon are the 100 meter run, long jump, shot put, high jump, 400 meter run, 100 meter hurdles, discus, pole vault, javelin, and 1,500 meter run. The decathlon data were analyzed using factor analysis based on principal axis factoring using a varimax rotation."

Narrative for the BF Results Section

"Three factors were selected using the criterion of retaining factors associated with eigenvalues greater than 1. The three factors can be interpreted as (1) leg speed/spring, (2) arm strength, and (3) a factor focusing mainly on the 1,500 meter run. Factors 1–3 accounted for 24.3%, 22.5%, and 10.2% of the variance respectively."

SUMMARY

In this chapter, we have discussed methods for using factor analysis to summarize the information into a smaller set of features or factors.

Throughout this book, we have endeavored to provide explanations of techniques and procedures that allow you to "find the message" in a data set so that you can use the information for description, decision making, or prediction. Along with these explanations, we have also provided specific ways to assess whether your data fit into a particular analysis. Our purpose is to provide more than cookie-cutter statistical examples. It is to provide you with clear explanations of statistical procedures so that you can use them effectively and correctly. Our hope is that this book will help you increase your expertise and confidence in performing statistical analyses.

REFERENCES

Gardiner, H. (2006). *Multiple intelligences: New horizons*. New York, NY: Basic Books.

Johnson, D. E. (1998). *Applied multivariate methods for data analysts*. Pacific Grove, CA: Duxbury Press.

Johnson, R. A., & Wichern, D. W. (2007). *Applied multivariate statistical analysis* (6th ed.). Englewood Cliffs, NJ: Pearson Prentice Hall.

Stevens, J. P. (2002). *Applied multivariate statistics for the social sciences* (4th ed.). Mahwah, NJ: Lawrence Erlbaum.

Tabachnick, B. G., & Fidell, L. S. (2013). *Using multivariate statistics* (6th ed.). Boston, MA: Allyn and Bacon.

Appendix A

A Brief Tutorial for Using IBM SPSS for Windows

The SPSS program has been around since 1968. Its origins are in social science (thus the original name Statistical Package for the Social Sciences), but it is now used in a wide variety of application areas of statistics and data analytics. IBM purchased SPSS in 2009, and it was renamed IBM SPSS. (Because of a name dispute, for a short time in 2009–2010, it was called PASW (Predictive Analytics SoftWare). Throughout this book, we will refer to the program as IBM SPSS or (more frequently) simply SPSS. Although this book (and, in particular, this appendix) is not meant to teach all the ins and outs of SPSS, this brief introduction provides enough information for you to use the examples in *IBM SPSS by Example*. (There is also a built-in tutorial in SPSS that can be accessed by selecting **Help/Tutorial** from the main SPSS menu.) The examples throughout this book are based on SPSS Version 23 or above, although most of the examples work in the same way for earlier (and probably later) versions of the program.

When you first start up SPSS, the screen in Figure A.1 is displayed. If a preliminary dialog box appears asking "What would you like to do?" click Cancel. The main SPSS screen looks a lot like a spreadsheet, but there are differences. Notice the two tabs at the lower left of the screen labeled "Data View" and "Variable View." These two views will be used in the upcoming examples to illustrate how to enter and manipulate data in the program.

The SPSS menus at the top of this window will be referenced throughout this book to describe how to select an SPSS option or analysis. (They may differ slightly according to what modules you have installed.) Briefly, typical main menu items are as follows:

SIDEBAR
Although the examples are analyzed using SPSS for Windows, all of the examples could be similarly analyzed using other versions of SPSS, including SPSS for Apple Macintosh.

> **File**: Create a new data file, open an existing data set, import and export data.
>
> **Edit**: Edit data in the SPSS spreadsheet, including copy, paste, and undo.
>
> **View**: Select options about how to view the SPSS data grid.

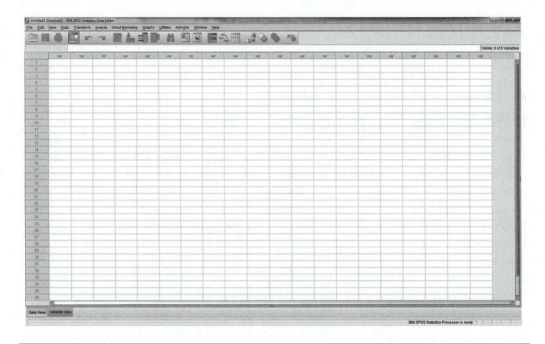

Figure A.1   The SPSS Data Editor Grid

Data: Manipulate data in the SPSS grid.

Transform: Create new variables.

Analyze: Perform a statistical analysis using the data in the SPSS data grid.

Graphs: Create a graph from data in the SPSS data grid.

Utilities: Select SPSS utility options.

Add-Ons: Provides a listing of add-on packages to which you do not currently have access.

Window: Manipulate windows.

Help: Access the SPSS help system, including tutorials.

In *IBM SPSS by Example*, we often refer to a series of menu choices using a command list such as **Analyze/Descriptive Statistics/Frequencies** . . . , which means to select the **Analyze** menu from the main SPSS menu followed by selecting the **Descriptive Statistics** submenu and then the **Frequencies** sub-submenu.

Working With Data in SPSS

Before performing any type of analysis, you must enter data into SPSS. There are three typical ways to make data available for use by SPSS. They are the following:

1. Open an existing SPSS data file (such as the example data files that are associated with the examples in this book).

2. Enter data into the SPSS spreadsheet using the keyboard.

3. Import data from another program such as Excel.

Whether you create your own data set or open or import a previously created data set, you should pay some attention to each variable name and type. Variable names and types were introduced in the section "Guidelines for Creating Data Sets" in Chapter 1. The information for naming variables in that discussion is sufficient to get you started, however the following is additional information concerning data types available in SPSS. For each variable in SPSS, you will need to select among the following list of data types.

- *Numeric*. Variables whose values are meaningful numbers. Subcategories of numeric variables in SPSS include the following:

  o *Comma*: numeric variables that are displayed with commas delimiting every three places and with the period as a decimal delimiter

  o *Dot*: numeric variables displayed with periods delimiting every three places and with the comma as a decimal delimiter (a numeric format used in some countries)

  o *Scientific notation*: numeric variables displayed with an imbedded E (single precision) or D (double precision) and a signed power-of-ten exponent such as 1.22D3 (meaning 1220) or 1.22E-2 (meaning 0.0122)

  o *Custom currency*: numeric variables displayed in accordance with a definition in the Currency tab of the Options dialog box

- *Date*: A variable that represents a calendar date or clock time.
- *String*: Categorical/text variables whose contents are not numeric. This can include text descriptions such as "Has the Flu," categorical designations such as "Male" and "Female" or "M" and "F," or noncalculated numbers such as a patient ID number. However, before you create a categorical variable

SIDEBAR

Before using the examples in IBM SPSS by Example, you should follow the procedures in Chapter 1: Introduction for downloading the example data files and placing them on your computer so you can use the hands-on exercises in this book.

that uses text instead of numbers, be aware that some procedures in SPSS (such as regression) do not allow text variables to be used in the analysis. If you choose to code categorical data using numbers (e.g., 1 and 0) instead of text (e.g., Y and N), you will be able to specify the meaning of your numeric code in the SPSS data editor using value labels.

- SPSS also identifies a "Measure" type for each variable. These can be Scale (indicates a continuous numeric variable), Ordinal (indicates a categorical variable that is ordered such as small, medium, and large), and Nominal (indicates categories that are not ordered). This was described in more detail in Chapter 1: Introduction.

- The following sections provide examples describing how to enter data into SPSS.

SPSS Step-By-Step. EXAMPLE A.1
Entering Data Into the SPSS Data Sheet

This example shows how to create a new data file in SPSS (using the information in the Data Dictionary shown in Table A.1 as a guide) and how to enter data into the SPSS data sheet.

Table A.1 Data Dictionary for Example A.1

Variable Name	Type (Width)	Label	Value Codes	Missing Code
ID	String (4)	Identification number	None	Not allowed
Age	Numeric (3.0)	Age on January 1, 2015	None	−99
Female	Numeric (1.0)	Patient is female	1 = Yes 0 = No	9
Tdate	Date (10) (mm/dd/yyyy)	Test date	None	"." Or 11/11/1111
Score	Numeric (6.2)	Initial test score	None	−99

1. On the main SPSS page, select **File/New/Data**. Click the "Variable View" tab at the bottom of the screen. Figure A.2 shows the displayed grid. Enter variable names and information into the Variable View grid beginning with the variable ID.

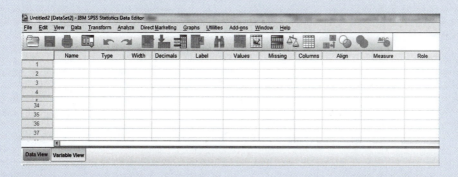

Figure A.2 The SPSS Variable View Grid

2. In the "Name" column, enter ID.

3. In the "Type" column, click on the ellipsis (. . .), select "String," and change the Character Width value to 4.

4. In the "Label" column, enter "Identification Number." Ignore the other columns.

5. Enter the descriptions for the other variables by using the information in the data dictionary in Table 1.3 (Chapter 1: Introduction). Using these criteria, perform the following steps:

   a. Define the variable *Age* as 3 digits with no decimal places and a missing value of –99. To set the missing values code, click on the ellipse (. . .) in the Missing column, select "Discrete Missing Values," enter –99 as a missing value and click OK. In the Measure column, indicate "scale."

   b. Define the variable *Female* as string variable 1 digit wide with a missing value code of 9. To enter the values for the *Female* code, do the following:

      (1) Click in the Values cell, then on the ellipse (. . .).

      (2) Type in 1 as the value and Yes as the value label and click Add.

      (3) Type in 0 as the value and No as the value label and click Add. Indicate Nominal in the Measure column.

      (4) Click OK.

   c. Define the variable *Tdate* as a date variable using mm/dd/yyyy date format, which automatically sets the width at 10 characters. Indicate the label Test Date and leave the missing value code as blank. Indicate Scale as the measurement.

   d. Define the variable *Score* as a numeric variable six digits wide with two decimal places (accommodates the maximum possible score of 999.99). Indicate Initial Test Score for the label, a missing value code of –99, and Scale as the measurement.

The resulting variable definitions are shown in Figure A.3.

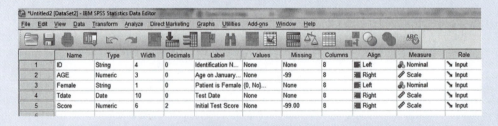

Figure A.3   The SPSS Variable Grid Showing Entered Definitions

Once your variables are defined, click on the "Data View" tab at the bottom of the SPSS screen and enter the data in Table A.2.

Table A.2 Sample Data

ID	Age	Female	TDate	Score
1001	23	1	10/22/2015	98.00
1002	43	0	10/23/2015	78.00
1003	24	0	11/03/2015	90.00
1004	36	1	11/06/2015	89.00
1005	29	0	11/10/2015	82.00
1006	26	0	11/15/2015	75.00
1007	19	1	11/20/2015	94.00
1008	32	1	11/23/2015	89.00
1009	35	1	11/30/2015	99.00

After you've entered the data, save the data file by selecting **File/Save As**. . . . Save the data using the filename MYDATA1.SAV in the C:\SPSSDATA folder. These data are now ready to analyze.

SPSS Step-By-Step. EXAMPLE A.2:
Importing a Data File From Microsoft Excel

Data are sometimes entered and stored in a program other than SPSS. When you are ready to perform an analysis, you will want to import these data into SPSS. For example, it is often useful to import a Microsoft Excel file (.xlsx file) into SPSS. The procedure is similar for other file types such as SAS (.sasb7dat), Systat files (.sys or .syd), and Lotus (*.w*).

Before importing Excel data into SPSS, review the guidelines in Chapter 1: Introduction, in the section "Preparing Excel Data for Import." The following example uses the spreadsheet named EXAMPLE. XLSX, located in the SPSS examples folder for *IBM SPSS by Example*. This file is already in the proper format for importing into SPSS, discussed in Chapter 1, and is shown in Figure A.4.

	A	B	C	D	E	F	G
1	GROUP	AGE	TIME1	TIME2	TIME3	TIME4	STATUS
2	A	12	22.3	25.3	28.2	30.6	5
3	A	11	22.8	27.5	33.3	35.8	5
4	B	12	22.8	30.0	32.8	31.0	4
5	A	12	18.5	26.0	29.0	27.9	5
6	B	9	19.5	25.0	25.3	26.6	5
7	B	11	23.5	28.8	34.2	35.6	5
8	C	8	22.6	26.7	28.0	33.4	3
9	B	8	21.0	26.7	27.5	29.5	5
10	B	7	20.9	28.9	29.7	25.9	2
11	A	11	22.5	29.3	32.6	33.7	2
12	B	12	23.4	29.2	30.4	35.1	2
13	B	14	22.5	29.3	33.4	34.8	5
14	B	9	19.3	25.5	26.2	25.1	3
15	B	10	18.5	24.4	26.5	26.7	4

Figure A.4 Data in Excel for Import Into SPSS

You do not need to open the Excel file to be able to import it into SPSS. To import this Excel file, use the following steps (in SPSS):

1. Select **File/Open/Data**.... (make sure you are viewing the C:\SPSSDATA folder).

2. In the "Files of Type" option in the Open dialog box, select files of Excel (*.xls, *.xlsx, *.xlsm) type.

3. Select the file named EXAMPLE.XLSX located in your C:\SPSSDATA directory (or wherever you stored *IBM SPSS by Example* examples files). The dialog box, as shown in Figure A.5, appears.

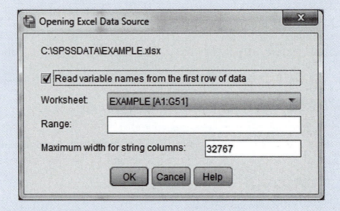

Figure A.5   Dialog Box for Excel Import

4. Since the data in this file are formatted for import, you may accept all the defaults in this dialog box to import the data. (If there is information in columns and rows that you do not want to import, you will need to enter a specific range of cells to import.)

5. Click OK to import the data into SPSS. The SPSS file will automatically be opened in the SPSS Data View mode, as shown in Figure A.6.

6. Click on "Variable View" and change any data definitions (labels, values, missing value codes) that were not properly imported.

7. Once your data file has been imported and you have added any "Variable View" changes, you should save the data as an SPSS data file. For this example, click on File/Save As . . . and save the file as IMPORTED.SAV in the C:\SPSSDATA folder.

8. The data are ready to analyze.

	GR	AGE	TIME1	TIME2	TIME3	TIME4	STATUS
1	A	12	22.3	25.3	28.2	30.6	5
2	A	11	22.8	27.5	33.3	35.8	5
3	B	12	22.8	30.0	32.8	31.0	4
4	A	12	18.5	26.0	29.0	27.9	5
5	B	9	19.5	25.0	25.3	26.6	5
6	B	11	23.5	28.8	34.2	35.6	5
7	C	8	22.6	26.7	28.0	33.4	3
8	B	8	21.0	26.7	27.5	29.5	5
9	B	7	20.9	28.9	29.7	25.9	2
10	A	11	22.5	29.3	32.6	33.7	2
11	B	12	23.4	29.2	30.4	35.1	2
12	B	14	22.5	29.3	33.4	34.8	5
13	B	9	19.3	25.5	26.2	25.1	3
14	B	10	18.5	24.4	26.5	26.7	4
15	B	7	20.2	28.8	33.5	28.1	5

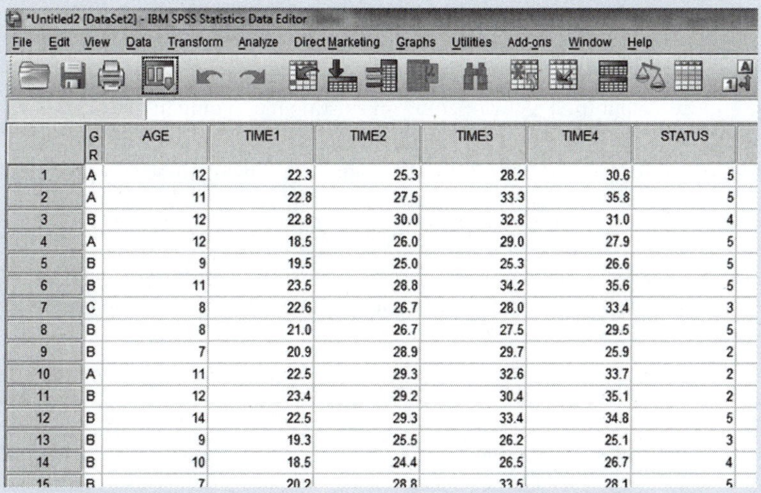

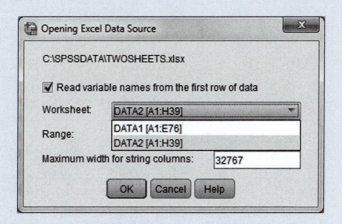

Figure A.6 Data Imported From Excel

When an Excel File Has More Than One Worksheet

When importing an Excel spreadsheet with more than one worksheet, SPSS allows you to select which worksheet to import. As an exercise, import the worksheet called DATA2 from the files TWOSHEETS.XLXS. When you select the Excel type (*.xls, *.xlsx, *.xlsm) to import, the "Opening Excel Data Source" dialog box shows more than one choice in the Worksheet pull-down menu as shown in Figure A.7. Select the worksheet you want to import. For this exercise, select the DATA2 worksheet.

Figure A.7 Selecting an Excel Worksheet to Import

SPSS Step-By-Step. EXAMPLE A.3: Performing an Analysis

Once you have entered data into SPSS by opening an existing file, typing in your data, or importing data, you can perform an analysis. For example, using the SPSS data file named TESTSCORES.SAV, you can calculate the means of AGE and SCORE for this data file following these steps:

1. Open the TESTSCORES.SAV data file by choosing **File/Open/Data**. . . .

2. From the main SPSS menu, select **Analyze/Descriptive Statistics/Descriptives**. . . . The dialog box shown in Figure A.8 appears.

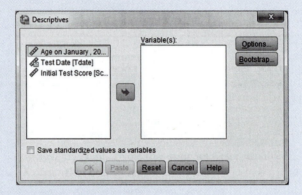

Figure A.8 Dialog Box for Descriptives Analysis

3. Drag the variables *Age* and *Initial Test Score* into the Variable(s) box.

4. Click OK, and the output shown in Table A.3 appears in the SPSS output window showing descriptive statistics for these two variables.

Table A.3 Output From Descriptives Procedure

Descriptive Statistics

	N	Minimum	Maximum	Mean	Std. Deviation
Age on January , 2015	9	19	43	29.67	7.550
Initial Test Score	9	75.00	99.00	88.2222	8.42285
Valid N (listwise)	9				

With these examples under your belt, you are ready to perform the analyses discussed in this book.

Transforming, Recoding, and Categorizing Your Data

Even when information is carefully entered into the computer, researchers often find it necessary to manipulate the data set to prepare it for analysis. This could include the following:

- *Creating a new variable using computation.* Suppose a data set includes height in inches, but the standard for an analysis is to work with centimeters. Using a conversion formula, you can use the SPSS Compute procedure to transform the inches measurement into centimeters. This technique may also be used to transform data that are not normally distributed, using a function such as a square root or logarithm to create a new variable that is more nearly normal in appearance.

- *Removing selected data from analysis using filtering.* If a data set includes information for people outside the ZIP codes appropriate for a project, you can use the SPSS "Select Cases" option to filter out the unneeded records.

- *Combining groups.* If a survey contains 14 different categories for race, but most categories include only a small number of entries, you can use the SPSS Recode procedure to combine the sparsely represented groups into an "other" category and thus reduce the number of categories for analysis.

Although not all data manipulation techniques can be covered in this brief discussion, the following examples illustrate some commonly used techniques for manipulating your data in SPSS.

NOTE: To get back and forth between SPSS windows, you can select the Windows menu and select the Window you want to be displayed (i.e., the data window or output window), or you can click on the SPSS logo (in some Windows versions) at the bottom of your screen and select the Window you want to appear.

SPSS Step-By-Step. EXAMPLE A.4
Creating a New Variable Using Computation

SPSS allows you to calculate new variables as a function of current variables. This section illustrates how to perform this calculation and place the result into your data set. For example, suppose you want to compute an age-adjusted *Time1* variable from the EXAMPLE.SAV database in your analysis by creating a new variable, named *Time1adj*, defined by dividing *Time1* by the square root of *Age*. This can be accomplished using these steps:

SIDEBAR
Be Aware: Unlike a Microsoft Excel Spreadsheet (which updates your calculations when you change a value involved in the calculation), a calculation in SPSS is a one-time event. If you go back to your data set and change a value of *Time1*, for example, the corresponding value for *Time1adj* will not change unless you perform the **Transform/Compute** procedure again.

1. Open the EXAMPLE.SAV data file and click on **Transform/ComputeVariable**. . . .

2. In the Target Variable text box, enter the new name *Time1adj*.

3. In the Numeric Expression text box, enter the following mathematical expression to perform the desired calculation: (This dialog box is shown in Figure A.9.)

$$TIME1/SQRT(AGE)$$

4. Click OK, and a new variable (column) appears in the SPSS data file, named *Time1adj*. For example, the value of *Time1adj* for Record 1 is 6.44, which is $22.3/\sqrt{12}$.

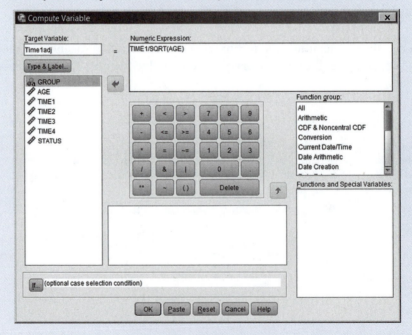

Figure A.9   Computing a New Variable

SPSS Step-By-Step. EXAMPLE A.5: Transforming Data to Make Data More Normally Distributed

Your data may be correctly entered but may still be in a form that is not ideal for analysis. In this case, you can transform the data using one of these techniques:

- Transform quantitative data into standardized z-scores or other standardized values.
- Transform data to induce normality by creating new variables that are functions of current variables (using the Compute technique shown in the previous section).

For example, suppose you want to express the *Satisfaction* variable in the SURVEY.SAV data set as a standardized variable (z-score) by subtracting the mean and dividing by the standard deviation. The following procedure allows you to automatically create a standardized z-score variable in SPSS.

1. Open the data set SURVEY.SAV and select **Analyze/Descriptive Statistics/ Descriptives**. . . .

2. Select Survey Score (*Satisfaction*) as the variable and check the box labeled "Save standardized values as variables."

3. Click OK. When the analysis is finished, notice that a new variable has been added to your data set, *ZSatisfaction*, which is the z-score for *Satisfaction*.

If you want the data to be standardized with mean 100 and standard deviation of 15, you can create a new variable from calculation (as described above) using the following expression:

$$ZSatisfaction100 = (ZSatisfaction * 15) + 100$$

You may also want to transform your data to make their distribution more nearly normal before applying an analysis procedure that assumes normal data. For example, taking the logarithm or the square root of the values in a right-skewed data set can sometimes produce data that are more nearly symmetric. The following example shows how a logarithmic transformation can improve normality. The variable *Skewed* in the TRANSFORM.SAV data set is highly skewed, as shown in Figure A.10.

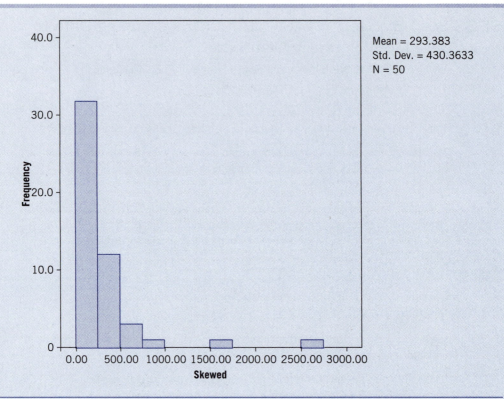

Figure A.10   Skewed Data

Transform the data by taking the natural logarithm (the LN function in SPSS) of this variable. Perform this calculation using the **Transform/Compute** . . . procedure in SPSS and entering the following expression:

$$Trdata = \text{LN}(Skewed)$$

A histogram of the transformed data (*Trdata*) is shown in Figure A.11, which appears to be much more "normal-like" in appearance than the histogram of the original data in Figure A.10.

> After transforming a variable for purposes of performing an analysis using the transformed data, the results reported should usually consist of statistics that have been transformed back into the original units.

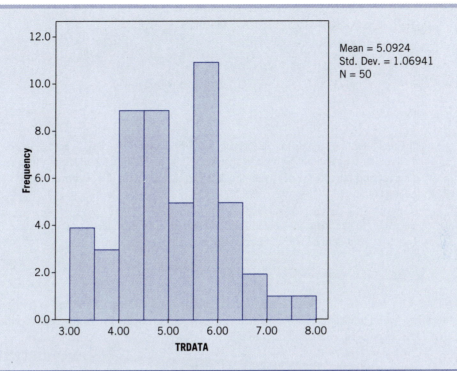

Mean = 5.0924
Std. Dev. = 1.06941
N = 50

Figure A.11 Transformed Data

SPSS Step-By-Step. EXAMPLE A.6: Removing Selected Data From Analysis Using Filtering

Sometimes a data set contains records that you choose to exclude from your analysis. To exclude these records, you can filter them out (i.e., exclude) using the **Data/Select Cases** procedure in SPSS, as illustrated in the following example.

Filtering data in SPSS temporarily removes records from analysis. In the CARS2014.SAV data set, for example, suppose the analysis calls for cars with strictly combustion engines. Using Select Cases, you can define a filter that will exclude cars with hybrid electric engines from an analysis. To create such a filter, you must come up with some method of defining exclusion criteria. For example, the *Battery* variable in the CARS2014 data set indicates if the vehicle has a battery/electric motor (hybrids). This variable can be used to filter these cars from the list. The following steps accomplish this:

1. Open the data set CARS2014.SAV, and select **Data/Select Cases**.
2. Click on the radio button option titled "If condition is satisfied . . . ," and click on the "If . . ." button.

3. In the "Select Cases: If" dialog box, enter the following expression:

$$Battery = 0$$

(That is, we want to use only vehicles that are NOT electric or hybrids.)

4. Click on Continue, and click OK.

Once you define this filter, the records for the electric or hybrid models have a slash across the row label. This indicates that they will not be used in analyses as long as this filter is in effect. The filter should have detected and filtered out 12 cars in the data file, including the Toyota Prius, Honda Civic Hybrids, and several others.

Suppose you also want to eliminate any vehicles with more than eight cylinders from the analysis. You would use the same steps described above, but you would use the expression

$$Cylinders < 9$$

as your filter, which selects only those records with eight or fewer cylinders. If you want to use both of the criteria (not hybrid and eight or fewer cylinders), you would string the two expressions together with a "&" (AND) sign between them. For example,

$$Battery = 0 \ \& \ Cylinders < 9$$

This tells SPSS to include only those records that meet *both* criteria. To specify an OR condition instead of AND, you would use the vertical bar symbol "|" in the expression instead of the "&" sign.

To verify that the combination filter has worked correctly, you can perform the following check using the filtered CARS2014.SAV data.

1. Select **Analyze/Descriptive Statistics/Descriptives**. . . .

2. Select *CityMPG* as the variable to analyze, and click OK.

3. The analysis (where *Battery* = 0 and *Cylinders* < 9) should use only 1,071 of the 1,155 records in the calculations.

Note: To revert back to the nonsubsetted (nonfiltered) data file,

1. Choose **Data/Select Cases**. . . .

2. Click on the "All Cases" radio button.

3. Click OK.

All of the slash marks in the row designations are removed, signifying that all the data in the data file will now be used for future analyses.

> It is important to remember to remove any filtering you may have done before running any analyses where you intend to use all of the cases in the data set.

SPSS Step-By-Step. EXAMPLE A.7:
Combining Groups and Creating
Categories From Quantitative Data

At times, the categories of a categorical variable may be ill defined or too numerous to use in an analysis. In this case, you might want to recode the data into a more usable set of categories. Examples include the following:

- *Race.* Suppose you observe a number of Caucasians, African Americans, and Hispanics but very few Asians, American Indians, Eskimos, Pacific Islanders, and so on. As a result, you may consider recoding the sparse categories into an "other" category.

- *Income bracket.* Suppose more than half of your sample falls in a particular income bracket (High), and the rest are scattered among other lower brackets. It might be appropriate to combine the other brackets and create a binary variable indicating subjects in HIGHINCOME or not.

- *Type of trauma.* Suppose your original categories include penetrating wounds, blunt wounds, and burns, but there are very few burns in your data set. If, for your purposes, burn wounds are similar to penetrating wounds, you may want to combine burn and penetrating wounds into one category and analyze your data looking at blunt wounds versus all other types.

You must be careful when combining categories to ensure that the combination makes sense in terms of your needs. It is good practice to describe any recoding you perform in your report or article.

Suppose you want to recode the variable *SBP* (systolic blood pressure) in the BP.SAV data set into two categories: hypertensive (coded 1) and nonhypertensive (code 0), where in this study hypertensive is defined as *SBP* ≥ 140. Follow these steps:

1. Open the data set BP.SAV and select **Transform/Recode into Different Variables**. . . .

2. Select *Systolic Blood Pressure* (SBP) as your input variable. (The Numeric Variable——> Output variable box displays the text "SBP- ->".)

3. In the Output Variable Name text box, enter *Hypertension*. Click Change. (This causes the information on the Numeric text box to read "SBP—- > Hypertension" as shown in Figure A.12.)

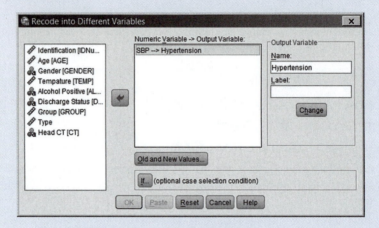

Figure A.12 Specifiying a Variable Recode

4. Click the button labeled "Old and New Values."

5. On the Recode dialog box, click on the "Range, Lowest through" radio button, and enter the value 139. For "New Value," enter 0, and click on the Add button. This defines *SPB* ≤ 139 as nonhypertensive.

6. To define hypertensive, click on the "All Other Values" radio button. For "New Value," enter 1, and click on the Add button. This defines *SPB* > 139 as hypertensive. (The information in the Old—- > New text box should now read Lowest thru 139—->0".)

7. To take care of missing values, click on the "System or user-missing values" in the Old Values section at the left of the dialog box. In the New Value section (right side of dialog box), enter –9 (or whatever missing value code you select) for the value, and click "Add." The resulting dialog box is shown in Figure A.13.

8. Click Continue. Click OK. Observe that the new *Hypertension* variable is included in the data set and contains the values 0 and 1. (Note: You might need to specify desired decimal places or other options in Variable View for new variables you create in this way.)

9. Click on the "Variable View" tab on the datasheet, and define the missing value code as –9 and your category values (0 = Nonhypertensive, 1 = Hypertensive) for your new *Hypertension* variable.

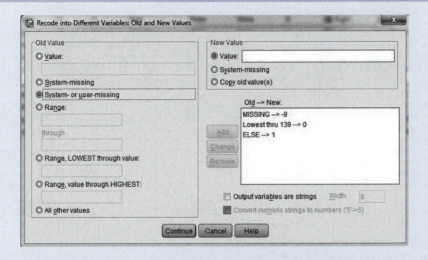

Figure A.13 Dialog Box Showing Selection of User Missing Values

You can now use the new variable in an analysis. The trick with recoding continuous data into categories is to find the cut-point (i.e., the point that defines the categories into which the observations will be placed). A cut-point could be an obvious break in the data, a point that makes logical sense, or one that you can otherwise justify.

> Royston, Altman, and Sauerbrei (2006) argue against dichotomization of a continuous variable stating that "simplicity achieved is gained at a cost; dichotomization may create rather than avoid problems, notably a considerable loss of power and residual confounding," p. 127. Therefore, care must be taken when using this technique, and if used, should be used when there is a previously acceptable cut point recognized in the literature.

SPSS Step-By-Step. EXAMPLE A.8:
Transposing Data

Data for analysis are usually set up with one subject (or entity) per row and variables as columns. This was discussed in the Chapter 1 section titled "Planning a Successful Analysis." However, it is not uncommon for data to find their way into SPSS in just the opposite fashion (i.e., in which rows are variables and columns are subjects). In this case, you must transpose your data set before you can analyze it. The following example shows how this can be accomplished. For example, suppose your data set in SPSS looks like the data in Figure A.14.

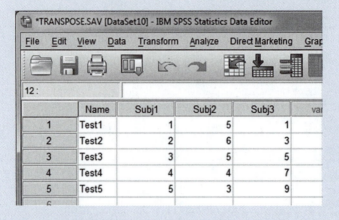

Figure A.14 Data Prior to Transposing

To transpose this data set, follow these steps:

1. Open the data set TRANSPOSE.SAV and select **Data/Transpose**.
2. Place all three subject variables in the Variables list.
3. Place the *Name* variable in the Name Variable list and click OK. See Figure A.15.

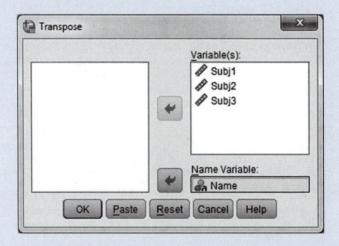

Figure A.15 Transpose Dialog Box

The resulting data set is shown in Figure A.16. Notice that each row is now a "subject" and columns are variables. After transposing, you might need to use the Variable View to adjust the variable definitions for the reconstituted data.

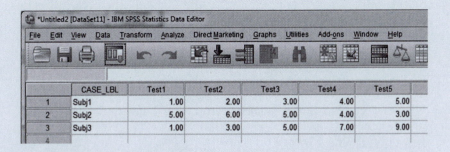

Figure A.16 Data After Transposing

Using the SPSS Syntax Editor

When SPSS runs a procedure, it is actually sending a series of programming code statements to a computer program that then acts on those statements to create results. People who use SPSS extensively may want to learn this code so they can program SPSS without having to use the point-and-click menu system. This book does not teach you how to program in the SPSS language, but this section shows you how you can take advantage of this code in certain cases to simplify your work when using SPSS (without having to learn syntax programming). The following are three situations where knowing a little about SPSS syntax comes in handy:

A) When you are doing several of the same analyses over and over again with only minor changes.

B) When you do the same analysis on a regular basis, and you'd like to save time and also make sure you do the same analysis this time that you did last time.

C) When you want to have an audit trail of an analysis you performed. In other words, you want to save the analysis so you can return to it later.

To illustrate how you can create and save SPSS syntax, follow this example:

SPSS Step-By-Step. EXAMPLE A.9a
Creating and Saving Syntax

1. Open the data set CARS2014.SAV.

2. Select **Analyze/Descriptive Statistics/Descriptives** . . . and select *CityMPG* as the variable to analyze.

3. Instead of clicking on OK, click on the button labeled Paste. The SPSS Syntax window is displayed as shown in Figure A.17. It contains the following lines of SPSS programming code. (Yours may be slightly different.)

   DATASET ACTIVATE DataSet3.
   DESCRIPTIVES VARIABLES=CityMPG
   /STATISTICS=MEAN STDDEV MIN MAX.

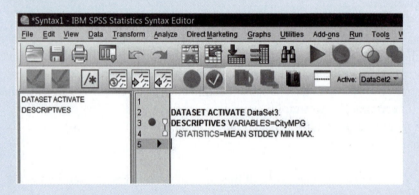

Figure A.17   SPSS Syntax Window

This SPSS syntax is code that tells SPSS to run the analysis that we previously selected using the SPSS menu system. Briefly, the code says to use one of the open data sets in SPSS (in this case, DataSet3) but your may be different and calculate descriptive statistics on the variable CityMPG. (If the Syntax Editor does not appear on your screen, you can get to it by clicking on the Window menu and select the Syntax option, or (on some Windows versions) click on the SPSS icon at the bottom of your screen and select the Syntax window.)

To explore how you can use this syntax, consider the first possibility—using the same code over and over again with minor changes.

4. In the SPSS Syntax Editor, copy the following code (using the same techniques you would use to copy in a word processor).

```
DESCRIPTIVES VARIABLES=CityMPG
/STATISTICS=MEAN STDDEV MIN MAX.
```

5. Paste the copied code below the current code, and change the variable *CityMPG* to *HwyMPG* in the second set of the code. Take out the DATASET line since you already have the data set opened. The lines of code now read:

```
DESCRIPTIVES VARIABLES=CityMPG
/STATISTICS=MEAN STDDEV MIN MAX.
DESCRIPTIVES VARIABLES=HwyMPG
/STATISTICS=MEAN STDDEV MIN MAX.
```

6. Using click and drag, make sure all of this code is selected (highlighted). Find the green arrow triangle at the top and middle of the Syntax Editor. This is the "Run" button. This tells SPSS to run the selected code. Once you click the green run icon, SPSS will display the descriptive statistics as instructed by the code. Although this is a simple example, it illustrates how you could do one analysis (it could be much more complex), then copy and paste the code into the Syntax Editor, make minor changes, and then run a series of analyses. Once you learn how to do this, it can be easier than going through the menu choices, and it can save you time.

7. To illustrate situation "B" from the previous list, we'll save this code, then bring it back and do the analysis again. To do this example, go back to the Syntax Editor (as described in Step 3). In the Syntax Editor, select **File/Save as** . . . and save the syntax using the name DESC1.SPS (the SPS extension is for SPSS syntax). Make sure you save this file to the C:\SPSSDATA folder (or whatever folder you are using for your examples).

SPSS Step-By-Step. EXAMPLE A.9b: Reusing SPSS Syntax Code

The second (B) reason you might use SPSS Syntax is "When you do the same analysis on a regular basis, and you'd like to save time and also make sure you do the same analysis this time that you did last time." This example illustrates the procedure. If you do the same analysis over and over again, this examples shows you how you can save the syntax as shown in the previous example, then rerun the analysis (even using a different data set). This is particularly helpful if you have a complex analysis that you want to duplicate for future analyses. This can be handy if, for example, you want to redo the analysis using slight modifications. Instead of recreating the complex analysis from scratch, you might be able to make a slight modification of the code and rerun the analysis quickly. To see how you could reuse SPSS syntax code, follow these steps:

1. Close SPSS and begin a new session. From the main SPSS window, select **File/Open/Syntax** . . . and open the DESC1.SPS file you created in the previous example. The code you've previously saved is displayed. However, there is a problem. The data set you had opened when you created this code is no longer available in the SPSS data window. Before you can continue, you'll need to open the desired data file. (You could do this within the SPSS code, but we'll not cover that now.)

2. Go back to the main SPSS data window, and open the file CARDATA2014 (**File/Open/Data**. . .). Take note of what data set number is assigned to this file. At the top of the SPSS data window, you should see information such as "CARS2014.SAV [DataSet1]." This tells you the data set number. Go back to the Syntax window, and make sure the code indicates the correct data set number, such as

DATASET ACTIVATE DataSet1.

3. Once you have verified that the data set number is okay, select all of the code, and click the green "Run" triangle (or select **Run/All**). SPSS will perform the requested analysis.

SPSS Step-By-Btep. EXAMPLE A.9c: Capturing SPSS Syntax Code

The third (C) reason you might use and save SPSS Syntax is to create an audit trail of the analyses you have performed. In other words, suppose you have performed an analysis and you want to preserve how you did it for future reference. To capture your analysis syntax, you can either save the information from the syntax window or use the SPSS Journal. Follow these steps:

Depending on the options set up in your SPSS program, you may have noticed that SPSS displays the syntax code in the output window when you perform an analysis.

1. To control the option to display syntax in the output window, go to **Edit/Options**, and click on the Viewer tab in the Options dialog box. At the bottom left of the window is a checkbox labeled "Display commands in the log." When this box is checked, the SPSS syntax is displayed in the Output window when you perform an analysis. (Leave it checked.)

2. To capture an entire SPSS session, you can collect the syntax into a "Journal." While still in the Options dialog, select the File Locations tab. Make sure the option "Record syntax in Journal" is checked, and make note of (or change) the location of the .jnl file. Select append or overwrite according to your preference. Click OK to exit the Options dialog box. (Note that your journal file is originally empty. It will not contain any information until you perform some analysis.)

3. Before attempting to open the journal files, run some SPSS analyses. After you have run some analyses, view the Journal file by using a program such as Word (or any other text editor) to open the journal.jnl file (that is in the folder where you specified it should be stored). You should see a record of whatever analyses you have performed. You can save this information for later use, or cut and paste it back into the Syntax Editor to redo an analysis.

Having a copy of your SPSS syntax code provides you with a precise audit trail of the analyses that were performed.

We recommend that you "turn on" the option to display syntax in the SPSS output window (as shown in the above example) so you can document analyses that you perform and keep copies of your code.

SUMMARY

After going through the tutorials in this appendix, you will have the skills to use the SPSS program to perform the statistical analysis examples in *IBM SPSS by Example*.

REFERENCE

Royston, P., Altman, D. G., & Sauerbrei, W. (2006). Dichotomizing continuous predictors in multiple regression: A bad idea. *Statistics in Medicine* 25.1, 127–141.

Appendix B

Choosing the Right Procedure to Use

The ideal time to choose the type of analysis you will perform on your data is during the planning process. Knowing the analyses that will be performed is crucial in designing your data collection strategy and determining a sample size. However, many times it is true that data are collected first, and only then is consideration given to the analyses that should be performed. In either case, this appendix will help you determine which analyses fit your needs. Remember, however, the earlier you address these statistical issues, the better.

To select a proper analysis, your experimental question must be well defined. The following guide leads you through a series of questions that will assist you in deciding which statistical procedure or procedures will address your research questions. Begin by deciding which of the following scenarios addresses your analysis type:

1. Are you performing a *descriptive* analysis, a *comparative* (*inferential*) analysis, or a *correlation/association* analysis? These analyses are described in the section in Chapter 1 titled "Planning a Successful Analysis."

2. What types of variables are you analyzing? Are you using quantitative (numeric or scale in SPSS terminology) or qualitative (categorical: nominal or ordinal in SPSS terminology) data? Are your response (dependent) variables normally distributed? These are the types of questions that you will need to be able to answer to decide on the appropriate analyses. For more details, see Chapter 2: Describing and Examining Data.

Once you can answer these questions, the following decision tables help you decide which analyses are appropriate. This is not an all-inclusive decision-making tool and cannot substitute for the thoroughness that a professional statistician would apply to your experimental question and goals. If your data and hypotheses do not conform to these simple rules, then your analyses may be more complex than those covered here, or you may not have properly defined your analysis questions.

> If you do not know what hypotheses to test, then you cannot know the proper statistical analyses to apply.

How to Use the Tables

To use the following tables, first consider the type of analysis you want to perform. This topic was described in more detail in the section in Chapter 1: Planning a Successful Analysis.

1. *A descriptive analysis.* Is the purpose of your analysis to summarize your data into a few numbers?

   For example, this would be the case if you want to characterize quantitative data using descriptive statistics (such as a mean and standard deviation) or you want to summarize information in a categorical variable using a frequency table or graph.

   If yes, go to Table B.1, "Descriptive Statistics."

2. *A comparative analysis.* Is the purpose of your analysis to compare one or more groups to each other or to a standard? Examples are comparisons of means or determination if categories in one group are in the same pattern as in another group.

   If yes, go to Table B.2, "Comparison Tests."

3. *Association and correlation.* Is the purpose of your analysis to determine if there is a relationship between variables, or do you want to predict one variable using one or more other variables? Examples of this would be a correlation or regression analysis as well as crosstabulation of categorical variables.

   If yes, go to Table B.3: "Relational Analyses (Correlation and Regression)."

For example, suppose you have collected information from two independent groups of subjects and you have measured some characteristic for each subject. Suppose further that you want to know if the means of the measured characteristic are different for the two groups. This scenario fits the description of the second option. Therefore, you would go to Table B.2 and, in the left-hand column, select the item labeled "You are comparing data from two INDEPENDENT groups." If you have determined that a normality assumption is plausible, then in the second column, you should select "Normal" as your data type. In the third column, you see that an appropriate analysis is a two-sample *t*-test. You can go to Chapter 4 and look over the hypotheses, assumptions, caveats, and description of a two-sample *t*-test to verify that this type of analysis is appropriate. If so, proceed with the analysis as described in Chapter 4.

If none of these options relates to what you want to accomplish, you should reexamine your analysis questions or consult a statistician to see what type of analysis best fits your goals. We emphasize that these tables contain only commonly used procedures and are not intended to provide an exhaustive listing of statistical techniques.

Table B.1 Descriptive Statistics

Make a decision by reading from left to right.		
You want to describe a single variable.	*What Is the Data Type?*	*Analysis Procedure to Use (Chapter)*
	Normal	Mean, SD, and so on, using the Descriptive or Explore procedure (Chapter 2)
	Quantitative	Median, histogram, and stem-and-leaf plot using the Explore procedure (Chapter 2)
	Categorical	Frequency table (Chapter 2)
You want to describe two related or paired variables.	Both are normal	Pearson's correlation (Chapter 5)
	Both are at least ordinal	Spearman's correlation (Chapter 8)
	Both categorical	Crosstabulations (Chapter 2 or 6)

Table B.2 Comparison Tests

Make decision by reading from left to right.		
You are comparing a SINGLE SAMPLE to a norm (gold standard).	*What Is the Data Type?*	*Procedure to Use*
	Normal	Single-sample t-test (Chapter 4)
	At least ordinal	Sign test (Chapter 8)
	Categorical	Goodness-of-fit (Chapter 6)
You are comparing data from two INDEPENDENT groups.	Normal	Two-sample t-test (Chapter 4)
	At least ordinal	Mann-Whitney (Chapter 8)
	Categorical	$2 \times c$ test for homogeneity/chi-square (Chapter 5)
You are comparing PAIRED, REPEATED, or MATCHED data.	Normal	Paired t-test (Chapter 4)
	At least ordinal	Sign test (Chapter 8)
	Symmetric quantitative	Wilcoxon signed-rank test (Chapter 8)
	Binary (dichotomous)	McNemar (Chapter 6)

(Continued)

Table B.2   (Continued)

More than two groups: INDEPENDENT	Normal	One-way ANOVA (Chapter 7)
	At least ordinal	Kruskal-Wallis (Chapter 8)
	Categorical	$r \times c$ test for homogeneity/chi-square (Chapter 6)
More than two groups: REPEATED MEASURES	Normal	Repeated-measures ANOVA (Chapter 7)
	At least ordinal	Friedman's test (Chapter 8)
	Categorical	Cochran Q (not covered)
You are comparing means where the model includes a covariate adjustment.	Normal	Analysis of covariance (Chapter 7)

Note: In this table, the term *Normal* indicates that the procedure is theoretically based on a normality assumption. In practice, normal-based procedures can be used if you have data for which a normality assumption is plausible or your sample size is sufficiently large that the normal-based procedures can be appropriately used. The term *At least ordinal* indicates that your data have an order. This includes ordinal categorical data and any quantitative data.

Table B.3   Relational Analyses (Correlation and Regression)

Make decision by reading from left to right.		
→		
You want to analyze the relationship between two variables. (If regression, one variable is classified as a response variable and one a predictor variable.)	*What Is the Data Type?*	*Procedure to Use*
	Normal	Pearson correlation, simple linear regression (Chapter 5)
	At least ordinal	Spearman correlation (Chapter 8)
	Categorical	$r \times c$ contingency table analysis (Chapter 6)
	Binary	Logistic regression (Chapter 9)
You want to analyze the relationship between a response variable and two or more predictor variables.	Normal	Multiple linear regression (Chapter 5)
	Binary	Logistic regression (Chapter 9)

Note: In this table, the "data type" applies to the dependent variable for regression procedures. For assessment of association (e.g., correlation, cross tabulation, etc.), the variable type applies to both variables. See the footnote to Table B2 for a discussion of the normality assumption.

INDEX

⑤SAGE research**methods**

The essential online tool for researchers from the world's leading methods publisher

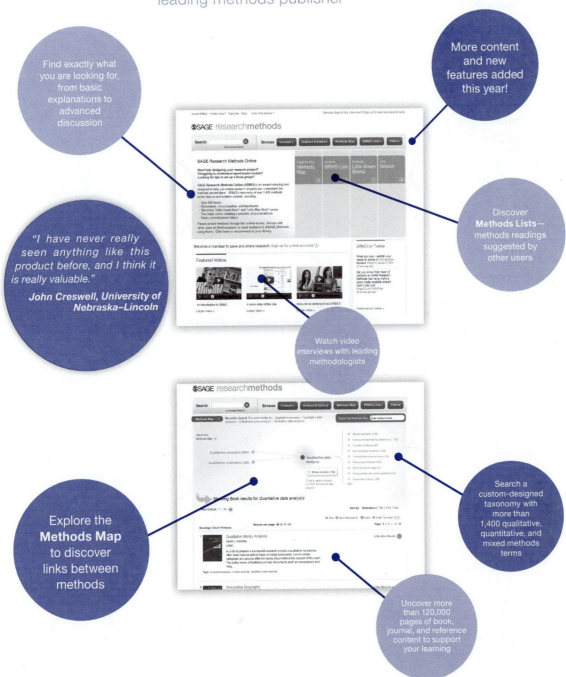

Find exactly what you are looking for, from basic explanations to advanced discussion

More content and new features added this year!

"I have never really seen anything like this product before, and I think it is really valuable."

John Creswell, University of Nebraska–Lincoln

Discover **Methods Lists**— methods readings suggested by other users

Watch video interviews with leading methodologists

Explore the **Methods Map** to discover links between methods

Search a custom-designed taxonomy with more than 1,400 qualitative, quantitative, and mixed methods terms

Uncover more than 120,000 pages of book, journal, and reference content to support your learning

Find out more at
www.sageresearchmethods.com